THE CHRISTIAN
INTERPRETATION
OF RELIGION

THE MACMILLAN COMPANY
NEW YORK • BOSTON • CHICAGO
DALLAS • ATLANTA • SAN FRANCISCO

MACMILLAN AND CO., LIMITED
LONDON • BOMBAY • CALCUTTA
MADRAS • MELBOURNE

**THE MACMILLAN COMPANY
OF CANADA, LIMITED**
TORONTO

THE CHRISTIAN INTERPRETATION OF RELIGION

*Christianity in Its Human
and Creative Relationships with the
World's Cultures and Faiths*

BY

EDWARD J. JURJI

THE MACMILLAN COMPANY

New York   1952

This Book Is Inscribed

TO MY WIFE

PREFACE

THE burden of this book is to sketch along Christian lines an interpretation of religion in its universal manifestations, taking into account the global crisis and the rising powers in Asia and the Middle East. For a decade or more, the author's interest has centered in the field of comparative religion. With a panel of eight distinguished contributors, he edited in 1946 *The Great Religions of the Modern World*, a symposium published by Princeton University Press. Like its forerunner, the present volume is addressed to the general reader, scholar, and layman, although it differs in being an attempt to depict the religions—extinct and living, primitive and advanced—in the light of the Gospel.

The central theme in short is that the message of Christianity has a direct bearing upon the history of religion and a distinctive validity for modern man; its propagation in East and West illumines the religious phenomena of the race, setting in sharp focus the manifold of man's spiritual consciousness.

I owe Princeton Theological Seminary an indescribable debt. More than they themselves perhaps realize, colleagues of the Faculty have oriented and nourished my thought on the subject here treated. Students of successive years, particularly John Crew Tyler, now of Edinburgh, and Roland Mashat Frye, of Princeton University, made invaluable criticisms. Dr. Kenneth S. Gapp, Librarian, and his staff, rendered the theological treasures of a first-class collection more readily accessible. By his vision and ecumenical discernment, President John A. Mackay delivered many a concept from possible ambiguity.

To all these, as well as to the editors and readers of The Macmillan Company, New York, notably Mr. Guy Brown, my profound gratitude.

EDWARD J. JURJI

Princeton, N.J.

CONTENTS

CHAPTER I

THE VISIBLE STRUCTURE
OF RELIGION

Few will dispute the fact that the essence of religion exceeds in significance what men think or write about it. That in its widest range and connotation religion defies the attempt at precise definition adds weight to the verdict that it is infinitely more subtle and profound than any human formulation of its reality.

Yet in its perennial impact upon men and nations, its increasing influence upon the hurrying generations, as well as upon culture and the historical process, and its capacity to mold character, save man from disorder, inspire faith and confidence and transform society, religion stands absolutely alone, peerless and incomparable. It therefore lays claim upon our attention and calls for searching self-criticism and sober judgment.

Less obvious perhaps is the fact that the essence of religion really transcends the classic statements of its nature which detached erudition produces. True religion may be said to annihilate the barriers between primitive and historic faiths. It blends the differences that separate the extinct religions from those of the modern world. And it touches the heart of man's existence where, all too often, the formal observances of worship fail to inspire.

Despite their peripheral character, however, the common expositions and varieties of religious experience merit careful scrutiny. They need to be probed if a proper approach to the inner making of religion is to be undertaken.

I. The Nature of Religion

Authorities are not agreed on what constitutes religion. J. H. Leuba (1868–1946)[1] offered some fifty definitions, drawn from

---

[1] In *A Psychological Study of Religion*, New York, 1912, see index and elsewhere.

almost as many eminent authors. The multiplicity and divergence of scholarly opinion in the field may be illustrated by the citation of a few current conceptions.

The French philosopher Emile Durkheim (1858–1917), on the basis of researches in the primitive religions and totemism of central Australian tribesmen, developed a concept which identified religion with the idea of the sacred as distinct from the profane. He observed religious beliefs and rites, and by an intensive study of the mentality of groups and communities, advanced the knowledge of sociology. A serious objection to this approach was raised, however, by the psychologists of religion when they argued that modern religion is too complex and elusive to be explained on the basis of findings in primitive religion.[2]

During the nineteenth century, a conception of religion combining naturalism with rationalism and grounded in the evolutionary hypothesis of Charles Darwin came to the fore. It was gradually adopted in the fields of philosophy, anthropology, and general culture. Herbert Spencer (1820–1903)[3] proposed the view that the vital and constant element of religion is the sense of mystery. He suggested that religion is awe in the presence of the cosmic forces and pointed to the "rhythm of motion" as one of the fundamental laws of the material universe. In his view, religion was derived from manism, that is, belief in mana, the extra-physical power that is inherent in nature, and produces the order of the universe.

Edward Burnett Tylor (1832–1917)[4] sought to determine the limits of animism, intending it to include "the general doctrine of souls and other spiritual things"; according to Tylor, religion was derived from animism. In 1890, James George Frazer (1854–1941) worked out a comprehensive study of ancient cults, folklore, and culture which he incorporated in *The Golden Bough*.[5] He described religion as "the despair of magic," maintaining that historically it merely succeeded magic.

[2] James Bissett Pratt, *The Religious Consciousness*, New York, 1930, pp. 4–5.

[3] *First Principles of a New System of Philosophy*, New York, 1864.

[4] *Researches into the Early History of Mankind and the Development of Civilization*, London, 1870.

[5] 12 vols., London, 1911–1927; *Aftermath: A Supplement to the Golden Bough*, New York, 1937.

Robert Ranulph Marett (1866–1943) and Wilhelm Max Wundt (1832–1920) held that religion actually grew out of magic. All these variations on the central evolutionary theme were later challenged. In 1917 the American ethnologist, John R. Swanton (1873–   ),[6] proclaimed the real existence of several parallel and independent lines of religious development, demonstrating at the same time that religion is one of the primary components of human nature and is not to be connected with any such specific origins as magic, death, dreaming, mana, or animism.

The exacting anthropologist, A. L. Kroeber,[7] in his reconstruction of the native Indian culture of California was cautious on the significance of his results. In his investigations of the growth of primitive religion, he noted a gradual change from a personal to a communal aim. Under external stimuli and internal variation, ceremonies grew more numerous as well as more elaborate. Yet as regards an ultimate explanation of the facts concerned, Kroeber was satisfied to refrain from comment, leaving the data in the hands of the psychologist.

Other specialists and philosophers have advanced many additional conceptions of religion. Its moral aspect was emphasized by Immanuel Kant (1724–1804) [8] who defined religion as the recognition of all duties as divine commandments. Friedrich Schleiermacher (1768–1834) [9] found the essence of religion in "the feeling of dependence."

The celebrated psychologist, William James (1842–1910),[10] speaking of the individual character of religion, described it as "the feelings, acts, and experiences of individual men in their solitude so far as they apprehend themselves to stand in relation to whatever they may consider the divine." Others found in religion the totality of man's yearning for worldly and other-worldly stability. Still others, taking a materialistic view, declared religion to be nothing more than a figment of the imagination.

[6] "Some Anthropological Misconceptions," *American Anthropologist,* New Series, vol. XIX, no. 4, 1917, pp. 459–470.

[7] *Anthropology,* New York, 1923, pp. 293–325.

[8] *Critik der reinen Vernunft,* Leipzig, 1818; tr. and ed. Lewis White Beck, *Critique of Pure Reason,* Chicago, 1949.

[9] *On Religion: Speeches to its Cultured Despisers,* London, 1893, pp. 26–101.

[10] *Varieties of Religious Experience,* London, 1911, p. 31.

Henri Louis Bergson (1859–1941), representative of those who distinguish between intellect and intuition, adopted a more subtle approach: his closed and open societies, the one mechanical and the other mystical, suggest that intellect is the source of morality and that intuition is the source of religion.

There is no immediate answer to the question of the origin of religion. Many of its roots can be traced, but the fundamental reality is not in such individual roots, but in the purpose that underlies religion.

The theistic conception of religion presupposes a superhuman Being who has a purpose for man, and with whom man may have communion. Thus, William Adams Brown (1865–1943) [11] quoted with approbation W. W. Clark,[12] who defined religion as "the life of man in his supernatural relations," adding that the words meant man's "relation to the power on which he finds himself dependent, the authority to which he deems himself responsible, and the unseen being with whom he is capable of communion."

This emphasis on the supernatural also points to revelation, that is, to actual implementation of the divine purpose in nature, scripture, and prophecy. In Christianity, the Incarnation is the center of the whole scheme of revelation. Nathan Söderblom (1866–1931) [13] defined the portals of revelation in human personality as three: the intellect or understanding, the intuition of infinity, and consciousness of the ideal.

II. Core of Religious Power

Although the true core of religious power eludes precise definition, it is possible to describe in broad outline certain channels through which religion has made its power felt.

A. *Worship*

The nature of worship in a given religion is generally governed by the meaning attached to the Supreme Being. Magic, totemism, manism, and fetishism among primitive peoples gave rise to a pe-

[11] *Christian Theology in Outline,* New York, 1906, p. 29.
[12] *An Outline of Christian Theology,* New York, 1898.
[13] *The Nature of Revelation,* tr. Friedrich E. Pamp, New York, 1933, p. 106.

culiarly rude pattern of worship. In the religions of Greece and Rome, gods in the likeness of men were worshiped in a strongly anthropomorphic style.

In Hinduism, the Brahman—a great impersonal oversoul—demanded awe and adulation. In Buddhism, contrary to the founder's injunctions, the Buddha came increasingly to be adored. The Confucianists centered their cult on the worship of ancestral spirits.

In total submission before the Almighty, the Moslem worships Allah, the merciful, the compassionate, Lord of heaven and earth, who begat not nor was begotten, and with whom no one is coequal. The Jew bows in worship before the Lord God, the King of the universe, "the God of our Fathers, the God of Abraham, Isaac, and Jacob." Yet no matter where, how, and what it is that men worship, they almost invariably give their assent to a supernatural power. This is the hallmark of religion; this is the grip that holds the human spirit.

In the case of Christianity, religious experience, centered in worship, evokes the will to serve God, and culminates in the faith that enables men to move mountains. When Christ taught His disciples to pray, He offered them, through Himself as mediator, a direct access to the Father. The Lord's Prayer, as the quintessence of worship, is unique in that it shows the limitation and lisping uncertainty of every other form of adoration.

The Christian comes to God in prayer, believing that only in Christ can he find his maker.[14] And in so doing, his communion with God culminates in faith nourished by the Giver of all life. For God's unfailing love—revealed supremely in the figure of Jesus Christ—offers personal regeneration and the redemption of all who come in penitence seeking the forgiveness of their sins that they may lead a righteous and holy life.

B. *Scripture*

A religion is strengthened by sacred texts, spoken by prophets and seers, written by countless scribes, surviving in many commentaries.

The scriptures of the great religions embody the wisdom of the

[14] Dietrich Bonhoeffer, *The Cost of Discipleship*, New York, 1949, p. 140.

ages. Whether they are the Analects of Confucius, the Tao Te Ching of Laotzu, or the Veda and Bhagavadgita of India, these hallowed writings exercise a tremendous influence on worshipers and are transmitted from generation to generation. They are judged as repositories of the truth and as the pilgrim's companion.

The theistic faiths ascribe the truth of scripture to a divine origin and, in different ways, identify the prophetic voice of scripture with that of the eternal God.

The Christian accepts the Old and New Testaments as the Word of God which was inspired by the Holy Spirit and conveys the Good News of what God has wrought in Jesus Christ. The Scriptures of Christianity are the norm of doctrine and the supreme authority of faith and work.[15]

C. *Ethics*

In ethics, the great religions have an apparent common ground. It is true that modern medical, psychological and sociological research has shed new light on human behavior and has suggested that actions once condemned as immoral deserve instead to be treated with due allowance for their natural or physical causes. But the development of personality and the cultivation of character, which are outside the sphere of the exact sciences, are linked with ethics as ethics is allied with religion.

Ethics renders a unique contribution in bridging the gap between the law of nature and the hazy optimism of philosophers. Within the religious orbit, it provides a safety zone across the tempest and tragedy of existence. The fundamental difference between Christian and non-Christian ethics will be dealt with subsequently in connection with the individual religions.

D. *Theology*

Taken in its specific relation to thought, theology may be said to treat ultimate reality apart from the categories of philosophy and the detachment of science. The major religious systems of East Asia tend to identify the divine with an impersonal, indeterminate and

[15] See Emil Brunner, *The Christian Doctrine of God: Dogmatics,* vol. I, tr. Olive Wyon, London, 1949, pp. 22, 44.

hence utterly unknowable principle. The monotheistic religions, on the other hand, accept the divine as a self-revealing being, a creator, and an arbiter of ends. The sovereign God is thus the God of the decrees.

Predestination forms an important part of theistic theology, but the freedom of man to choose is also admitted. Here we meet the great paradox of theology—belief in a sovereign God and the admission of man's free will. Man is responsible for his actions, good and evil. God, though in no way the cause of evil, is by His foreknowledge aware of the evil men do. Within the confines of Jewish, Christian, and Islamic theology, Greek reason and Hebrew theism are drawn upon, creating perhaps the most powerful system of religious thought that the world has ever known.

What is distinctive about Christian theology is its understanding of dogmatics as grounded in Scripture. Dogma may be defined as church proclamation, so far as it agrees with the Bible which is the Word of God.[16] A theology may be said to be Christian when it persistently seeks through the guidance of the Holy Spirit to understand and interpret the Word of God and to bring dogmatics into close conformity with the essence of Scriptural teaching.

III. Primitive and Historic Religions

Despite the lack of written records, organization, or a cultural heritage, certain primitive religions continue to be practiced to the present day, while some historic faiths have vanished, even though they had literary authority, priestly orders, and institutional traditions. Investigation of the basic and related aspects of such perseverance and failure is revealing.

A. *The Prelogical Mentality*

A striking feature of primitive mentality was described by Lucien Lévy-Bruhl (1857–1939).[17] Having studied "savage" thought and noted its fluidity and incoherence, he reached the conclusion that it was prelogical. In other words, lacking correlation and sequence, primitive concepts were drawn independently of logic.

[16] Karl Barth, *The Doctrine of the Word of God,* vol. I, tr. G. T. Thomson, Edinburgh, 1936, p. 308.
[17] *Primitive Mentality,* tr. Lilian A. Clare, London, 1923, pp. 59–63.

Early man did not pay much attention to the law of causality; events and phenomena were explained on the grounds of superficial concomitance; man was not distinguished from the forces, objects, and other forms of life which surrounded him. As a result, individuality was not clearly defined, man was lost in the mass, and the perplexing contradiction of such a scheme did not disturb anyone.

B. *High Gods*

Even with his prelogical approach to religion, primitive man probably believed in the existence of high gods and spirits, according to the opinion of Father Wilhelm Schmidt (1868–   ) [18] of Vienna, who classified a vast body of data dealing with primitive peoples. In forming his opinion, corroborated later in many quarters, Father Schmidt studied savage communities as widely separated as Australia and Africa, South America and India, discovering evidence that showed how prevalent was the worship of supreme deities, creative, cosmic, and celestial.

Father Schmidt's investigation showed that while the origin of religion remained shrouded in obscurity, the theory that monotheism is the result of evolutionary progress is no longer tenable. The positivism of Auguste Comte (1798–1857), which exalted humanity instead of God, began to recede as more knowledge came to light. A more adequate postulate arose which assumed that the several religious patterns now held among contemporary primitive peoples go back to an early belief in high gods; thus, from the belief in supreme beings there presumably appeared, by way of degradation, the various crude religious motifs that dominate animism, fetishism, polytheism, and the like.

C. *Mythology*

Although mythology flourished in a prelogical atmosphere, its importance to the science of religion is paramount and it is necessary that three steps be taken by the investigator if he is to appraise this importance. First, the myth proper must be separated from its expression in art, literature, and theology; second, with the aid of comparative mythology, light can be shed upon the common mytho-

---

[18] See his more recent *Rassen und Völker in Vorgeschichte und Geschichte des Abendlandes*, 3 vols., Lucerne, 1946–1949.

logical heritage of primitive peoples, as distinguished from individual national developments; third, it must be recognized that the rise and growth of myths cannot be explained by instinct alone, for only as myths satisfied the norms of reason were they likely to survive. By these steps one arrives at an idea of the inner substance of mythology which may be described as the tendency of all myths to indicate nearness to the Unseen, to sharpen the difference between good and evil, to portray the supernatural as real, not illusory. In short, mythology bridges the gap between prehistoric primitivism and the religions of historic times.

D. *History*

Even more noteworthy than mythology, in the study of religion, is history, oral and written. The centers of ancient culture, Egypt, Babylonia, Greece, Rome, India, and China, have yielded massive archaeological data which illumine the origin, growth, and decay of great faiths.

These evidences lend support to the belief that there is a continuity of religious tradition among all races, a continuity coming down from the earliest times. Although history in the orthodox sense did not come into being until the advent of writing, there was, nevertheless, a wealth of oral history, antedating and accompanying it, and the first use of writing, as W. F. Albright [19] has pointed out, was mainly as an adjunct to memory. Oral tradition crisscrosses the boundary line between history and prehistory. This oral tradition broke out in verse, crystallized in prose, was adopted in the well-defined techniques of narrators and story-tellers, and in due course emerged in the saga, epic, and hymn. History and prehistory, the primitive religions and the higher, are thereby intimately connected.

IV. THE EXTINCT RELIGIONS

Within recorded history are a number of religious developments of great antiquity, the study of which, though they are no longer practiced, constitutes a necessary approach to the study of contemporary religions.

[19] *From the Stone Age to Christianity*, Baltimore, 1940, pp. 33–34.

A. *Their Ethnic Character*

These ancient religions were associated with a number of well-defined groupings of the human family; though these groups were not always racially homogeneous, cultural and moral standards within each group made for ethnic unity. Each of these ancient religions was in reality a combination of cults, mysteries, and syncretisms, bound together by a few overriding principles.

The fields of these combinations coincided with the geographical dimensions of early Egypt, Babylonia, Phoenicia, Iran, Greece, Rome, Peru, and Mexico, as well as regions in which Semites and Indo-Europeans jostled each other in their restless groping for self-assertion. Especially during the three thousand years preceding the Christian era, the Near East loomed as a melting-pot of cultures and as the home of religious enthusiasm.

In Egypt, Phoenicia, Babylonia, and the adjoining areas, such elements of nature as rain, sun, storm, fertility, heaven and earth were deified. Humanized, these deities, together with household, tribal, and city gods, summed up in themselves the character and longings, the triumphs and defeats, the wisdom and folly of their adherents. When at last the great empires of antiquity lay in ruin, the gods they had cherished fell with them and were buried in the dust from which their glory had sprung.[20]

B. *Patterns of Religious Thought*

The meaning of the ancient religions is illustrated by a number of intellectual patterns bequeathed by antiquity, Egypt and Babylonia providing two arresting examples. Egypt is noted for the monophysite quality of her thought,[21] according to which there is only one substance shared by gods, men, and all other beings. The Egyptian texts suggest that the many gods were all in reality manifestations of the one god, and into this scheme were fitted not only the gods, but also the nature of all observed phenomena.

Babylonia affords another example of the dynamic quality of ancient religion, in its concept of the cosmos as a state in which the

[20] A. Eustace Haydon, *Biography of the Gods,* New York, 1941, pp. 29–56.
[21] John A. Wilson, *The Intellectual Adventure of Ancient Man,* Chicago, 1946, p. 66.

gods were the only first-class citizens.[22] This concept is in line with the tendency to relate the facts of nature to a cosmic state, which is represented as sovereign over such great and conflicting forces as earth and water. In accordance with this broadly interpreted pattern, man was created for the benefit of the gods, his institutions subservient to their purpose and serving their welfare; the national state, a mere detail in the cosmic order, was a police force to discharge the injunctions of the world state of the gods.

C. *Western Motifs*

The articulation and vitality of the Teutons, the law and order of the Romans, and the rationalized philosophy of the Greeks are important and distinctive motifs of the ancient West.

Tyr, greatest god of the Germans, was a specialist in war; Odin, his successor, led the Anglo-Saxons in their invasion of the British Isles. Enterprise, adventure, and action—noble virtues when coupled with a humane and constructive spirit—make up the Teutonic contribution to higher religion.

The heritage from Rome is no less impressive; identified with the political ascendancy of Rome, the sky-god, Jupiter Optimus Maximus, rose as emblem of the Imperial City.

From Greece came a purgative motif. The philosophers, among them Socrates, Plato, and Aristotle, set out to expunge superstition and idolatry and fulminated against the characteristics ascribed to the gods by epic poets, myth makers, and dramatists. Plato sought to purify the gods and make them into perfect beings; the Stoics recognized the deities as embodiments of the divine logos; the Epicureans, though they did not deny the celestial beings, had no use for them in their system. The gods could not long endure with no support other than philosophic tolerance, and as they passed from view as objects of worship, they made room for a higher religion.

V. RELIGIONS OF THE MODERN WORLD

There are eight principal religions in the modern world. Shinto is an expression of the national consciousness of Japan. With all

[22] Thorkild Jacobsen, *The Intellectual Adventure of Ancient Man*, p. 137.

its offshoots and variations, Hinduism sums up much that is particularly Indian. In East Asia Confucianism and Taoism may be considered the product of China's religious experience. Though Indian in origin, Buddhism long ago became a universally accepted faith in the lands of the Far East. Three religions had their inception in the Near East: Judaism, and its two "daughter religions," Christianity and Islam, both of which in due course established universal claims and were practiced on a worldwide scale. A ninth religion, Zoroastrianism, though Iranian in historic connection, is at present primarily the faith of the Parsi community centered upon the state of Bombay in India.

As faster means of communication and the contacts of war and peace brought the religions of the modern world into closer proximity, the exchange of religious insights proceeded on a vast scale. The thirst of the Eastern soul for reform and modernization was held in balance, however, by an unbending resistance to radical change and a firm attachment to old moorings.

Nor was the ascendancy of Western Christian culture left unquestioned. The havoc and agony of two world wars, the rising tide of secularism and the impact of materialistic philosophies—Fascism, Marxism, and naturalism—have had a staggering effect on the churches.

The fear of an apocalyptic end to civilization, occasioned by the development of ever more powerful instruments of destruction, has accelerated among the leaders of many religions the desire for concerted effort toward peace and human welfare. Jews, Moslems, Buddhists, Vedantists, Christians, and others, are engaged in a reëxamination of their respective positions. While preserving the claims of their own faiths, they seek to draw from their basic differences a measure of harmony and good will.

A. *Nontheistic Systems*

As distinguished from the theistic religions, which inculcate belief in the existence of one God, the nontheistic religions lay major stress upon some other aspect of worship. Though in some respects similar, each nontheistic religion puts forward its own integrating idea.

1. An ethnocentric nationalist emphasis inspires Shinto. Known for its devotion to the emperor and worship of the legendary imperial ancestress, Amaterasu Omikami, this system is reminiscent of ancient theocracies. In its claim to the possession of a manifest destiny, and other respects, Shinto bears some resemblance to theistic religions, though it lacks their emphasis on integrity, the idea of the holy, and the universal mission.

2. An eclectic genius may be said to typify Hinduism, which is tolerant of all creeds or none, all theologies or no theology at all. Dharma (religious law and wisdom), karma (the law of causality based on deed), the caste system, negation of individuality, and belief in transmigration, are elements in this rich heritage, which to many thinkers must seem nonetheless confused, purposeless, and empty of a positive word on human destiny.

3. A socio-ethical principle prevails in Confucianism. Blending the ancient ancestor-worship of the Chinese with the wisdom of the classics and the sages, especially Confucius, this system is primarily concerned with the civic, temporal and purely ethical sides of existence. The main problems are human relations, the family, and the sources of constitutional government.

4. A mystical strain runs through Taoism, a belief that the good life is one which conforms with the Tao, the way of nature; a somewhat deistical naturalism makes for spontaneity and prescribes willing obedience to the laws of the universe as a sacred duty.

5. Attainment of bliss through self-mortification and the elimination of craving and desire is at the bottom of Buddhism. There are many variations on this central theme, however. Pessimistic as regards individual destiny, Buddhism exalts the whole, that is, the universe. Though practically extinct in India, its cradle, Buddhism is widespread in the Far East where, wedded to other cultural traditions, it developed its protean universality and became in reality a family of religions instead of just one.

B. *Theism*

Although theism is usually related to the Near East and to the Semitic religious genius in particular, in simple form it is encountered at almost all human levels. The three classical forms of theism,

Hebraic, Islamic, and Christian, stem from the revelation and ethical monotheism of the Old Testament. Large divergences, however, divide these three traditions from each other.

1. The Hebrew religion is grounded in the faith that the God of Abraham, Isaac and Jacob is a righteous God and that He elected Israel as His own people and made them a light unto the nations. The total picture of Israel's sufferings, through Egyptian captivity, Babylonian exile, and worldwide dispersion, deepened the faith of the Jews in their destiny as a chosen people, a kingdom of priests, and a holy nation.

2. Islam may be regarded as a repercussion from Judaeo-Christianity. The original Torah and Gospel are revered as holy books, though not in the form in which they now exist. The Virgin Birth and the Second Coming of Christ are upheld in the Koran, but not the Incarnation and the Resurrection, nor the Trinity. Mohammed stands, in Moslem belief, at the close of the prophetic line, the seal of prophecy and messenger of Allah. Without being in any way responsible for its content, Mohammed brought forth, as every Moslem believes, the Holy Koran, God's uncreated and eternal truth for all who heed.

3. Historically, Christianity grew out of the Hebrew tradition. It is the culmination of Biblical faith in the self-revealing God who made Himself known in Jesus Christ. Through Christ, man makes contact with the divine power "which is able to overcome not only the ambiguity in which all human life and history is involved, but also the evils of history which are due to man's abortive efforts to overcome them himself by his own resources." [23]

Thus the divine drama, beginning with creation and the incidence of sin, is climaxed in the birth, ministry, death, resurrection, and ascent of Jesus Christ, the God-man. Christians believe that in Christ are realized the desires and longings of all men across all the ages; that by His conquest of death and through the working of the Holy Spirit man walks in newness of life.

Based on the New Testament, the doctrine of the Trinity, as Christians believe, opens up the infinitude of God to human understanding. It is implicit in the redemptive purpose of the one God

[23] Reinhold Niebuhr, *Faith and History,* New York, 1949, p. 126.

who, having created man in His own image, set out to save him from sin and death.

VI. THE INNER MAKING OF RELIGION

No aspect of human experience which has left so indelible a mark on man's total endowment, as has religion, can be explained away on the basis of fear, imagination, or quest after the truth. Its nature suggests an inner constitution and meaning which thoughtful men over the ages have striven in vain to discover. It is a fundamental tenet of most believers that seeking and striving, in themselves, lead nowhere, that the truth that sets men free is other than, and apart from, all human striving. Among the approaches to the subject of religious truth that bring some measure of understanding of it are those afforded by the study of comparative religion and the examination of such concepts as grace and faith, the image of God, and the solidarity of mankind.

A. *Comparative Religion*

Cultivated though it was by the ancient Greeks and medieval Arabs, the science of comparative religion, which promises to unlock the hidden treasure of religion, has not yet come to maturity. Its preliminary task is to gather and disseminate accurate information on past and present religions. Attainment of this goal is dependent, among other conditions, on the careful marking of the line between religion and culture, between religion and the social order, and also between religion and mechanical progress.

The canons of the study of comparative religion are basically three. First, any given religion is studied objectively; it is set forth in the light of its own affirmations, dogmatics, claims, apologetics, and the ethical performance that it fosters; its philosophical implications in society are fairly treated.

Second, the comparative study of religion proceeds on the basis of a thorough grounding in history, theology, and social dynamics, to describe the radical differences between the several faiths. The proper study of these differences, which are established as a necessary step toward better understanding and sounder judgment in the field, presupposes a reverent attitude, sympathy, and appreciation. Each religion is viewed as a bridge to the truth, as an evidence of man's incurably spiritual nature.

Thus only after compliance with the first and second canons will it be possible to formulate a philosophical critique showing both the limitations and the excellences of a living religion as compared with another.

It is obvious, therefore, that a maximum of religious liberty and scientific inquiry is desired in this discipline. Yet neither freedom of conscience nor the scientific method allows an investigator to prejudge the merits of a given religion or to state in advance its superiority over another. To stigmatize a faith as sterile or inferior before it has been dispassionately considered is contrary to the true spirit of religion.

Equally invalid from the standpoint of the study of religion would be the presupposition that all religions are equally true or that their differences do not really matter. In this connection, the findings of scholarship and criticism are indispensable. The Greeks, who found the world "full of gods," were yet by the power of reason and rational thought bound to rid themselves of much superstition and mythology.

In the history of religion, the emancipation of the mind from myth is crucial, and marks the end of one era and the beginning of another. In reality, myths have not yet lost their grip; dependence on them continues in the minds of many who have seen the modern world without being part of it.

B. *Grace and Faith*

Grace and faith constitute the underpinning of religion. Transcending history and prehistory, the truth of religion finds justification in the gift of grace, and in faith the means of articulation. Release from rebirth, salvation from sin, freedom from the bonds of misery and the shackles of ignorance must in the end depend upon a miracle. No one can accomplish this miracle by himself.

Religion depends upon God for the illumination of the dark recesses of the heart and for the revelation of the truth of heaven to solitary souls. Hindu *bhakti* or devotion is an intense experience of gratitude for the gift of grace; in appreciation of the Creator's mercies, the pious Moslem turns a "slave of Allah."

St. Augustine of Hippo (354–430) [24] was constrained by his consciousness of this gift of grace to adopt an attitude of humility and contrition.

> How is it then that miserable men dare to be proud, either of their free will, before they are freed, or of their own strength, if they have been freed? ... But if they have been freed, why do they vaunt themselves as if it were by their own doing, and boast, as if they had not received?

The inward religious crisis is reached when, overwhelmed by God's gift of grace, a man like St. Paul surrenders in submission and faith, saying:

> I am crucified with Christ: nevertheless I live; yet not I, but Christ liveth in me: and the life which I now live in the flesh I live by the faith of the Son of God, who loved me and gave himself for me.[25]

Walter Lippmann [26] illustrates, in a discussion of the birth of Christianity, what happens when the gift of grace is taken seriously. He describes the old structure of the Hebrew religion, which was represented by the law and the prophets and was converted by the scribes and Pharisees into a set of rites and ceremonies, and shows that it was displaced by Christianity when Jesus set His message against the "letter" of the synagogue, and Paul proclaimed the grace of God and the riches of Christ. For the gift of grace, accepted by faith, acts like a leavening agent, making old things new; but with the weakening of faith the flame of even this dynamic concept of religion has very often flickered and finally burnt itself out.

C. *The Image of God*

A constituent of religious truth which has long agitated the minds of men is the affirmation that man was created in the image of God. Intimately related to the concept of grace and its response in faith,

---

[24] *Nicene and Post-Nicene Fathers,* ed. Philip Schaff, New Series, vol. V, New York, 1887, "On the Spirit and the Letter," ch. 52, p. 100.

[25] Galatians 2:20.

[26] *A Preface to Morals,* New York, 1929, p. 12.

this Scriptural affirmation carries great weight in the world of Christian thought and requires careful elucidation.

There is, to begin with, the underlying assumption that apart from the gift of grace, human perfectibility in itself is unthinkable. To be sure, ingenuity and enterprise, diligence and persistent effort have brought about considerable intellectual and technological progress, and no true religion could underestimate the values bestowed by modern experimentation and scientific invention. Yet the distance separating man from the attainment of perfection remains constant despite all scientific and cultural advancement.

Thomas Aquinas [27] maintained that the "image of God," as man's relation of obedience and love to God, was destroyed by the fall of man from the state of perfection. In his opinion, the "image of God" cannot be construed as part of man's original nature but rather as a supernatural gift.

The issue thus can be reduced to the argument that, conscious of his being created in the divine image, man refuses in the end to worship a God created in his own image.[28] In so transcending his own personality man begins to touch the true meaning of religion. As he sets his gaze upon what lies behind the horizon and beyond himself, the thought dawns on him that the truths of religion must be sought outside the framework of the intellect, for a creature is unwilling to worship a mere projection of his own fallible nature.

D. *Human Solidarity*

No interpretation of religion can ring true that turns man against man or fails to foster brotherhood among all men; and yet differences in men's understanding of religion often militate against the cause of human solidarity.

F. S. C. Northrop,[29] the Yale philosopher, building on profound cultural and philosophical foundations, attempted a synthesis of the thought of the East and West, religion figuring as a primary

[27] *The Summa Theologica*, tr. Fathers of the English Dominican Province, pt. I, no. 3, question 95, London, 1912, pp. 309–311.

[28] Reinhold Niebuhr, *Nature and Destiny of Man*, vol. II, New York, 1943, pp. 62–67.

[29] *The Meeting of East and West: An Inquiry Concerning World Understanding*, New York, 1946.

consideration in the treatment. Northrop's central thesis was that the Eastern religions, with their intuitive and aesthetic component of knowledge, and the Western religions, with their theoretical posited component, are both necessary for a full understanding of religion's inner meaning. Yet one flaw in this apparent oversimplification of the truth is inherent in its planned nature.

The intricate mysteries of man, matter, and God are not rendered less mysterious by the pooling of Eastern and Western insights. Religion has generally emphasized the idea that man, the finite, is incapable in himself of comprehending the Infinite, and when he seeks to know the Unknowable, philosophical categories prove inadequate. In the words of Arnold Toynbee,[30] "The prayer '*My* will be done' stands self-convicted of futility."

The contribution of religion to the unity of all human beings is made, then, not in the intellectual but in the spiritual realm. In the memorable adoration of St. Augustine: "Thou hast created us, O God, for Thyself, and restless are our souls until they find their rest in Thee." God is acknowledged not only as the ally but also as the spiritual leader of mankind.

The contribution of religion to human solidarity is inherent in its making as the sum and substance of action and reaction between the Infinite and the finite. As such, it is the holy register of every transaction between the spirit and the physical organism, the matrix of goodness, light, and life.

[30] *A Study of History,* Abridgement by D. C. Somervell, New York, 1947, p. 524.

CHAPTER II

THE CHRISTIAN STRUCTURE
OF RELIGION

THE Gospel of Jesus Christ sets in sharp focus the entire structure of the world's religions. Or, to change the metaphor, it is the apex of a triangle at whose base one corner represents Christianity, the other the remaining religions.[1] Whereas a Christian interpretation of religion will take into account the data offered by the science of religion, it cannot equate the Gospel even with the noblest monuments of the religious phenomena of history.

Christianity in essence is not a culture, nor a body of ideas. It is the Gospel. Its central theme and its clue to religion consist in the Incarnation, "The Word became flesh and dwelt among us." The transcending power is that of the creator God who in Christ offers an infallible criterion by which the religious heritage of a given people is to be evaluated. This is the criterion by which the free man's worship of Bertrand Russell, the humanism of Walter Lippmann, the naturalistic philosophy of John Dewey, the various fascisms and communisms of our era, as well as the non-Christian religions of the twentieth century are brought under judgment.[2]

But there can be no interpretation of religion in general that did not begin with some religion in particular. We are of necessity thrown back upon the study of the several religions, one by one, and of Christianity's core, the main thesis being that God revealed Himself in nature; for in the light of the Gospel, a general revelation is manifest, despite many disqualifying features, in almost all the religions of mankind.

[1] Heinrich Frick, *The Gospel, Christianity and Other Religions,* tr. James Haire, Oxford, 1938, pp. 46–47.
[2] Nicol Macnicol, *Is Christianity Unique? A Comparative Study of the Religions,* London, 1935, pp. 26–142.

These religions have failed to conform with the truth already disclosed to them. They evolved, instead, their own ways of obscuring the eternal verities and set up standards which throttled true religion. Involved in our task are three distinct categories which will help determine the Christian structure of religion. First, the definition of religion and an analysis of its perversions in history. Second, the essence of general revelation and a brief recapitulation of the degrading factors which appear in the several great religions. Third, the incomparable validity of the Gospel in relation to the non-Christian religions and in relation to Christianity. We must now examine each of these categories.

I. Religion and Its Perversions

Religion may be defined, according to the Christian understanding of it, as the response of man to the holy and righteous call of the Eternal. Rudolf Otto formulated in *The Idea of the Holy,* and developed in later studies, a concept of religious autonomy which constitutes an original and enduring contribution to modern theology.[3] That the science of religion records a variety of definitions of religion is to be explained on the grounds that the response of men to the call of the Eternal is not a constant, but a variant. In addition to spiritual blindness, there are two forms of perversions which become effective in primitivism and anthropocentrism. In the wake of these perversions, a variety of definitions arose.

Further complications arise when students of the science of religion formulate their definitions in the light of whatever they deem to be the likely origin of man's religions. Their opinions bear the imprint of their varied fields of specialization and are naturally conditioned by the particular modes of their inquiries, as well as by their professional bias.

Where the Eternal is lost sight of and a religion emerges which knows not His name, is it still possible to think of a basic, perennial, and ultimate origin of religion derived from the call of God? Yes, for as we shall presently see, there is evoked in man a certain homesickness for the Divine which, no matter how hideous the distortion

[3] Robert F. Davidson, *Rudolf Otto's Interpretation of Religion,* Princeton, 1947, pp. 13, 14.

of religion may be, persists in the form of a longing for the Father of our spirits who revealed Himself in nature.

A. *Primitivism*

As it is here used, primitivism means the religion of primitives. In its past and present expression, primitivism is a prelogical, tribalistic, and often animistic response to the call of the Eternal. Despite its crudity, debasement and simplicity, primitivism provides a striking evidence of general revelation. It ought to be remembered that its perversions are to be observed not only among primitive peoples, but also within the confines of the advanced religions.

Primitivism becomes a perversion when its righteous faith suffers decadence. The symptoms of decadence may consist in peculiar conceptions of the spirit world, pagan priesthoods and shamanism, ancestor-worship, cannibalism, human sacrifice, and secret orders. A common feature of this perversion is animism, that is, the appeal to the forces of nature and the spirits which are ostensibly resident in them. In the pre-animistic phase, the religious phenomenon known as mana appears, its potent energizing fluid being attributed to persons and objects. Molded by animistic beliefs, rituals, sacrifice, and magic, the response of the primitive to the call of the Eternal is stunted.

A plausible explanation of this decadence rests on the assumption that the abstract conception of God is beyond the grasp of primitive mentality. In order to bridge the gap between the yearning of his soul for the High God and the concept of the Infinite, the primitive turns to symbols, metaphors, parables, and anthropomorphic devices. Soon he finds himself alienated from the holy and compassionate Lord by a world of evil spirits, witchcraft, and sorcery. Alongside these, however, a deeper spiritual consciousness is evident in the veneration, among many primitive peoples, of an originator God, a Supreme Being.

The pioneer effort of Father Wilhelm Schmidt [4] and his associates in the field of primitive monotheism, represents a valiant

[4] See especially *The Origin and Growth of Religion,* tr. H. J. Rose, London, 1931; *Primitive Revelation,* St. Louis, Mo., 1939.

attempt on the part of a Roman Catholic scholar, hitherto un-
matched in Protestant quarters, to take the offensive in the study of
primitive religion on a purely scientific level. The interpretation of
Christianity in relation to the non-Christian religions, the nature of
primitive religions, the origin of religion, as well as the very possibility of a universal comprehension of religion among primitive
peoples are issues involved in this important phase of the science of
religion.

To the credit of primitivism is its testimony to the unity of mankind and the general revelation of God. Closely affiliated with the
tribal state of existence, it preserved religion within the family and
as a sacred human bond. Around the hearth and altar, arose the
means of all human beliefs and the common tie of all early societies.
The differences which separate the various groupings of mankind
seem to inhere in distinctions of culture and environment. More
apparent than real, they depend on variations in the poetic impulse
of races and the degree of abasement of the human spirit. The true
religious aspect of primitivism points to the fundamental unity of
the human family.

Stripped of all its appendages of myth, superstition, and magic,
primitivism shows the marks of general revelation. G. K. Chesterton's essay, "The Wind and the Trees," depicts a violent wind which
causes the trees to wave like a huge fan. "Nothing could be more
human," says Chesterton, "than the belief that it is the trees that
make the wind, and this is the belief of about ninety-nine out of a
hundred of the philosophers, reformers, sociologists, and politicians
of the great age in which we live." But this is not true of the
primitive who is quite convinced that the visible effects are produced by unseen forces, and that the material world is acted upon
by the spiritual.[5]

B. *Anthropocentrism*

The perversion of religion also stems from anthropocentrism, the
general assumption that man is the only center of importance in the
world and that he is worthy of being made the ultimate object of
thought and striving.

[5] R. R. Young, "Christianity, Secularism and Tribal Religion," *The Triumph of God,* Max Warren, ed., London, 1948, pp. 306–324.

There is, of course, a proper sense in which man may be regarded as of central importance. As an individual, he possesses freedom of will and action under God who endows him with power over nature. As a creature of destiny, man is capable of contemplating eternity. And as an object of divine affection and grace, he is sought after by God who determines to redeem him from sin and restore him to everlasting knowledge of God and communion with the heavenly Father. "For ye know the grace of our Lord Jesus Christ, that, though he was rich, yet for your sakes he became poor, that ye through his poverty might become rich." [6]

But when this order in the redemptive purpose of God is reversed in a manner to make man, rather than God, the prime actor on the stage of history, the perversion of religion immediately follows. The sovereign Lord is then relegated to the periphery of man's existence, and man becomes the measure of all things, the chief arbiter of ends. In that case, it may be said that anthropocentrism comes to assume the menacing proportions of an abomination which distorts religion and deprives man of general revelation.

This anthropocentric evil often operates in secrecy, behind the curtain of culture and in the name of humanism, rationalism, and naturalism. It inevitably leads to the enthronement of man and the exaltation of his talents, attainments, discoveries and inventions. Held in honor above the glory of the Eternal, man by his very enthronement will eventually suffer the loss of his true manhood—the divine image—sink into the dark abyss of estrangement from God, and surrender to carnal cravings.

Common to both East and West, because it is inherent in the basic human tragedy, this typical perversion is almost universal. It lifts its head not only in the myths and legends bequeathed by the various ethnic traditions of Europe and Asia, Africa, and the Americas, but more particularly in the idealization of race, history, reason, culture, and human welfare as ultimate objects of devotion.

In more recent decades, many of these constituents of civilization were grouped under a virtual ethnocentrism, the centrality of one's race, nation, and cultural heritage, and commanded the admiration and devotion of great peoples. Ethnocentrism offered what was

[6] 2 Cor. 8:9.

hailed as a lofty and perfectly legitimate plane for the pursuit of ideological warfare and armed conflict. Man's revolutionary will, backed by military science and national pride, meant the restriction of his religious growth.

The history of Japan, as a case in point, leaves little doubt that Shinto [7] in its ethnocentric and militant expression, marred the culture of a highly gifted people. As Nazism and Fascism brought chaos to Europe and confusion to Western Christianity, likewise Japan's worship of itself ushered in incalculable grief and frustration to the Japanese and spiritual futility to the Far East.

The cult of the sword, which has already made the twentieth century the bloodiest in history, has been pressed into the service of ethnocentrism. This was part of a grand strategy designed to strangle religion and eliminate its strongholds. Within this domain the perversion of religion proceeded apace, attaining new levels in Marxist materialism. "Atheism is a natural and inseparable part of Marxism, of the theory and practice of scientific socialism. In accordance with their fundamental philosophical outlook, Marx and Engels always called themselves materialists." [8]

In the guise of their peculiar brand of messianism, the Communists threatened, under an anthropocentrism of their own, to brutalize both Eastern and Western man. Much of the strength of Communism was derived from the fact that it was a faith with a dogmatic system rooted in the teaching and character of Karl Marx. As such, Communism meets its only real rival in the Christian faith.[9]

Marxist materialism achieves the perversion of religion and the corruption of man wherever its seven leading affirmations are made effective. These affirmations, together with their Christian repudiations, are:

(1) That ultimate reality is matter. The truth is that besides matter, and utterly irreducible to it, there is an independent and superior reality, namely, mind and spirit.

(2) That the proper attributes of reality are strife and change. The truth is that a stable order of existence, on which the mind can surely depend, is available.

[7] D. C. Holtom, *Modern Japan and Shinto Nationalism,* Chicago, 1943.

[8] V. I. Lenin, *Religion,* New York, 1933, Introduction, p. 3.

[9] H. Ingli James, *Communism and Christian Faith,* London, 1950.

(3) That there is no objective and eternal truth. Christians know, however, that such a truth exists in revelation.

(4) That only the immanent and temporal exist. The truth is that there is a whole dimension of transcendent norms and precepts fully open to the mind, heart, and soul.

(5) That there is no God. The truth is that there is a God, our gracious Father, Maker of heaven and earth, the God and Father of our Lord Jesus Christ.

(6) That man may attain perfectibility through his own self-sufficient efforts. The truth is that man's disorder, because of original sin, can only be healed by the Redeemer.

(7) That the human person is for the sake of society. The truth is that society is for the human person whose chief end is to glorify God and worship Him forever.[10]

Despite the gigantic political and social upheavals of our era, the real contemporary crisis centers in the perversion of religion at the hands of certain intellectual leaders and secularizing statesmen. Their commitment to anthropocentric goals and ideals discourages the proper response of men and nations to the call of the Eternal and reduces the cathartic effectiveness of religion in a free society.

But history warns against despair since these restrictions on religion are not final. For military power, conquest, empires, as well as the entire scope of political theory and practice, do not constitute the full meaning of history. The great Palestinian scholar and church historian, Eusebius (*ca.* A.D. 260-*ca.* 339),[11] contemporary of Constantine and admirer of his action in recognizing Christianity (A.D. 312), wrote that the true makers of history are those who fight for the peace of the soul:

Other writers of historical works have confined themselves to the written tradition of victories in wars, of triumphs over enemies, of the exploits of generals and the valour of soldiers, men stained with blood and with countless murders for the sake of children and country and other possessions; but it is wars most peaceful, waged for the

[10] Cf. Charles Malik, "War and Peace," *United Nations Press Release,* New York, PM/1598, November 23, 1949, pp. 15–16.

[11] *The Ecclesiastical History,* tr. Kirsopp Lake, London, 1926, vol. I, pp. 405–406; cf. George Sarton, *The History of Science and the New Humanism,* Cambridge, Mass., 1937, pp. 170–171.

very peace of the soul, and men who therein have been valiant for truth rather than for country, and for piety rather than for their dear ones, that our record of those who order their lives according to God will inscribe on everlasting monuments: it is the struggles of the athletes of piety and their valour which braved so much, trophies won from demons and victories against unseen adversaries, and the crowns at the end of all, that it will proclaim for everlasting remembrance.

The discontinuities that separate holy history from the secular leave no doubt that in limiting its perspective to the latter, anthropocentrism fails to produce an adequate view of ultimate reality.

For our purpose two propositions may be inferred from the vast sweep of history. First, if primitivism in its distortions jeopardized religion by an appeal to physical objects and by a fear-inspired program of appeasing and coercing the spirit world, likewise the appeal of modern man to culture, race, and human security as ultimates constitutes defection from his divine origin and is calculated to submerge him in the ignorance of God. Second, if in the great religions of antiquity there were nature deities, animal forms, and human figures which served as idols in a manner prejudicial to the true knowledge of the Eternal, it is also true that the anthropocentric and ethnocentric themes and predilections of the modern world constitute an idolatry which is inimical to religion.

II. GENERAL REVELATION AND ITS MISREPRESENTATION

Religion, then, is the response of man to the holy and righteous call of God. If so, general revelation may be defined as precisely that holy and righteous call of the Eternal which discloses His truth and is received through the portals of reason, intuition, conscience and faith.

That the faithful God who perfected man's salvation in Jesus Christ had not left Himself without a witness [12] was Paul's way of stating the reality of general revelation. The first eleven chapters of the Book of Genesis, depicting the prehistoric and primitive epochs, do not support the notion that prior to the covenant between God and Israel all mankind was lost in iniquity without any knowledge of God. Abel, son of Adam, was a righteous man. In subsequent

[12] Acts 14:17.

generations, when apostasy became rife, righteous men like Noah and Enoch were still to be found. The classic example of a non-Hebraic monotheist acclaimed in the Bible is the figure of Melchizedek, whose priestly order is hailed in the Epistle to the Hebrews as of supernatural inception.

Specifically what the Greeks and with them all who had access to general revelation lacked, Paul set forth on Mars Hill.[13] For all their syllogism, philosophy, art, science, and tragedy, the Greeks did not understand that the Word must become flesh. Without this clue to revelation, their religion tended to atrophy, wasting away in insidious primitivism and anthropocentrism.

In the case of primitive peoples, the degradation of religion amounted to a falsified response to general revelation. In the advanced religions of antiquity and the modern world the misrepresentation of religion followed two patterns: (A) The disregard of general revelation and the adoption of a substitute therefor; (B) Acquiescence in revelation, general and special, but its forfeiture through the intrusion of some anthropocentric standard.

A. *Disregard of General Revelation*

The disregard of general revelation is clearly reflected in Hinduism, Confucianism, and Buddhism. In each of these, a substitute for general revelation occurs. Taken respectively, the three substitutes are: (a) reflective genius, training in wisdom, and practice of the occult (Hinduism); (b) humanism and social equilibrium (Confucianism); (c) psychological ethics and protean universality (Buddhism).

1. *Hinduism.* The general revelation of God, evident in the ascetic ideal, faith, and devotion of Hinduism, is disregarded by undue emphasis on the discipline of the mind, works, training in wisdom, and practice of the occult.

The whole religious pattern of Hinduism is climaxed in the philosophy known as Vedanta, the end of knowledge. A monism systematized by the eighth-century commentator Shankara, Vedanta teaches the need for achieving unity between the individual self and Brahman, the universal, impersonal Oversoul. This is the com-

---

[13] Acts 17:16–34.

mon religious basis of Hindu contemplation. Instead of faith in the self-revealing God, Hinduism adopts a man-made substitute which tends to reduce man to a nonentity.

Representing an unbroken continuity from the Stone Age to the twentieth century, Hinduism took form in the last pre-Christian centuries. This is the Hinduism of the Vedic texts, a polymorphism —a variety of forms and characteristics—of infinite capacity to assume new shapes and to adopt contradictory meanings. It blossomed in Vedanta and a social system of caste. The determining factor of Hindu piety—birth and social conduct—seems to relegate the intrinsic worth of man, as a child of God, to the limbo of pessimism.

But the subconscious Hinduism of the masses, ninety per cent of the 350 million Hindu people, knows little of the technical literature and the reflective disciplines of India. Theirs is a degraded primitivism which but vaguely apprehends the theistic and incarnate Krishna of the Bhagavadgita, the so-called New Testament of Hinduism. Fakirs, illiterates, and mystics have made India primarily the land of animal-faced, octopus-limbed gods and goddesses. The primitive cults form a world of fantasies, impulses, and powerful emotions to which even a Mahatma Gandhi had to bow in his bid for the soul of India.[14]

In substituting reflective discipline and social function for simple faith in God, Hinduism came very close to the denial of man, his destiny and dignity. The masses, hungry for the living God, turned to degraded primitivism with its shabby aberrations.[15]

2. *Confucianism.* China's substitute for general revelation is a humanism suffused with the ideals of social equilibrium. China matured a worldly system of ethics and statecraft steeped in the worship of ancestors and filial piety. The very name of Shangti, Lord of Heaven, however, is a reminder of general revelation which in the case of the Chinese was emptied of meaning by an endemic obsession with human relations and the everyday problems of the community. What China gained in the realm of political integration she forfeited in the realm of the spirit.

[14] E. Stanley Jones, *Mahatma Gandhi, An Interpretation,* New York, 1948.
[15] On the relations between Christianity and Hinduism today, Sabapathy Kulandran, *The Message and the Silence of the American Pulpit,* Boston, 1949, pp. 146–156.

The basis of China's culture is the philosophy of Confucius (551–479 B.C.) and his followers, consisting in filial piety, benevolence, justice, propriety, and belief in the original goodness of man. The total impact of Confucianism on China was to produce a system of morality, a religion of humanism, naturalness, and social balance.[16]

The plain fact is that Confucius was neither a prophet nor a mystic. The sixth-century Laotzu, traditionally recognized as founder of Taoism and an elder contemporary of Confucius, was the liberal expounder of China's religious heritage. Moti (fifth and fourth century B.C.) promoted the ultra-conservative natural polytheism of China. But Confucius himself followed a narrow path between these two extremes.

Confucianism's disregard of general revelation is, therefore, well attested. Confucius refused to discuss spirits, the supernatural, and immortality. He confined himself instead to human affairs and the art of living. He encouraged, nevertheless, the worship of Heaven and ancestors as a course conducive to morality and social stability. The ultimate objective was keyed to central harmony, adjustment, and a general give-and-take in personal, national, and universal relations. A number of Chinese scholars, of whom Mencius (*ca.* 371-*ca.* 289 B.C.) was a forerunner, explained, augmented, and interpreted the original humanism of their master. There was never a question, however, but that these sages founded their teaching on the way of the gods.

Despite the lofty conceptions of Confucius, the system which he bequeathed was a chief ally of bureaucracy. It gradually became a composite of anthropocentric presuppositions mingled with superstition and idolatry. Today, Confucianism ranks numerically as first among the non-Christian religions, claiming the adherence of more than 370 millions in China alone. The Chinese continue to be Confucianists, with a leaning towards Taoism and Buddhism. Yet this religio-ethical heritage of China is in full dissolution, the abetment of humanism and naturalism by the Communists notwithstanding. Obscured by the cult of nature, ancestor-worship, archaic tradition,

---

[16] Francis C. M. Wei, *The Spirit of Chinese Culture,* New York, 1947, pp. 69–94.

and the materialist bent of the people, the Lord of Heaven, Shangti, is all but lost to the Chinese masses as he is lost to the materialists and intellectuals.

3. *Buddhism.* The substitute for general revelation which Buddhism offers is a psychological ethics which inculcates the annihilation of all desire, both good and evil, leaving man without that spiritual dynamic which comes from God and which makes clear the meaning of personality. By means of easy compromises, peculiar to its genius of protean universality, Buddhism won over many local cults. With this in mind, the far from simple history of Buddhism may be clearly understood.[17]

A protest against, and an offshoot from, Hinduism, the religion of the Buddha attained its ascendancy in the Far East. Practically extinct in India, its cradle, it assimilated itself to the major cultures of East Asia, such as those of China, Japan, Tibet, Thailand and Ceylon where, despite its decadence, Buddhism continues to exert considerable social and political influence.

Gotama the Buddha (563–483 B.C.), the founder, abandoned his aristocratic Hindu caste and became an ascetic. He organized early Buddhism with its order of wandering monks. Release from suffering and mortality was the object of his psychological ethics. It consisted in a purported release from misery, achieved by the renunciation of desire and the attainment of nirvana, a state of self-extinction. Nothingness and void loom large at the heart of Buddhism's ideal bliss.

The disregard of general revelation is obvious. Into the foreground of his teaching, the Buddha put no thought about the Divine and man's relationship to Him. Nor did he claim any revelation from above. He did not speak as a prophet but as a seer who had discovered the truth about the nature of human misery and the means of escape. He neither prayed nor taught his followers to pray. Following his death, the order which he instituted began to change. Hinayana (small vehicle) Buddhism, close to the original precepts of the Buddha, spread in Ceylon, Burma, Siam, and Cam-

[17] For an illuminating exposition of Buddhism, see A. K. Reischauer, *Great Religions of the Modern World,* Edward J. Jurji, ed., Princeton, 1947, pp. 90–140.

bodia, a nontheistic and monastic cult. The verities of Buddhism, such as forgiveness, love, and renunciation of the world, are evidences of a general revelation which is marred by the disregard of their origin in God.

The overwhelming majority of the Buddhists belong to the family of sects collectively known as Mahayana (great vehicle). By the protean quality of their religion, the adherents of this branch multiplied through central, eastern, and southeastern Asia. Within the confines of Mahayana, the Buddha was deified and an elaborate pantheon was developed. The tendency toward theism, detectable in Mahayana, is an evidence of rudimentary faith in God. But it never was more than a sideshow. Theistic thought and worship were thwarted by the strictly agnostic nature of Buddhist metaphysics. The speculation of Buddhist teachers is shot through with skepticism. All truth is conceived as relative and, before it was mediated to finite human understanding, it often had to pass through contradictory processes of accommodation.

B. *Acquiescence in but Forfeiture of Revelation*

Acquiescence in revelation, general and special, but its forfeiture through the intrusion of an anthropocentric standard of interpretation is evident in two great religions, Judaism and Islam.

1. *Judaism.* Judaism begins on a high level, accepting the call of the Eternal and the choice of Israel as a blessing to the nations. Historical Judaism demonstrates, however, the intrusion of an anthropocentric standard for the interpretation of religion. Thus, the vision of God, mediated for the benefit of mankind through the revealed Book, observance of the Law, and the historical experience of a chosen people assume humanistic and rationalized meaning. Each of the modern expressions of Judaism—Orthodox, Reform, and Conservative—has its special emphasis. Orthodoxy is greatly concerned with the Torah, Reform with the vision of God, and the Conservatives with Israel.

The essence of Judaism may be illustrated from the life of the Apostle Paul. His conversion on the road to Damascus made him a new man. This newness of life, consisting in allegiance to Jesus Christ, cannot be explained completely in terms of the Torah and the noblest insights of Pharisaism. In fact, the history of religion demonstrates that devotion to a Person creates a religious consciousness and vitality which transcend the nature of any faith steeped in devotion to doctrine, tradition, or a national experience.

Precisely at this point comes the parting of the road between the Gospel and Judaism. Whereas the writings of the Rabbis, the Talmud, and the Mishna instilled devotion to a superb teaching, the New Testament brought sinful man into an encounter with a Saviour. Judaism brought man to a Book, a Law, a tradition, all marked by acquiescence in revelation and almost simultaneously by the intrusion of an anthropocentric interpretation. In searching the depths of his religion, the Jew, therefore, found himself, his people, and his nation. In following Jesus Christ, the Revealer and Redeemer, the Christian found the living God. Personal devotion to Jesus Christ, thus, replaced the study of the Torah as the central reality of existence and the determining factor in receiving God's revelation.

2. *Islam.* Islam's loss of revelation may be attributed to a nonredemptive view of Allah's sovereignty, the Koran's finality, the prophetic role of Mohammed, and the ultimacy of theocracy. The religion of some 300 million inhabitants of the world, Islam ostensibly throve as the embodiment of revelation, interpreted in the light of Biblical truth and fashioned in keeping with the celestial revelation delivered to Mohammed (*ca.* A.D. 571–632).

The science of religion, however, recognizes Islam as a repercussion from Judeo-Christianity, a defection from revelation, and a peculiar blend of anthropocentric and spiritual elements. The history of Islam has been rightly described as that of an Arab religion in a non-Arab world.

In defiance of textual criticism, the Koran is conceived to be the uncreated word of God, and the Bible is scorned as a falsification of what God originally revealed to Israel and the Church. Whereas Jesus is recognized in the Koran, his Godmanhood and Resurrection are dismissed. Mohammed emerges not only as the chief exemplar of perfection but as the main architect of religion.[18]

Actually, Mohammed replaces Jesus Christ as the supernatural

[18] Samuel M. Zwemer, *The Moslem Christ,* New York, 1912, pp. 155–173.

channel of grace and of communication with God. Although orthodox Islamic theology dwells laboriously on the theme that the
Prophet was a mere man, popular fancy and mystical piety have
found in him their refuge and the object of their contemplation. For
all who are familiar with the details of Mohammed's biography, the
unwholesome outcome of this idolization evokes hardly any surprise.

The real threat to the true Islamic heritage stems in the twentieth
century from the archaic emphasis on the theocratic order in the
guise of unmistakable nationalism. Thus the temporal and political
outlook of Islamic peoples is made a substitute for the worship of
the sovereign God. Among the fundamentalist Moslems of Arabia,
Pakistan, and Egypt, the sovereignty of Allah is construed as a
theological determinism. As such it blocks all sound progress and
marks the loss of revelation in the abyss of fatalism.[19]

III. THE INCOMPARABLE GOSPEL

That the Gospel is the sure guarantee of Christianity's superiority
over all other religions is neither a discovery of Christian minds nor
a purely intellectual deduction. It is a God-given power unto salvation which in order to be comprehended must be received in faith,
and in order to be appreciated must be tried on the anvil of piety and
worthy living. In his own inimitable way, Albert Schweitzer [20]
wrote:

There are two kinds of naïveté: one which is not yet aware of all
the problems and has not yet knocked at all the doors of knowledge;
and another, a higher kind, which is the result of philosophy having
looked into all problems, having sought counsel in all the spheres of
knowledge, and then having come to see that we cannot explain anything but have to follow convictions whose inherent value appeals to
us in an irresistible way. Compared with the logical religions of the
East, the Gospel of Jesus is illogical. It presupposes a God who is an
ethical Personality, and who is, therefore, so to speak, outside the
world. . . . It must (also) hold fast the belief that God is the sum-
total of the forces working in the world—that all that is, is in God. . . .
Again and again, in the course of the centuries, Christianity has sought

[19] Cf. H. A. R. Gibb, *Mohammedanism: A Historical Survey,* Oxford, 1949,
pp. 165–191; also his *Modern Trends in Islam,* Chicago, 1947, a critique of
Islam's modernism.

[20] *Christianity and the Religions of the World,* London, 1923, pp. 74–75, 84.

to harmonize the philosophical and the ethical conceptions of God, but it has never succeeded. . . . Christianity must, clearly and definitely, put before men the necessity of a choice between logical religion and ethical religion, and it must insist on the fact that the ethical is the highest type of spirituality, and that it alone is living spirituality. Thus Christianity shows itself as the religion which, penetrating and transcending all knowledge, reaches forward to the ethical living God, who cannot be found through contemplation of the world, but reveals himself in man only. And it is thus that Christianity speaks with all the authority of its inherent truth.

Whether in the interpretation of the science of religion, in the evangelistic and missionary outreach of the Church, or in the comparative religious encounter between Christian and non-Christian, it is the Gospel of Jesus Christ that constantly renews the strength of Christianity and empowers it to triumph over sin and unbelief.

What in particular does this Gospel achieve to merit the attribute incomparable? It achieves two things which are of momentous significance to the Christian structure of religion. First, as regards the non-Christian religions, the Gospel summons their adherents to the true meaning of general revelation and its corroboration in the Person of Jesus Christ. Second, as regards Christianity itself, it quickens the believer's faith that only as the Gospel is preached among non-Christians unto the ends of the earth will the light of the knowledge of the glory of God in the face of Jesus Christ shine out of the world's darkness.

A. *The Gospel and the Non-Christian Religions*

That a general revelation is manifest in the non-Christian religions forms part of the Gospel proclamation (kerygma). The Gospel is the good tidings of what God wrought in His Son in order to save sinners. The unique character of Christianity inheres in God's love made known in Christ who sums up in Himself all that God said and did in nature and Scripture as well as in the sacred story of His people and the witness of those who know His name.

To non-Christians of diverse persuasions, the Gospel brings a confirmation of general revelation, an extraordinary reconciliation with God, and sanctification. For those in the grip of degraded primitivism, the Divine Being is made known in personal devotion to the Redeemer who displaces the degradation of art and magic. The spiritual opportunity which the Gospel offers the devotees of the several ethnic religions springs from the vindication in Christ of the inner cry of the soul, the primary affirmation of general revelation, namely, that God is close to each one of us, for it is in Him that we live and move and have our being.

Those who accept the truth of revelation only to forfeit its essence are likewise taught by the Gospel. Christ enters their lives as the solitary clue to religion, displacing all standards which conjure up goodness, reason, and nation, as absolutes. What God has done of old and His manifest will behind all faiths form the common ground between Christianity and all other religions. But there is a point at which this common ground breaks down.

It is the non-Christian religions themselves which actually are to be held responsible for this break. Invariably, they take the accidental which cannot be made commensurate with Providence and build it up into a concept of fate. This fate in which the dread of the non-Christian has its object, is, of course, nothing.

The pagan cannot come into relation with fate, for one instant it is necessity, the next instant it is chance. Nearer to fate than this, the pagan cannot come. The attempt paganism made was penetrating enough to cast a new light upon it. He who was to explain fate must be just as ambiguous as fate is. And this too the *oracle* was. But in turn, the oracle might mean exactly the opposite. So the relation of the pagan to the oracle is again dread. In this fact lies the profound and inexplicable tragedy of paganism. . . . The concept of guilt and sin does not in the deepest sense emerge in paganism. If it had emerged, paganism would have foundered upon the contradiction that one might become guilty of fate. This indeed is the supreme contradiction, and in this contradiction Christianity breaks forth.[21]

Christianity operates in two ways. It proves the dread of fate to be a dread of nothing; it shows that the dread of guilt is well-founded and that freedom from dread is vouchsafed through repentance and the power of the Saviour to renew life.

Hence the discontinuity of the Gospel with all other forms of piety

[21] Søren Kierkegaard, *The Concept of Dread,* tr. Walter Lowrie, Princeton, 1944, p. 87.

and religion is self-evident. The Gospel of Jesus Christ, involving a Christ-centered faith in God the Father, victory over sin, and fellowship with the risen Lord who gives life and immortality, requires a complete break with all other forms of religion.

B. *The Gospel and Christianity*

Recognition of the science of religion as a prerequisite for the interpretation of Christianity in the modern world is vital to the understanding of the superiority of the Gospel. But even as general revelation is meaningless apart from the Gospel, so too is a Christianity which fails to take the Gospel as everlasting guide.

This failure has marred the works of eminent scholars who penetrated the depths of man's religions but through indifference to the Gospel of peace missed the heart of the science of religion. Nor can Christianity long live by the Gospel and its proclamation without constant examination of the affirmations, literature, ideals, religious thought and practice current among the hundreds of millions of non-Christians.

Henry Drummond (1851–1897), the Scottish clergyman, scientist, and evangelist, held that the scientific principle of continuity extended from the physical world to the spiritual. His essay, "The Relation of the Will of God to Sanctification," [22] contains these Scriptural references:

This is the will of God even your sanctification (I Thess. 4:3). As He which hath called you is holy, so be ye holy in all manner of conversation; because it is written, "Be ye holy, for I am holy" (I Pet. 1:15, 16). Lo, I come to do thy will, O God. . . . By the which will we are sanctified through the offering of the body of Jesus Christ once for all (Heb. 10:9, 10).

But the voice of God, saying to us: "Be ye holy, for I am holy," is something more than the voice of literature, poetry, music, and drama. It is the will of God manifesting His nature in the Incarnation.

What the Incarnation means for humanity is beyond computation. In the lands where the non-Christian religions prevail, we can see far more clearly than can be seen in a Christian country, the extent

[22] *The Greatest Thing in the World,* London, n.d., p. 297.

to which human nature is diseased. Yet Christ became man to under-take and accomplish the whole cure, the healing and the renewal of the race. He became man to do far more than repair the ravages caused by sin. He came to pour into the race abundance of life, the life that fallen man needs in order to renew his strength like the eagle.

In his Epistle to the Romans,[23] Paul may be said to sum up the teaching of the New Testament on this subject, and his watchword is "wherein sin abounded, grace did abound more exceedingly." The Incarnation reveals the capacity and original destiny of human nature. It declares that man, made in the divine image, was meant to have a life of direct communion with God. Thus God accomplishes the atonement of man, that is, the bringing together of the whole fallen creature to be at one with Himself in and through the Incarnate Lord.[24]

The Christian structure of religion is upheld by the firm belief that if the Church is not to become a mere temple made with hands, and therefore unfit as a tabernacle of the Holy Spirit, the mystery of the Gospel must remain an ever-present challenge to faith. Great faith in the hearts of Christians will, by the sheer force of their testimony, spread the truth of God. For the One, whom by a heavenly voice God called His Son with whom He was well pleased, instructed His disciples that repentance and the remission of sins should be preached unto all nations.

[23] 5 :12–21.
[24] E. L. Strong, *Lectures on the Incarnation of God,* London, 1920, pp. 72–78.

CHAPTER III

THE RELIGIONS OF PRIMITIVES

Perhaps it is sanguine and odd to refer to the message of primitive religions. Yet these religions are not abstractions, nor are they to be properly understood along abstract lines. They actually bear the imprint of objectivity and concreteness. For primitive man, religion was bound to employ physical forms and symbols, born out of a deep desire to translate the spiritual realities of worship into tangible, visible results. The core of its message was the consecration of life and the stimulation of the will to action.[1]

The worship of the central Australians, for instance, exhibits a phenomenon known as *churinga,* a closely guarded tablet whose rectilinear and curvilinear designs represented the soul. The tablet exercised a mystic influence upon the native mind of the worshiper, imparting confidence in battle and penetrating insight in the crucial moments of life. This inwardness which typifies primitive cults is further verified by our knowledge of the primitive whether in the historic or prehistoric stages of his religion.

Primitive religion had for its focus a belief in the supernatural, vindicated through an appeal to the natural forces of the spirits which allegedly dwelt in them. Under the general heading of animism, this phase of early religion witnessed the emergence of priests, shamans, and necromancers, who often, through the wizardry of their craft, offered their devotees the prospects of healing, divination, and protection from evil powers. Among the Crow Indians, visions were ascribed to the mediators between the worshiper and the divine.

Contributing to the religious process thus set in motion, was the belief in mana, dating to preanimistic days. Ritual, sacrifice, exorcism, and prayer were, at a very early stage, manifest in the primitive religions. The use of spells, amulets, and incantations

[1] R. R. Marett, "Religion," *Encyclopaedia Britannica,* 14th ed., New York, 1929, p. 105.

followed. Tabus, and other restrictions on behavior, militated against contact with certain objects. But alongside such distortions of religion, there was a deeper consciousness frequently implicit in the veneration of an originator god.

The fundamentals of primitive religion include an assurance of the sovereignty, eternity, and justice of the creator; an awakened faith in the existence of a deathless soul and a hereafter; the acknowledgment of sin, suggested by the innumerable proscriptions and commandments; a vivid memory of the ideals of morality, chivalry, and honor; and a living consciousness of the validity of service, sacrifice, unity, and love.

Through alliances with other clans, the family fortified itself and extended the intellectual horizon of its members. Animism, fetishism, naturalism, magic, and idolatry are not adequate explanations of primitive religion in its germinal and abiding essences. It is no exaggeration to state that man—in all his errors and confusion—never quite lost his resources of reason, will, and conscience. With the grace of divine wisdom to guide him, he acquired a capacity to challenge the darkness. That his failures did not altogether separate him from the Lord of conscience is a thesis which needs to be tested in the light of our knowledge of primitive man, the witness of Scripture, and the primitive ideas of God.

I. Our Knowledge of Primitive Man

The existence of religions, more or less developed, among all the peoples known to history is a proven fact. Little is known, however, of man's religious career in the long period extending from the first manifestation of intelligence down to the dawn of history. A few bones and some crudely fashioned implements are the only remains of prehistoric man. The number and range of these objects increase as one approaches the time of the earliest written documents. But the obscurity that shrouds the prehistoric primitive as he sets out on his arduous spiritual journey is not easy to penetrate.

In their deep desire to lift the veil that hides the prehistoric past, investigators have sometimes resorted to the study of contemporary primitive societies. It is a grave error, however, to apply the discoveries that are brought to light in the study of native Australians and African pygmies to their remote ancestors; or to equate the religious practices of modern primitives with those of Grimaldi man, the Cro-Magnon and the Neanderthal. The possibility may not be overlooked that modern primitive societies might represent degeneration from a higher and more spiritual level.[2]

A. *The Races of Mankind*

Man's religions are embedded in a medley of cultures whose leading carriers are the several races. Of the three leading stems of the human tree—Caucasian, Mongoloid, and Negroid—the first deserves special notice for its record in religious and cultural history.[3]

Thus to the Caucasians must be assigned the art of Upper Paleolithic Europe; the foundations of modern civilization which were laid along the banks of the Nile and the Tigris-Euphrates; such ancient efflorescences of culture as those of the Minoans in Crete; the theistic effulgence among the Semites and their neighbors; and the phenomenal advance of the West during the last twenty-five centuries.

Though not as creative in a religious sense or as universal in its making, the culture of the Mongoloids is remarkable in its own right. The main structure of Chinese wisdom and ethics bears the marks of great originality. In some of its derivatives such as the culture of Japan, the Mongoloid family attained a high degree of organization and refinement. In its East Indian branch, the Mongoloid stem showed a magnificent power of assimilation, appropriating for itself in the past two thousand years from Hindu and Islamic sources as the North Europeans had appropriated in the period 1500 B.C. to A.D. 500, from the Mediterranean peoples, the elements of culture and religion.

Moreover, with nothing more than a late Paleolithic or earliest Neolithic culture as a basis, and in complete isolation from the centers of higher civilization in the Mediterranean and Eastern worlds, the American Mongoloids produced a noteworthy civilization in Mexico and Peru.

[2] G. Bardy, *Les Religions non-Chrétiennes,* Paris, 1949, pp. 11–36.
[3] A. L. Kroeber, *Anthropology,* New York, 1923, pp. 41–48.

As regards the Negroids, if one is to set aside their present-day achievements in the Western Hemisphere, it may be said without overconfidence that their best productivity seems to be in the future. With closer geographic proximity to the centers of Mediterranean culture than that of most Nordics, the African Negro has nevertheless evoked a distaste for higher religious values and cultural creativity. Writing, the use of iron, and higher religion, until fairly recent epochs, seemed to stop dead at his threshold.

Yet when we recall that the Mediterranean and Alpine peoples, whose creative records go back six thousand years, were definitely surpassed by the Nordics, who until the last three hundred years were regarded as newcomers in the realm of culture, the destiny of the Negroids cannot of a certainty be designated as dark. A future of bright cultural achievement may well be in store for these and many others of the so-called primitive peoples of the modern world.

B. *Prehistoric Man*

Behind the races and their religious history is the relatively ambiguous record of prehistoric man. A reappraisal of the dark ages of prehistory in the light of the evolutionary theory has been often undertaken. But the history of religions, while taking stock of the evolutionary hypothesis, will guard against the danger of setting the problems of man's early faith in a purely biological perspective.

As a theory of natural selection, the sole factor in the development of species, Darwinianism is but an assumption. Science offers no positive answer to the question of human origins. All that it posits is that the historic races are foreshadowed by fossils dating back to the late Stone Age, that is, from twenty to twenty-five thousand years ago. Although the so-called Grimaldi type possesses Negroid affinities, and the Cro-Magnon as well as the Brün types evince Caucasian features, we know neither the origin nor the precise descendants of these fossil races.[4]

That the teaching of Darwin has scientific validity and may be accepted on its own merits subject to the reservations and later findings of specialists in the field is to be admitted. Insofar as this teaching goes, it offers in the biological domain a parallel to the

[4] A. L. Kroeber, *op. cit.*, pp. 33–34.

contributions of Copernicus, Kepler, and Newton in physics. Its basic tenet is that the species now inhabiting the world have been preceded by countless others from which they are descended. It affirms, furthermore, that man is part of that long-enduring succession. Biology demonstrates that the peculiar organism, known as man, has evolved from lower organisms by natural means, that all life is part of a single process, and that life must have developed from "not life" during a peculiar phase of the planet's history.[5]

As regards this dictum of science, religion need have no qualms. Although the purpose of religion goes beyond that of scientific research, it would hardly seem to follow that the two realms are mutually exclusive. Galileo's suggestion was right: The aim of Scripture is much higher than that of teaching us the wisdom of this world. Not how the heavens are made, but how man may look upward to God is the chief burden of religion. Whereas research has the world for its object, the eyes of faith are fixed upon spiritual and moral reality.[6]

Were man to neglect the findings of modern science, however, spiritual and moral reality would lose its full meaning for him. Springing directly from the fundamental import of Scripture with regard to redemption, the distinctive character of Christianity among world faiths is inherent in the fact that while it is timely, it is also timeless.

Whereas the Bible offers no cosmology or philosophy of history, it leaves hardly any doubt as to the universal and everlasting character of its message. Biblical truth lends itself to combination with the modern scientific temper as it once did with the prescientific mentality. For despite the marvels of science, the modern world has not outgrown the revealed truth that "God created man in his own image." Nor does the lapse of ten thousand years since the first burials change the disclosure that "in the beginning God created the heavens and the earth."[7]

The very simple truth is that the burials of early man were deliberately made, and rank as our first intimations of religious belief.

[5] T. H. and Julian Huxley, *Touchstone for Ethics,* New York, 1947, p. 36.
[6] Emil Brunner, *Revelation and Reason,* tr. Olive Wyon, Philadelphia, 1936, pp. 279–280.
[7] Gen. 1:1.

To be sure, the funerary rites which some have read into the remote epoch of China man are highly colored. Yet there can be little doubt that Neanderthal man practiced burial of the dead and that thereafter the rite took on added significance and popularity.[8]

The whole point is that man stands out as the only living being who buried his dead and that the rites of interment gain in scope and complexity with the passage of time. In striking contrast with the animals which ignored the corpses of their kind, the high antiquity and intricacy of the cult of the dead, among all branches of the human race known to anthropology, suggest belief in the immortality of the soul and the reality of the unseen world; for in holding the physical organism in awe and tenderness, original man signified his regard for the individual as the child of eternity. In short, while on purely scientific grounds, judgment regarding primitive monotheism must be reserved, the findings of anthropology in the sphere of early burials allow for more precise deductions.

C. *The Historic Primitives*

It is not always permissible to equate paganism with primitivism. A number of primitive religions, such as those of the Amerinds, Negroes, and Polynesians, have claimed a revelation, which may be described as inferior less for its essence than for its procedure.[9] If primitive supernaturalism is revolting, it is primarily because of the incoherence and base purposes which it frequently serves. And for that matter, the inconsistencies of religion are not limited to primitivism alone, for they also crop out in the advanced religions. With all the blessing of sacred revelation at his disposal, Western man has waged wars, in this highly sophisticated age, demanding a heavier toll of victims than all the human sacrifices of the primitive peoples combined.

This continuity of degradation, joining primitive and higher religions, stems from the attributes of fallen creatureliness. Yet the simplest tribes uphold conceptions that are of ethical and intellectual worth, detectable in an ordering of the data of reality and in un-

[8] F. M. Bergounioux and A. Glory, *Les Premiers Hommes,* Paris, 1945, p. 172.

[9] Robert H. Lowie, *An Introduction to Cultural Anthropology,* New York, 1947, pp. 324–328.

questionable ability to distinguish between good and evil. The Indian hunters of California and Nevada evinced an appreciation of righteousness in their recognition of the coyote and the wolf, the first as the symbol of saving power friendly to man, the second as one bent upon destructive ends.

Monotheistic notions are common to a variety of primitive peoples belonging within the pale of history. Conceived as overlord of history, the deity was the object of emotional outpouring and devotion. The Ewe of West Africa, for example, regard their priests as emissaries of a benevolent sky-god, to whom they address their prayers. Where a belief of this kind fuses with an ethical life-centered program, the result is monotheism.

Without putting an end to crude worship, this primitive monotheism, attested by the data of competent authorities, is a well-established reality and in essence exists among some of the least progressive orders of tribalism. Although accompanied by forms of doubtful value, if not rank degeneration, the monotheistic consciousness of primitive folk is the genius around which many of the realities of their behavior and human needs are built.

Careful study of the populations indigenous to central Africa, Oceania, the Americas, and Northern Asia reveals striking physical and mental discrepancies. Since their religious peculiarities also differ widely, it is nothing short of naïve to speak of the primitives as though they shared the same fundamental beliefs and cults.[10] The variety of primitive religions notwithstanding, the most contradictory materials that have been brought to light may be said to illumine the real feelings, ideas, aims, and modes of thought current within the societies concerned. Even fairy tales, according to G. K. Chesterton,[11] are marked by some cultural theme, "that peace and happiness can only exist in some condition. The whole happiness of fairy land hangs upon one thread."

In the Biblical account of creation, the mythical mentality of primitive man is lifted to a sublime height. The stories of Eden and the Tower of Babel express a revealed truth regarding the unity, personality, and holiness of God. By a divine inculcation even while

---

[10] Robert H. Lowie, *Primitive Religion,* New York, 1924.
[11] *All Things Considered,* London, 1908, p. 256.

the mythological framework is preserved, the crucial difference between the natural and the supernatural is emphasized. Here we encounter a differential of true religion.[12]

The capstone of primitive religions, as it is disclosed in their mythologies, is that man confronts a *Thou* in nature, giving emotional, imaginative, and intellectual expression to an overwhelming religious experience.

Now the Greeks are deservedly lauded for their contribution to man's intellectual stature in substituting the It of nature for the Thou of primitivism. It is the hallmark of our scientific outlook that we explain rain, for example, in terms of atmospheric change. Lacking the quality of scientific analysis, the Babylonians explained the break of a drought and the downpour of rain-showers as the intervention of the gigantic bird Imdugud which allegedly came to their rescue bringing relief from drought. Imdugud covered the sky with the black storm clouds of its wings and devoured the Bull of Heaven whose hot breath had scorched the crops.[13]

Despite its unscientific character, the Babylonian interpretation of rain has an imperishable something which even the man of science can ill afford to disparage. For in predicating the manifold phenomena of nature upon a physically tested causality, the mystery and the actuality of the unconditioned are sacrificed. In its essence, mythology bridges the gap between primitivism, on the one hand, and the rational faith and reasoned religion of scientific man, on the other. It breaks the wall of partition between history and prehistory, and links the widely dispersed experiences of God which, despite their ephemeral nature, have served their purpose in enriching and sustaining man and his religious faith.

Thus, the primitive religions, which stand in the blaze of history, are part of a process which is interminably related to the eternal God and the subject of evil, to the Kingdom of God and man's fear of death, to life now and uncertainty regarding the future.

Whether oral or literary, true history consists in something more than a mere narrative or tale. History as a process reflects primarily

[12] Stanley A. Cook, *The Study of Religions,* London, 1914, pp. 259–260.
[13] H. and H. A. Frankfort, *The Intellectual Adventure of Ancient Man,* Chicago, 1940, p. 6.

the human consciousness and personality. The history of an aristocratic family may go back three or four hundred years. Its record might include the careers of warriors and princes, professional giants, sages and saints. All that is not history unless it imparts a continuity of influence and meaning in terms of human creativity and goodness. The essence of history, therefore, must be discovered in the social activity of the human group as a communal, moral, and creative reality.[14] And to the extent that this reality is related to the Eternal is it a constituent of religion in history.

In order that it may have meaning, history must be conceived as an immanent-transcendent process marked by events in time born out of eternity. The mythology of primitives serves as a source of history in that it mirrors man's destiny and reflects his ambitions and longings. It vaguely indicates his vital relation with God, his misery, and his vision of freedom. And it is precisely from these profound, though sometimes ambiguous intimations of the unknown, that history, when conceived as a part of eternity, draws its major themes.

What light does history shed upon the profound problems that constitute its process? Within the context of ancient Oriental history, the Old Testament discloses God and nature; it develops the basic theme of man's sin and the fall; and while regarding God's wrath with fear, it recognizes him as the God of Israel, the Lord of mankind.

But the God of Abraham, Isaac and Jacob, the God of history, reveals himself more fully, as the New Testament declares, in the person of Christ and the subsequent record of Christian history. The key to all the spiritual drama that followed and the key to history, as such, is this new freedom which is given in Christ.[15]

The new freedom means liberation from the yoke of idolatry and all the degradation of primitive religion. With the new freedom, Christianity introduced a new concept of history. For not only was man free from the demons and spirits of the ancient and primitive worlds, he was free from tribalism, the political fetters of race, empire, and the family. He was free from the bonds of hate, the

---

[14] Luigi Sturzo, *The True Life,* Washington, 1943, pp. 198 *sqq.*
[15] Nicolas Berdyaev, *The Meaning of History,* London, 1936, pp. 63 *sqq.*

shackles of superstition and the ambiguities of mysticism. The remote and melancholy power of some unknown god—arbitrary and tyrannical—was superseded by the God of Jesus Christ.

History as a process thus comes to be understood as a redemptive purpose with the living God as the loving Father ever in sovereign control. Through this majestic concept of time and man, history redeems the victims of primitive religion and joins them to itself in the great epic of freedom.[16]

II. IN THE LIGHT OF SCRIPTURE

The historian of religion will note that considerable areas of ancient Hebrew life and worship re-echo primitive cults. Animal sacrifice and the veneration of sacred places, to single out two well-known features, figure among the primitive elements of the Old Testament. These echoes of earlier religious stages and lower levels of worship help us to comprehend the higher truths and the unique revelation which shattered them. They also shed light on the revival and recrudescence of analogous phenomena in the historic religions of primitives.

A. *Purity of Worship*

Viewed as God's revelation, as reported in the words of men, the Bible assumes supreme importance in relation to primitivism. It comprises not only a historical record of primitive religion but a critique of history formulated in the light of divine purpose. The Bible gives us an interpretation of primitive religion in its twentieth-century expression in pew and marketplace, in the jargon of emotional religion, and in the depraved metaphors of the chancelleries and battlefields.[17]

It is indisputable, furthermore, that the Bible not only re-echoes primitive religion, but also rebukes its falsehood. In the category of ancient accounts wherein the Old Testament reproduces the concept of an impersonal force, wielded in diverse ways, the distinctive stamp of revealed truth is unreservedly borne. This is true when mention is made of superior persons, animals, and ob-

[16] Herbert H. Farmer, *God and Man,* New York, 1947, pp. 116, 156.

[17] Millar Burrows, *An Outline of Biblical Theology,* Philadelphia, 1946, pp. 4–5.

jects which exercise a so-called mysterious power in a manner parallel to the imagined potency of mana among the Melanesians or the function of the medicine man and village priest among the primitives of Africa and Indian America. Within this category are said to fall the earliest conceptions of God's spirit such as that of a mysterious wind,[18] calling through the burning bush,[19] appearing in dreams, or waking, to individuals,[20] speaking in a pillar of cloud and smoke,[21] and causing His fire to fall.[22]

With regard to all such phenomena and metaphors, the Bible teaches that God is one and invisible. "Hear, O Israel, the Lord our God is one." [23] Also, "And he said, Thou canst not see my face; for man shall not see me and live." [24]

The Bible, moreover, prohibits the worship of images and idolatry. "Thou shalt have no other gods before me. Thou shalt not make unto thee a graven image, nor any likeness of anything. Thou shalt not bow down thyself unto them, nor serve them. . . ." [25] And above all, the impersonal conceptions of gods bequeathed by heathenism and primitive religions are overshadowed in the Old Testament by the teaching that the Lord had a personal way of dealing with men.[26]

B. *Repudiation of Magic*

The offerings of Cain and Abel, the building of altars, the offering of sacrifices by Noah and Abraham, and rites such as circumcision, reflect the primitive religions of Israel's polytheistic ancestors and neighbors.

To the extent that these practices were attempts to control automatically the operation of nature and coerce the divine power they re-echoed man's weakness to magic. But to the extent that they represented the divine being as superhuman, they indicated the faith that only God can do for man what man in his impotence can only discern without ever achieving.

Taken in their positive and unique spiritual challenge, the Old

[18] Job 4:9; Judges 14:6.
[19] Ex. 3:4.
[20] I Sam. 3:10; I Kings 3:5.
[21] Ps. 99:7; Deut. 29:20.
[22] I Kings 18:38.
[23] Deut. 6:4.
[24] Ex. 33:20.
[25] Ex. 20:3–5.
[26] Burrows, *op. cit.,* pp. 26–27, 60–61.

and New Testaments set a standard for the repudiation of magic. A central Biblical affirmation, lifting the Scriptures above their primitive and idolatrous environment, consists in the belief that the self-revealing God refuses to be appeased and placated by man, although He readily forgives the penitent sinner whose confession comes out of the heart. Corruption in worship and formalism were condemned.[27]

Since the Creator is neither human nor infrahuman, but transcendent and superhuman, His divine essence and righteousness are not open to human manipulation. The sovereign and loving Father refuses to be cajoled into action as He despises all forms of patronage. Whether in worship, ritual, ceremony, or festival, therefore, the people of God could only perform an act of devotion when they stood in penitence and adoration before the God of the ages, the redeeming and sanctifying Lord whose holiness and divine purpose are ever unfolding. "God is a spirit: and they that worship him must worship him in spirit and truth." [28]

III. PRIMITIVE IDEAS OF GOD

As has already been indicated, darkness hides the daily life of prehistoric man from our vision. With regard to the science of primitive man, Christianity makes three affirmations. First, at least prior to the Fall, a primitive revelation disclosed to man a number of general supernatural verities. These were necessary for his peace and comprised faith in the sovereign God, rewarder and revealer, who draws men to His friendship, to His likeness, to immortal life, and to peace through the Mediator who was to come in the fullness of time. Second, an elevated knowledge of God was enunciated in the verities of natural morality, involving the unity of nature and raising the life of man above the lower creatures; in the indissoluble bond of marriage the foundations of society were laid by the establishment of the family. Third, a certain degree of knowledge was disclosed concerning the range and consequence of the sin which man was free to commit.[29]

---

[27] Is. 1:11–20. [28] John 4:24.
[29] A. Verrielle, *Le Surnaturel en nous et le Péché Originel,* Paris, 1932, p. 149.

Subsequent to the Fall, men lost that light which had once illumined their outlook and therefore their hearts became hardened, their spirits confounded. And "knowing God, they glorified him not as God, neither gave thanks: but became vain in their reasonings, and their senseless heart was darkened. Professing themselves to be wise, they became fools, and changed the glory of the incorruptible God for the likeness of an image of corruptible man, and of birds, and four-footed beasts, and creeping things." [30]

Despite their survival in the memory of the races, these elements of knowledge belong to prehistoric times and the attempt to prove their traces in prehistory is futile. Belief in primitive revelation is belief in the veracity of Scripture re-enforced by the teaching of the Holy Spirit and the witness of the Church. The unquestioned verdict of history and prehistory is that men are prone to sin, that is, to pride, ignorance, and undue anxiety over death. That, despite these encumbrances, the primitives known to history tended to uphold monotheistic ideas is a basic contention of Christian anthropology. But those monotheistic ideas can hardly be judged on the basis of modern man's secular habits and concepts. Nor would it be instructive to subject the cults and mysteries of peoples, who are strangers to the patterns of our social and spiritual organization, even to the standards of Western Christianity alone.

The interpretation of primitive religions solely on the basis of magic, animism, and psychology is the direct result of our one-sided approach. Nothing more could be expected from a treatment of these systems that rested primarily on the standards of sociology, anthropology, and biology—almost to the total exclusion of the presuppositions of theology and divine revelation.

A. *The Evidence of Geology*

In the language of geology, the Quaternary Period, that is, the Age of Man, was marked by the advent of glaciers, comprising the Pleistocene (Glacial Epoch) of about a million years. The brief twenty-five thousand years since the last retreat of the ice sheets is called the Recent Epoch.[31]

[30] Rom. 1:21–23.
[31] Rollin T. Chamberlin, "The Origin and History of the Earth," *The World and Man,* F. R. Moulton, ed., Chicago, 1947, p. 88.

Paleolithic (Early Stone Age) Man, judged by his remains in Africa, Northern Europe, and Australia, lacked neither intelligence nor morality. Throughout this Age, which included the four Ice Ages with the three warmer inter-glacial periods in between when the ice retracted, man was a hunter and food-gatherer.

Then, after the last retreat of the ice and the beginning of the modern climatic conditions, there came the encroachments of forest upon plain, the vanishing of the animals which had been hunted by Paleolithic man, and the reduction of the population to a cramped existence chiefly along seashores.

This is the Mesolithic phase of culture which, coming down almost to historic times, is known in the Near East, and later in Europe.[32] Mesolithic man produced nothing of the imaginative quality and artistic skill which typified the Paleolithic artist. In the absence of material evidence to show his creativity, it may be safe to assume that he sank into a degraded pattern of social and religious life. Yet the original monotheism, postulated by certain scholars and corroborated by natural theology, indicates that some idea of God survived.[33]

Indeed, the choice is not between primitive theism, on the one hand, and the denial that from the very first man had some access to the mysterious heart of things, on the other. Rather, in a very real and scientific sense, we might admit that from the outset and in the most primitive forms of religion, there was a recognition of a Supreme Being. This is understandable if it is remembered that man's primitive idea of God was not couched in the theological and philosophical language common to our way of thinking.[34]

B. *The Evidence of Anthropology*

Of the vast array of primitives known to history, two examples will here suffice, namely, the early Arabians and the Amerinds.

1. The religious history of primitive Arabia is revealing. Archaeological research leaves no doubt that there is no focus of early

[32] John Murphy, *The Origins and History of Religions,* Manchester, 1949, pp. 38–60.

[33] Nathaniel Micklem, *Religion,* Oxford, 1948, pp. 36–37.

[34] C. C. J. Webb, *Studies in the History of Natural Theology,* Oxford, 1915, p. 355.

culture fit to be compared with the lands of the Eastern Mediterranean in antiquity and activity. The Near East, a primary cradle of whose peoples was in the Arabian Peninsula, antedates in its ancient records any of the other foci of early civilization such as India, China, Central America, and Western South America.[35]

The testimony of Arabia with regard to primitive religion is significant. For it is now clear that monotheism was not unknown in Arabia long before the coming of Mohammed. Nor did the Prophet of Islam derive his idea of the one God solely from Jewish and Christian sources. Even less tenable is the presupposition that the precursor of Allah was the pagan god, Hubal, of pre-Islamic al-Kaabah.[36]

Evidence shows that Allah was conceived of in Arabian antiquity as creator of the world, sender of rain, absolute master of men, and lord of destiny. He was recognized by the primitives of Arabia as the guardian of their oaths, the supreme judge of their conduct, and the author of rewards and punishment.[37]

The belief of the ancient denizens of the desert is not always akin to the views of the other Semitic peoples, most of whom were pagan and culturally idolatrous. Semitic inscriptions do not reveal a deity comparable to the Allah of primitive Arabia. In fact, the theory of Ernest Renan concerning the original disposition of the Semites toward monotheism is generally discredited. But the existence among the primitives of the Arabian Peninsula of an old faith in an originator, Allah, seems to rest upon firm grounds.[38]

Here is the crux of the matter concerning primitive Arabian religion. The primary heartland of the Near East and scene of an early civilization, Arabia shows a marked inclination toward monotheism. And that in a definitely Semitic world. Yet whereas polytheism was rampant in Egypt, Syria, Mesopotamia, Greece, and Anatolia, the primitives of Arabia, in their simpler folkways,

---

[35] Albright, *From the Stone Age to Christianity*, pp. 4, 6.
[36] D. C. Brockelmann, "Allah und die Götzen der Ursprung des vorislamischen Monotheismus," *Archiv für Religionwissenschaft*, vol. XXI, Leipzig, 1922, pp. 99–121.
[37] W. Schmidt, *The Origin and Growth of Religion*, p. 193.
[38] Nathan Söderblom, *Das Werden des Gottesglauben*, Leipzig, 1916, pp. 118 *sqq.*

retained a belief in the unity of God. This belief was not derived from the polytheism of the ancient Orient. It was not the child of the wisdom of Egypt, Mesopotamia, and Greece, but an autochthonous faith in God, the forerunner of the Western religions.[39]

2. Although Amerindic culture attained heights comparable with the chief civilizations of the ancient world, the sweep of its history is that of an aboriginal primitivism and shows marked evidence of natural monotheism. All the more startling is the testimony of this field since the cultural history of native America constitutes the record of a civilization independent from the main Old World tradition, that is, the Euro-Asiatic nexus.[40]

The first Amerinds can hardly have come from any other continent than Asia. Their arrival in the Western Hemisphere probably took place about ten thousand years ago. In defining their racial affinities, it may be well to remember that they are akin to the Mongolians, that group of East Asian peoples of whom the Mongols are a part. But the main stem is known as Mongoloid, comprising the three subordinate branches known as Mongolians, East Indians, and Amerinds.

The Amerinds are, therefore, the far-removed kinsmen of the Chinese, and the latter, we are told, only acquired slant eyes at a relatively late period in their career as a separate people. When they made their way into North America, entering through Bering Strait, the Amerinds had characteristics which identified them more closely with the original Mongoloid stem of the human family.

That the Amerindic civilizations which subsequently arose were impressive in scope and structure, although the historical data on them lacks sufficient clarity, is generally conceded.[41] A monument to tropical nature in Central America, the Mayan culture emerged in the lands known to us as Guatemala and British Honduras. The earlier Maya age, represented in an inscriptional chronology which is internally certain, remains unplaced in terms of universal history.

[39] James A. Montgomery, *Arabia and the Bible,* Philadelphia, 1934, pp. 185 *sqq.*

[40] A. L. Kroeber, *Anthropology,* New York, 1923, pp. 327, 343, 350.

[41] A. L. Kroeber, *Configurations of Cultural Growth,* Berkeley, 1944, pp. 24–35.

Affiliated with it are the later societies of Yucatan and Mexico. In general, the early Mayan period was more resplendent than its successors. It suffered a rapid decline, however, in the seventh Christian century, leaving behind those records discovered in the ruins of Yucatan's great cities.

Discovered by Hernando Cortez (1485–1547), the Spanish conqueror of Mexico, the religious rites of the Aztecs are a grossly barbarized version of the early Maya religion.[42] Human sacrifice, maintained on a hideous and colossal scale, marred the ancient rites.

Then there is the Inca Empire of Peru, recognized as the climax of that other expression of Amerindic culture, the Andean civilization. It had already achieved the proportions of a universal state when it was overthrown by the Spanish conqueror of Peru, Francisco Pizarro (*ca.* 1471–1541) in 1530.

It would be hazardous to attempt an interpretation of the vast records of Amerindic religion on the basis of current research. A. L. Kroeber,[43] the distinguished anthropologist and specialist in the field, confirmed the view that the Indian tribes of Central California belong to the oldest and most primitive Amerindic societies in North America. More than any other Amerindic people, these tribes acknowledged a clearly defined Supreme Being. Theirs is a lofty conception of the Creator, although sometimes anthropomorphism intervened. In one instance, as already noted, the divine qualities are even merged with those of the crafty coyote.

Elsewhere, as in Aztec religion, terror seemed to fill the Indian soul—a dominant note in their representations before the deities and in their ceremonies.[44] In the case of the Incas of Peru, worship of the sun was the very marrow of their life. As children of the sun, they discovered a lost sense of dignity, and in the sun found a glorious dispensation for mankind.

More intricate is the worship of Mayan culture in which the deities stand as guardians of their dualist conception of divine power, good and evil. Itzamna, the creator god, had as counterpart

[42] Toynbee, *A Study of History, Abridgement,* pp. 33–34.
[43] *Handbook of California Indians,* Washington, 1925.
[44] Paul Radin, *The Story of the American Indian,* New York, 1934, pp. 84, 126.

a goddess whose primary function was destruction. His father, Hunab, was a kind of Mayan Zeus, adored at a certain level of worship as the one and only god.

This unsystematic story of Amerindic religion strangely enough fits into the general pattern of primitive society. Divided into patriarchal, matriarchal, and totemic cultures, the Indians of North America belonged to a humanity that was less ancient than the pygmies, Australians, and Arctic peoples. A fair proportion of them, particularly the most primitive, worshiped God, the powerful, righteous and unique Lord. To the North American Indian, Wilhelm Schmidt [45] devoted a learned volume containing an evaluation of their beliefs, and offering on the basis of anthropological data and psychological treatment, an insight into their mentality and place in religious history.

The naïve faith of the primitive Amerind excelled that of pygmies, Australians, and Arctic peoples inasmuch as it produced a deliberate and reflective conscience endowed with greater depth and delicacy. This commendable aspect of faith was not, however, free from perversion through admixture with degraded worship and the intrusion of false conceptions. Genuine belief in the Unseen gave way before the inroads of awesome forces. Nature and man's yearning for the supernatural met and clashed in perpetual conflict, a conflict which all too often made of religion a sham struggle for selfish advantage and preferment.

C. *African Ideas of God*

The uncertainty prevalent among scholars, regarding the belief of the African in an overruling Providence, lasted well through the first decade of the twentieth century.[46] Evidence which has since come to light, however, effected a radical change in the position of those responsible for this field.

In his Gifford lectures, Sir James G. Frazer [47] reached the conclusion that African Supreme Beings are not deified ancestors, but personifications of the great celestial phenomena. Schmidt advanced

---

[45] *Die Religionen der Urvölker Americas,* Münster, 1929.

[46] E. Sidney Hartland, "Bantu and South Africa," *Encyclopedia of Religion and Ethics,* London, 1909, vol. II, p. 363.

[47] *The Worship of Nature,* London, 1926.

the theory that the African pygmies (Bushmen), representing the oldest strata of mankind, were genuinely monotheistic.

Father Joseph J. Williams,[48] in a series of monographs, noted a general retrogression in religion among the tribes of Africa whose recent polytheism is often a clear indication of earlier monotheism. Formerly including, in some of their rites, human sacrifice and cannibalism, the obeah sorcery and magic rituals, especially of the Ashanti West African Negroes, have survived in the Voodooism of Haiti and other West Indian islands, with ophiolatry (snake worship) as a prominent feature.

Yet Hermann Baumann,[49] the German ethnologist, detected as the core of African mythology and magic, a creative principle often identical with the High Lord, accredited with the creation of man. Edwin W. Smith,[50] assisted in his study of African beliefs by a corps of missionary specialists, gave a survey of the ideas of God upheld by the several peoples studied at first hand.

On the basis of these and allied researches, the conclusion has been reached that the African idea of God, as distinct from cosmic mana, includes His personality, ultimacy, and divinity. Though generally conceived within the framework of tribalism and subjected to association with others, the idea of the Eternal was real and objective, implying the worship of God and the acknowledgment of His power as Judge in the affairs of men and their ethical relations.

D. *Christianity and the Primitive Ideas of God*

Christianity maintains in faith that from the beginning God revealed Himself to man created in the supernatural state. Whether this supernatural revelation has left any traces observable in prehistory it is hard to judge. Coming at a very early stage, original sin so corrupted the nature of man that of his first perfection he only preserved a faint recollection, sustained by an undying nostalgia for the paradise he lost.[51]

---

[48] See his *Africa's God,* New York, 1937.
[49] *Schöpfung und Urzeit des Menschen in Mythus der Afrikanischen Völker,* Berlin, 1936.
[50] Editor and Contributor, *African Ideas of God,* London, 1950, pp. 1–35.
[51] G Bardy, *Les Religions non-Chrétiennes,* pp. 35–36.

But the truth is that if man would find God, all he needed to do was to scrutinize the world around him and look within his deeper self. For He whose glory the heavens declare and who through the voice of conscience inspires man to goodness, moves him to acts of mercy and justice, checks his rebellious moods, and transforms his infirmities to strength, is the one true God. This supreme Lord of all being, far and exalted above the tragedy of existence, is near to all His children though oft ignored by men who in servitude to the passions of the flesh are divorced from communion with the living God.

Everywhere men grieve the Eternal and consciously offend the Holy Spirit: in associating others with Him, in seeking substitutes for His revealed truth, in worshiping the stars, the forces of nature, and four-footed beasts. Everything becomes to them God except God Himself. So rife was this degradation in historic times that monotheism was sadly obscured.

Only among the people of Israel was faith in God kept alive. We must hasten to add, however, that with the Babylonian captivity, the generality of men in Israel succumbed to the bewitching power of idolatry and that only a remnant remained faithful, guided by God's Spirit. This fidelity itself was assured only through the challenge of God's special intervention by the prophets. Nor is it idle to ask what the status of Israel's monotheism might have been but for the quickening of the Spirit, the constant unfolding of revelation and the fulfillment of all truth in the person and message of Jesus.

When the Jews of the Diaspora came in contact with Hellenic thought, they discovered in the writings of the philosophers religious truths which they themselves had learned from the Torah and the Prophets. The question arose as to where the pagans had acquired such knowledge of the true God if not from the Creator Himself. The same question was raised more acutely several centuries later, when the apologists sought to present the truths of Christianity to the Greeks.

Plato had emphasized the existence of the unique and incorporeal God; and the early Christians taught that if in a corrupt and ignorant world, Plato was able to expound so elevated a doctrine, it was because he had obtained it from the Old Testament through an indirect and secret tradition. Paul in writing to the Romans,[52] however, indicted the Gentiles as sinners on the grounds that while possessing the truth of God they nevertheless lived unrighteously. "For the wrath of God is revealed from heaven against all ungodliness and unrighteousness of men, who hold the truth in unrighteousness; because that which is known of God is manifest in them; for God manifested it unto them. For the invisible things of him since the creation of the world are clearly seen, being perceived through the things that are made, even his everlasting power and divinity; that they may be without excuse." It is patent, therefore, that the idea of God is the spiritual patrimony of all mankind which possesses the spiritual means of coming to the Saviour.[53]

Neither Philo, Justin, nor Augustine had access to the data indispensable for the resolution, on a historical basis, of the problem posed by primitive monotheism. To the modern student of comparative religion, however, the world, at once enlarged and shrunk, unveils a diversity of races which practice many cults amidst a bewildering variety of impurities and perversions. These discoveries in the realm of primitive religions have too often been communicated to the non-specialist by a science of religion which looks askance upon the belief in God.

Thus it was formally asserted, and the attempt was made to prove, that man, having no inkling of the Eternal, began with the practice of magic but that in the course of long stages, he developed polytheism out of magic which, upon being purified and narrowed down, led to the idea of God. If that line of reasoning were sound, the God of Christianity, as well as of philosophy, would be no more than the distillation of magic as it passed through a long drawn-out social process.[54]

Considerably more cautious than the science of religion, positivist sociology won the merit of recognizing in religion an essentially

[52] 1:18–20.

[53] Gaston Rabeau, *Dieu, Son Existence et Son Providence,* Lille, 1933, pp. 33 *sqq.*

[54] For a treatment of primitive religion written in a scholarly vein, yet skeptical of skepticism, see William Howell's *The Heathens: Primitive Man and His Religions,* New York, 1948, pp. 283–293.

social phenomenon and, in religious thought, a mode of knowledge acquired through the spontaneous participation of those who form the social unit. But even this sociology held fast to the position that mankind began with the lowest forms of religion conceivable; it saw in the God of Christians a purified abstraction descending from the collective representation of mana, that is, from the vital and persistent belief in the sacred forces that activate society and are constantly at work in nature.

In fairness to Father Schmidt and his adherents, it must be conceded that they explained the origin of religion on grounds that afforded greater understanding of the issues involved. While it is by no means true that the labors of this school have settled all the problems in the case, or met with universal acceptance, its findings are of considerable importance, nonetheless, since they make possible the formulation of a theory that accounts for the religions of contemporary primitives and possibly their forbears. With regard to the essential connection between human thought and monotheism, the case may be briefly outlined in what follows.

Six principles seem to be involved.[55] First, primitive societies do not constitute a homogeneous unity but differ widely among themselves. Yet wherever it has been investigated, the idea of God among primitives bears certain striking marks of resemblance. That the primitive idea of God is not metaphysical means that it does not rely upon such criteria as would define His subsistence and essence but is rather calculated to give a grasp of His spiritual being, omnipresence, perfection, and righteousness as author of morality and determiner of ends.

Second, this idea of God may be said to be precise insofar as it annuls contradictions derived from emotional and confused perception.

Third, primitive religion is theocentric in that its functional aspects revolve about God and not man.

Fourth, regardless of the fears and insecurity that encompassed him, the primitive was able to acknowledge the power and the holiness of the unique God.

Fifth, narratives and rites, and at times images and parables,

[55] Rabeau, *op. cit.*, pp. 35–36, 61–65.

were the primary means by which the primitive understood the things of God. Mythology was made to serve a high purpose in communicating the truth.

Sixth, anthropomorphism, that is, the representation of the conception of God under human forms, attributes, and affections, with all its aberrations, held the key to the disclosure of the plenitude of spiritual truth to the primitive.

Admittedly, the teachers of religious truth might lead their followers astray by making them think of God as a human being; but, antedating such teaching, the idea of God had a way of rehabilitating itself. Nor do the facts about primitive religion really dispose of the view that the conception of special creation stemmed directly from primitive revelation. Indeed, the presupposition that the religion of prehistoric man, inaccessible in detail as it is, was infinitely more spiritual than that of such historic primitives as the pygmies, the Arctic peoples, and the Algonkian Amerinds, is quite plausible though lacking demonstrable proof.

Nor is it absurd to assume that the religion of prehistoric man was relatively free from the abased narratives which in his further degradation man produced in order to explain the mystery of God and the universe. It is not awkward to think that the first men to tread this earth fashioned their narratives and myths in the light of primitive revelation instead of developing their idea of God from legendary lore.

In sum, our knowledge of primitive man permits us to think that belief in God is the normal exercise of human thought when it is not obsessed with the pursuit of pleasure and the love of self. In fact, the study of the most archaic cultural cycles gives sufficient evidence that this belief is a valid testimony to the existence of divine Providence.

CHAPTER IV

THE GREAT RELIGIONS
OF ANTIQUITY

Rᴇᴀʟ religion is contingent upon divine revelation. In art, science, and philosophy, when a new, grand idea dawns for the first time on the spirit, one may speak of revelation. But the word revelation belongs more properly in the vocabulary of religion.

Religious revelation is subjective and central in nature. But since it also points to God, the objective, absolute center of all things and beings, it fills the entire nature and heart of man. If we concede that revelation is related to the entire nature of things and of man, it would follow, then, that its manifestations impart to man a share in the divine life, not merely in the knowledge of the divine. In order to vindicate its truth and value, revelation must possess novelty or originality, continuity, and rationality.

The extinct religions of antiquity do not possess all these attributes. They do not stand comparison with Biblical revelation in its emphasis upon the holy, one, personal, and redeeming God who made man and continued to care for him even when he went astray. They demonstrate, nonetheless, the existence of divine agency and, in a broader sense, support the truth of revelation.

The first thing to note about the religions of antiquity is that in their fetishism, animism, polytheism, and dualism, the divine principle is finitized, circumscribed, and blurred. But the Old and New Testaments [1] teach that in God we live, move, and have our being, and that through nature, history, and conscience God did not leave himself without witness even among the heathen.

---

[1] That the Old Testament acknowledges religious truth outside the faith of Israel has already been noted. To the case of Melchizedek "priest of God most High" (Gen. 14:18) must be added that of Cyrus, "my shepherd" (Is. 44:28), and similar allusions in Job and Daniel.

"For when Gentiles that have not the law do by nature the things of the law, these, not having the law, are the law unto themselves in that they show the work of the law written in their hearts, their conscience bearing witness therewith, and their thoughts one with another accusing or else excusing them; in the day when God shall judge the secrets of men, according to my gospel, by Jesus Christ." [2]

This interpretation of the vanished religions of antiquity in their relation to Christianity rests, therefore, on Biblical foundation and sanction and was thus acknowledged among the early church fathers and writers.

Justin Martyr [3] (*ca.* A.D. 100–*ca.* 165), born in Samaria of a Gentile family in a Greek-speaking settlement, tested before his conversion to Christianity the various schools of heathen thought and philosophy. He left us a living picture of the relation of Christianity to Judaism and paganism. Though the Greek philosophers and poets did not know the whole Word, that is, Christ, they were right in many things, as bearing the seeds of the Logos in them; they taught the immortality of the soul, punishment after death, and contemplation of celestial objects.

In his *Exhortation to the Greeks,* Clement of Alexandria [4] (*ca.* A.D. 150–220), who had come to Christianity with a mind steeped in Greek learning, asserted that a real revelation had been made to the higher minds of Greece. By quotation from the philosophers and poets, particularly Plato and Homer, he showed that Greek thought had actually taught the unity, supremacy, and goodness of God. But the greatest witnesses of all were the Hebrew prophets, through whom God gave men His truth and promises.

Clement contended that the Greeks were prevented from accepting the truth by the dead weight of custom and tradition; his fearless acceptance of truth from every available source makes him an important interpreter of the vanished religions of antiquity. His wanderings through many lands and his acquaintance with the mystery cults, he himself having been initiated into some of them,

[2] Rom. 2:14–16.
[3] *Works,* Oxford, 1861, pp. 33–34, 68.
[4] Tr. G. W. Butterworth, London, 1919, pp. 5–6.

equipped Clement as a presbyter of the Church with confidence that Christianity offers the penitent soul something infinitely more substantial than the true mysteries and the true vision of the Eternal.

He described the priests, who managed the temples of antiquity, in words which were most revealing—while the higher religious minds of antiquity had the benefit of general revelation, popular morality and folk religion were nothing short of abominable.

"Let any of you look at those who minister in the idol temples. He will find them ruffians with filthy hair, in squalid and tattered garments, complete strangers to baths, with claws for nails like wild beasts; many are also deprived of their virility. They are an actual proof that the precincts of the idols are so many tombs or prisons. These men seem to me to mourn for their gods, not to worship them, and their condition provokes pity rather than piety. When you see sights like this, do you still remain blind and refuse to look up to the master of all and the Lord of the universe? Will you not fly from the prisons on earth, and escape to the pity which comes from heaven? For God of His great love still keeps hold of them, just as, when a nestling falls from the nest, the mother bird flutters above and if, perchance, a serpent gapes for it, 'flittering around with cries, the mother mourns for the offspring.' " [5]

In its interpretation of the great religions of antiquity, Christianity is not negative but offers a new angle of vision. As the Father of all men, God planted even in the heathen heart a quest for the Eternal. This quest of the pagans, He quickened and shaped by their training in religion. If so, the greatness of Christianity does not depend on the fact that there is no truth whatever outside of its historic scope, nor is it mandatory to suppose that the Hebrew religion borrowed its greatness from the utter futility of the neighboring cults.

The greatness of the Hebraic-Christian tradition is intrinsic and patent, making it unique without any necessity to disparage all that there is in the religious systems of the ancient world. Indeed, there is hardly any extinct religion in which relics and surmises of man's converse with God were totally absent. This common reli-

[5] Clement of Alexandria, *op. cit.*, pp. 199–200; the last sentence is a quotation from Homer's *Iliad* (II, 315).

gious heritage of the human race appears among the Hindus in Brahman; among the Teutons in Tiu (Zio, Zeus); among the Iranians in Ahura-Mazda; and among the Greeks and Babylonians in cosmic Fate.

The essence of polytheism, the underlying perversion of the great religions of antiquity, is that the foreground of consciousness is occupied by a plurality of deities. There is no warrant, however, that the true religion is thereby permanently eclipsed. On the contrary, there are evidences on record showing that amidst the deepest gloom of religious depravity, a decisive disposing of the heart by God continues to be in operation. The human response asserts itself in a constant and common longing after communion with Him in surrender of heart and mind and soul.[6]

I. RELIGIONS OF THE ANCIENT ORIENT

With the foregoing conception of religion as a frame of reference, the spiritual experience of the ancient Near East may be said to assume greater significance. In this part of Western Asia, from the Hellespont to Iran, and from the Caucasus to the Arabian Peninsula, a composite culture was achieved in high antiquity.

Here, probably more than five thousand years ago, autochthonous Indo-Europeans, Semites, and possibly Ural-Altaians were thrown together. Their common traditions, cultures, and religions enhance the importance of that part of the world which geography had already made the focal area of the Eastern Hemisphere.[7] Within the context of universal history, the priority of Egypt and Babylonia has been authenticated by the findings of archaeology. Linked together by the Fertile Crescent—a naturally favored territory constituting Syria, Palestine, and part of Northern Iraq— the valley of the Nile and that of the Tigris-Euphrates emerged as the two main centers of the Ancient Orient.

Shortly prior to 3000 B.C., in both Egypt and Babylonia, several startling developments occurred. Included among these were a system of partly phonetic writing, the use of copper, wheel-turned

---

[6] I. Dorner, *A System of Christian Doctrine,* vol. II, tr. J. S. Banks, Edinburgh, 1891, pp. 237–238.

[7] A. L. Kroeber, *Anthropology,* p. 440.

pottery, sun-dried bricks, architecture, organized government, a calendar, and a congeries of great gods with particular names and attributes. Temples for the worship of these gods made more inspiring the early strides in art and architecture.

On the North and East, the Anatolian Hittites and the Iranians built mighty empires and made lasting contributions to the religious development of the Ancient Orient. In due course, Syria, with her Canaanite, Phoenician, Aramaean, and later Hebrew populations, developed independent cultural and religious systems.

Finally, on the island of Crete, almost equidistant from Asia, Africa, and Europe, a civilization followed the introduction of bronze about 2000 B.C. Although most of its constituent elements were borrowed, the Minoan civilization of Crete did not lack originality. When Greek culture arose, it was charged with Cretan influences, Minoan, Aegean, and Oriental, to which the ingredients of beauty and reason were added by the Greeks themselves.

1. *The Essence of Divine Universality Obscured by Cultic Polytheism: Egypt.* In its classical development (3000–1000 B.C.), the religion of ancient Egypt, evolved in a prelogical setting, moved from an age of dynamism to a higher stage approaching pantheism. Among the masses, and in folk religion generally, as it expressed itself in the daily worship of the temple and the offerings, polytheism and magic were invariably dominant. Theology and ethics emerged early in the second millennium. Marked progress was made in the fields of mathematics, surveying, and medicine. Plato [8] urged that the free-born children of Greece should acquire as much of these new sciences as the generality of Egyptian children did. But he somewhat critically observed that the Egyptian priests drilled their scholars in arithmetic and geometry partly with practical ends, such as land measurement, in view.

As among all early races, religion in Egypt was the core of culture. The pharaohs of the early dynasties unified the many local faiths. There came into being a state religion with central deities. Its literature and ritual were systematized by generations of scribes, and molded by theological schools. The religious writings, such as the *Book of the Dead* which dealt with the fortunes of the soul in

[8] *Laws,* tr. R. G. Bury, London, 1926, vol. II, p. 105.

the hereafter, gave an epitomy of funerary religion. They were dominated by magic and reveal a thoroughly materialistic conception of the soul. The folk religion was communicated through a variety of myths and legends in which the gods remained aloof and austere.[9]

In a period of over a thousand years, the structure of Egyptian religion was established, conservatism and monophysitism, as already noted, being its most striking features. The corpus of Pyramid Texts (2400–2200 B.C.), among the oldest and longest religious texts known, supplemented by a variety of other writings, illustrated the genius of Egyptian religion.

But the origins of this religion are hidden by the dim past. Though frequently represented in animal form, the gods were neither fetishes nor numina, and it would be inaccurate to consider them the products of totemism as in the case of primitive Australia, Africa, and America. In their prehistoric antiquity, the Egyptians already had a complex religion, with triads consisting in father-mother-son and expanded into enneads inherent in the local pantheons which go as far back as predynastic times.

Theology followed the pattern set at Heliopolis (On, City of the Sun), in the vicinity of modern Cairo, in the fourth millennium B.C. Ra (Re), great sun-god, was principal deity of the city which even after the foundation of Memphis and Thebes remained the religious capital of the Nile valley. The pharaohs claimed to be incarnations of Ra, the god who was variously represented as lion, cat, and falcon, and who ordinarily wore a sun-disk. His other forms were Horus (rising sun), Khepere (morning sun), Tene (setting sun), Sokaris (evening sun), Shu (atmosphere), and Atum (sun-disk). This conflation of mythology and symbolism, particularly between Ra and Osiris, often was incongruous. Yet, throughout the vicissitudes of Egyptian history, Ra was not shaken from his anchorage in the people's affections.

A second center of theological ascendancy was Hermopolis in Upper Egypt where Thoth, god of the scribes and scribe of the supreme deity Ra, acquired a place in the cosmic scene. When the early rulers of the Eighteenth Dynasty expelled the Hyksos invaders and extended their power in Syria, Amon (the hidden)

[9] H. Frankfort, *Ancient Egyptian Religion,* New York, 1948, p. 81.

became the chief deity of Hermopolis. As Amon-Ra, he is depicted as a man wearing on his head a disk surrounded by two ostrich plumes. He suffered eclipse for a period of seventeen years while Akhenaton (1377 B.C.) glorified Aton as sole god and light of the world. But the religious revolution of Akhenaton was a passing phase and Amon soon gathered up the reins of his former power. The temples of Karnak testify to the grandeur of Amon, the great god of Thebes.

The theology of Heliopolis, as it was modified somewhat at the cult-center of Hermopolis, was not really threatened with eclipse until the rise of Memphis, capital of the First Dynasty. In order to justify the sudden rise of this town to importance, the Memphyte god, Ptah, was proclaimed as First Principle, invested with creative power, and thus held to be above all other creator-gods.[10] Thus going back to the dawn of Egyptian history and reflecting earlier traditions, Ptah stood at the head of the ennead, creator of eight deities. Whatever the other gods did was a manifestation of him, and his creativity, from about 3000 B.C., was considered continuous. He was usually represented as father of the gods and men, swathed like a mummy bearing the symbols of life, power, and stability. As Ptah-Seker-Osiris, he symbolized the mummified Osiris. Detectable in his character is a theological emphasis upon the creative word and through the conflation of the different gods under him the conception of an impersonal high god comes to the forefront.

These three main theologies were the result of reflection and the product of an intellectual process. Their communication in popular form was made possible by means of legends which may be grouped around two themes represented by the solar cycle and the cycle of Osiris.

The solar cycle was based on the belief current among the ancient Egyptians, namely that the world began with the gods as the rulers. This period was not a golden age, however, but rather a time of rebellions and jealousies, of turmoil among the gods themselves. Ra, the sun, lord of creation, was not safe from the assault of his enemies. According to the legend entitled "Deliverance of Mankind

---

[10] John A. Wilson, *Ancient Near Eastern Texts,* James B. Pritchard, ed., Princeton, 1950, p. 4.

from Destruction," [11] Ra had grown old and was grieved by the things which were being plotted against him by mankind. The theme is the sin of mankind, the destructive disappointment of the creator, and the deliverance of the race of man from annihilation.

The setting of the solar legend shows, however, that its purpose was magical protection rather than moral teaching. On the walls of the three royal tombs of the Empire, this legend accompanies certain charms intended to afford protection for the body of the dead ruler. The implication throughout is that the deliverance of men from destruction was valid for the common individual as well as for the ruler and the entire race.

In the cycle of Osiris, the deity is portrayed as god of the underworld and judge of the dead. Osiris is here conceived as the classical type of the dead king and god who possessed cosmic powers; and underlying the legend, enriched by popular fancy, one detects the recollection of the transitory sovereignty of Upper Egypt, represented by the god, Set, when its domination of the Delta was followed by the defeat of Set and his partisans and the triumph of Osiris, King of United Egypt. Repeated with numerous revisions and additions, the legend outlived the ages and received its final version from the pen of the Greek moralist and biographer, Plutarch (*ca.* A.D. 46—*ca.* 120).

Osiris figured in a creation story which formed part of the cycle. He was one of the four deities descended from Geb (Earth) and Nut (Sky). As father-mother of men, he combined in himself the fertility of the earth, the water of the Nile inundation, and the growing vegetation. As plant life died and revived, so did Osiris. Thus he became ruler and judge of the dead, imparting new life to his devotees.

Osiris was brother and husband of Isis (Ast), goddess of motherhood and fertility. He was brother-father of Horus and Anubis. Treacherously murdered by his brother Set, his corpse, which drifted to Byblos on the Phoenician coast, was recovered by Isis and brought back to Egypt.

The gods restored Osiris to life and immortality; and the fertility god, later identified by the Greeks with Dionysus who had

[11] John A. Wilson, *op. cit.,* pp. 10–11.

suffered, died, and been brought to life, emerged as divine sovereign of the living and dead. This parallelism with the Risen Lord of Christianity—despite the caricature aspect of the legend—is an eloquent testimony to the insatiable and ancient longing of men for a divine saviour who is able to deliver from sin and death and to secure life and immortality.

The principal center of Osiris worship was at Abydos although the whole of Egypt really bowed to him. He was represented as a mummified figure, wearing the crown of Upper Egypt and carrying a whip and a crook.

The common belief of the ancient Egyptians was that Isis bewailed Osiris when the river began to rise and that the inundation of the Nile was her tears. After the glory of Egypt was gone (*ca.* the sixth century B.C.), Osiris, Isis, and Horus, idealized by the people, gained in stature as the state gods failed. Osiris in particular fitted into the pattern of the other pagan gods who died and returned. Isis, too, was identified with the popular goddesses of the Hellenistic world, and her cult, combined with that of Horus and Serapis, became one of the chief religions of the Roman empire until the sixth Christian century.

Such was the broad outline of religion during the long course of history in ancient Egypt. An integral part of political and social life, religion invariably made the pharaoh divine, recognized him not only after death but even while he reigned as son of Ra. And in keeping with the prevalent Memphyte theology, the pharaoh was designated as Horus and his divinity was conceived of as a sharing of essentials with the god whose being was not exhausted, however, by his incarnation in the living ruler of Egypt.[12]

The symbol of Horus was the falcon, and he was generally called "the great god, the lord of heaven," which seemed to make him the god par excellence. On the First Dynasty couch he appears as the winged sun-disk; later, and in preference to a dozen or more Upper Egyptian deities, he was esteemed the animating spirit of the pharaoh. Research on the subject, it ought to be admitted, is vague and the exact nature of Horus has not been sufficiently elucidated.

His connection with the state seemed to rest in the main upon

[12] Henri Frankfort, *Kingship and the Gods,* Chicago, 1948.

his incarnation in the king, which identified him with the solar disk as Ra-Harakhti and, at a very early stage, elevated him to the rank of first god of the state. During the Fifth Dynasty, an attempt was made to substitute Set for Horus despite the power of Ptah, the god of Memphis. With the unification of Egypt under the Twelfth Dynasty, Amon, who was one of the gods of Hermopolis, was theoretically substituted for Ra. The Hyksos invaders looked to Set as their protector but their authority was restricted to Lower Egypt, and in Upper Egypt the Theban dynasty remained faithful to Amon. The Eighteenth Dynasty, which marked the height of Egyptian expansion and empire, gave Amon a universal character, and his high priest was second only to the pharaoh. To this period date the hymns, dedicated to Amon, which were almost exclusively solar.

Amon remained peculiarly Egyptian in essence and attributes. The question arose whether it was not better religion to address worship directly to the solar disk, Aton, without resort to an anthropomorphic image as an intermediary. That this was a direct thrust at Amon was made obvious when Akhenaton set up his monotheistic cult at the expense of Amon and his high priest. The reforms of Akhenaton brought Egypt closer to monotheism, but Tutankhamon lost little time in restoring Amon and his priesthood to their former leadership in the realm.[13]

In addition to its temples dedicated to the gods at Karnak, Egypt was the land of tombs. No other people of antiquity gave so forceful an expression to their belief in immortality or as moving a picture of the hereafter. Underlying the development of funerary religion and the belief in a future life were the social, personal, and strongly human motives of the Egyptian. To believe that death by no means ends all and that man possesses a spiritual principle similar to that which assured imperishability to the gods, meant that men had a common ground with each other and with the divine. In the hieroglyphics, *akh* denoted the supernatural being or spirit. The soul was known as *ba*, represented by a bird with human head; it left

---

[13] That the relation between the monotheism of Akhenaton and Hebraic theism is untenable was lucidly brought out in John A. Wilson, *The Burden of Egypt,* Chicago, 1951, pp. 221–229.

the body which, if preserved upon death, could look to the return of the soul, together with *khu* (intelligence) and *ba* (the genius of the body) to revivify it. The *ba* was conceived as immortal, eternal, and capable of becoming divine.

The mortuary god Anubis was in the image of a jackal who devoured the dead. With Thoth, he shared the function of conducting the dead through Amenti (hidden places, the west) where the soul appeared in the hall of Osiris to be judged. The *Book of the Dead,* composed under the pharaohs of the Fifth and Sixth Dynasties, was eventually incorporated in the Papyrus of Ani, a collection which sheds light on the religious beliefs of the middle Eighteenth Dynasty, and is a document concerned with the hereafter.

Chapter 125 of this papyrus depicts Ani, followed by his wife Tutu, bowing humbly in the great hall of judgment. In the center is the balance operated by the jackal-headed Anubis. On the left scalepan is Ani's heart while in the other is a feather, the symbol of truth and righteousness. Identified by the Greeks with Hermes, Anubis was commonly described as a son of Osiris in whose company he attained farreaching fame.

Beyond the legends, animal forms of the divinities, the mortuaries, and funeral rites, the religion of ancient Egypt manifests the universality of the divine essence. Although it was relatively ignored by the masses, this idea of ultimate reality was nevertheless established among the men of wisdom. When the writers of wisdom literature spoke of God they evidently did not think of one deity in opposition to another but rather of the general concept of the Eternal. It would appear that despite their spiritual anarchy and the confusion of their religious ideas, the ancient Egyptians had a view of the unique Lord who was capable of manifesting himself to men under different forms. Such was the nature of the Egyptian syncretism which led back to a monotheistic doctrine.[14]

But the religion which Egypt bequeathed was of a degraded order. Apis (Hapi), the sacred bull, was the embodiment of the god Ptah of Memphis and an image of the soul of Osiris. Passing to the world beyond, his soul became known as Osiris-Apis, hence

[14] J. Vaudier, *La Religion Egyptienne,* Paris, 1944, pp. 228–229.

Serapis; his worship was developed by the Greeks and subsequently spread throughout the Roman Empire. Actually, Apis was introduced to the Greeks as the equivalent of Hades, and the golden calf of the Hebrews may have been his symbol. In Rome, the temple of Serapis and Isis was a vast structure, on a site occupied now by part of the Church of Sant' Ignazio—a section of the Collegio Romano.[15]

The ascendancy of Egypt in art and architecture, in government and mathematics, suggested to her neighbors a greatness in ethics and religion, in wisdom and intellectual pursuits. The Old Testament recognized Egyptian learning, for Solomon "excelled the wisdom of all the children of the east, and all the wisdom of Egypt." [16] But Isaiah [17] warned Egypt that her culture was doomed even though she "shall seek unto idols, and to the charmers [whisperers] and to them that have familiar spirits, and to the wizards." These magicians enjoyed status in the royal palace at the time of Moses; the pharaoh "called for the wise men and the sorcerers: . . . the magicians of Egypt." [18] Like Moses himself, Egyptian religion at its best had but a glimpse of the Land of Promise; it never crossed the Jordan of faith.[19]

Though its golden era placed Egypt in a period long antedating the maturity of the Hebrews, Greeks, and Romans, a contemporary cultural growth of equal, if not superior, significance arose in Babylonia.

2. *The Cosmic Polytheism of Assyria-Babylonia.* As far back as we can go in history, Lower Mesopotamia, up to the latitude of what later became the site of Baghdad, was divided into two distinct zones: Akkad in the north and Sumer in the south. Arising on the coast of the Persian Gulf and the banks of the Euphrates, the chief cities of the Sumerians were Eridu, Ur, Larsa, Lagash (Tello), Umma, Uruk, Shurappak, and Nippur, the northernmost city which was the principal religious center.

To the north of the Sumerian country lay the land of Akkad with its chief cities, Borsippa, Babylon, Kish, and Sippar.[20] There

[15] Jack Finegan. *Light from the Ancient East,* Princeton, 1946, p. 293.
[16] I Kings 4:30. [17] 19:3. [18] Ex. 7:11.
[19] John A. Wilson, *The Intellectual Adventure of Ancient Man,* p. 19.
[20] L. Delaporte, *Le Proche Orient Asiatique,* Paris, 1938, pp. 6–7.

is evidence to show that the Sumerian civilization was not imported but grew on Mesopotamian soil. The Akkadians belonged, however, to the Semitic family of peoples, had entered Mesopotamia as conquerors, and as they settled on the land found it inevitable to accept the established culture.

Thus, whereas the Akkadians preserved their Semitic speech, they were unable to resist assimilation of Sumerian technology and religion. One may speak, however, of Akkadian deities and Sumerian deities, for when about the middle of the third millennium B.C. the Akkadians imposed their hegemony on the land of Sumer, they did not seek to obliterate the religion of the conquered territory. Instead, they adopted its deities and, having given them Semitic names, sought to discover their affinities with their own gods. The resultant Akkadian religion was of such a composite nature that, owing to its heavy indebtedness to Sumerian sources, one dare not classify it, and its Assyro-Babylonian offshoots, as a pure Semitic religion.[21]

This basic religious structure was not substantially altered at the beginning of the second millennium B.C. when the Amorite West Semites overran not only Sumer and Akkad but northern Babylonia and Assyria as well. They also inherited the religious traditions of Mesopotamia with which they reconciled their own institutions. Next in line were the Kassites who ruled Mesopotamia from the middle of the eighteenth to the middle of the twelfth century, and the Assyrians who followed thereafter; both regimes observed a similar policy of toleration and adjustment in religious matters. Indeed, when the Assyrians entered Babylon, they contented themselves with the substitution of the name Assur, their national deity, for that of Marduk, the great deity of Babylon.

In view of this unbroken continuity, the religion of Assyria-Babylonia, despite undisputed variations, might be regarded as one. Its essence was the concept of the divine, which found its expression in the forms of cosmic, astral, and nature deities, as well as in the general character of the national gods and the concomitant religious life.

As they appear in the cuneiform writings, the names of gods and

[21] E. Dhorme, *Les Religions de Babylonie et d'Assyrie,* Paris, 1945, pp. 3–4.

other supernatural beings are invariably preceded by the sign of a star. The supposition might, therefore, be in order that the first religion of Babylonia was astral. It is to be noted, however, that the sign was repeated thrice when a star or some celestial body was meant. If the sign represented the sky, it stood alone. The deity, therefore, was not conceived of as a star but rather as a celestial being, whereas the chief god was the sky.

This does not imply, however, that the gods did not resemble men. While in Egypt the deity was represented as a hybrid, with human body and animal head, the Assyro-Babylonian god was in human form. Depicted in the likeness of men, the gods of Babylonia were endowed, nevertheless, with immortality. They had wives, children, and maidens, yet required the worship of their devotees. Offerings and sacrifices were performed with consummate regularity, that is, if the anger of the deity was to be avoided.

The gods had a history, and Assyro-Babylonian mythology ranks among the richest on record. This phenomenal growth of mythology has been explained on the grounds that once the deity is humanized there is no limit to the development of the pertinent mythology. The gods intervened in the creation of the world, in the Deluge episode, and in all the legendary happenings related to the origin of the universe. Such were the cosmic deities of Mesopotamia which presided over the destiny of man and nature.

One looks in vain, as he examines the making of Babylonian religion, for the marks that might even remotely resemble monotheism. Undoubtedly, the god of a conquering race might pass for a supreme deity and, in assimilating the traits of divinities whose adherents were subdued, he might perhaps convey certain intimations of the living God. But such a case can only be made at the ost of justice to the facts.

Marduk became the supreme deity of Babylonia. His prestige as head of this pantheon was enhanced by the political ascendancy of Babylon under Hammurabi (1728–1686 B.C.). To him were transferred the attributes of the great gods of Sumero-Akkadian antiquity. He assimilated the powers of Bel (lord)—Akkadian successor to Enlil—in the great triad, Anu (Sky)-Enlil (Earth)-Ea (Water). In honor of Marduk, the Epic of Creation was composed. On seven tablets, it represented the revolt of Tiamat (goddess of the Deep), her destruction by Marduk who also created man and established cosmic order.

The astral deities included the moon-god, Sin, of the Sumerians and Akkadians, also known as Nannar, and the sun-god, Shamash. But of the astral divinities the greatest was the planet Venus whom the Sumerians knew as Ninanna, later Inanna or Ninni (mistress of Heaven), identified with Akkadian Ishtar.

Ishtar thus owed the origin of her myth and ritual to the Sumerians. Personified as the Earth-Mother, goddess of love and of the reproductive forces of nature, she was also regarded, particularly among the Assyrians who made Arabela her cult-center, as goddess of war. The destruction of Tammuz, her lover, and her descent to the underworld, seem to identify her with the great goddess (earth-mother) worshiped throughout Western Asia, especially with Astarte, the Phoenician goddess of fertility and sexual love. From Nineveh, her cult was carried by the Hurrians and Hittites into Egypt and Southwestern Asia Minor. The Hellenistic world knew Ishtar, together with Isis, Cybele, Demeter, and Semele, as a madonna figure.

Tammuz fitted into a cycle indicating similarity between Sumero-Akkadian, Anatolian, and Egyptian myths. In all of these, there was a tendency to group beliefs and practices around a central deity: Tammuz in Mesopotamia, Osiris in Egypt, Adonis in Syria and the Hellenistic world, and Attis in Asia Minor. Coming immediately prior to the summer solstice, the annual festival of Tammuz consisted of a mourning period followed by rejoicing over his return. Ezekiel [22] condemned the action of "the women weeping over Tammuz," at the north gate of the Temple, as a great abomination.

The Akkadians borrowed the Sumerian mythological cycles including the Gilgamesh Epic, that of Creation and the Deluge, as well as the Descent of Ishtar. They transformed these stories into veritable epics vested with dramatic movement and meaning unknown to the verbose and liturgical original. And the whole mythological tradition was set in sharp focus when Hammurabi (1728–1686 B.C.),

[22] 8:14.

great sovereign of the First Dynasty of Babylon, centralized the local cults in the worship of Marduk.

Hammurabi made it possible, through the union, stability, and prosperity of his rule, for scholars to devote their efforts to learned pursuits. Philology, lexicography, astronomy, mathematics, magic, and divination throve. For a thousand years, the lists of gods prepared during his reign remained canonical in Babylonia and its Western Asian outposts.

Other than the myths, epics, and lists of gods this literature, studied and translated by Western scholars during the past century,[23] included prayers, various types of wisdom composition, and legal material. In the wedge-shaped (cuneiform) script, it represents Sumerian literary genius as it was gradually molded by Babylonian scribes, poets, and scholars.

The Gilgamesh Epic, dating from the end of the third millennium B.C., is the most significant Babylonian composition. Less concerned with the activities of the gods, it dealt with man, his struggles and hopes, his need for friendship, instinct for loyalty, fear of death, and longing for immortality.

The Creation Epic, known in Akkadian as Enuma Elish ("when on high," after the opening words), is a remarkable expression of the religious literature of Mesopotamia.[24] In metric form and mythological vein, it is an account of the rise of Marduk to the headship of the Babylonian pantheon. The story of the creation of the gods forms the opening phase of the work, culminating in the victory of Marduk over Tiamat, primeval water-goddess and personification of chaos, from whose corpse he made the universe. With the universe created and organized, he went on to make man. A hymnal epilogue, devoted to Marduk's fifty names, concludes the work which in essence revolves around the struggle between cosmic order and chaos.[25]

---

[23] See Hugo Gressmann, ed., *Altorientalische Texte zum alten Testament,* 2nd ed., Berlin and Leipzig, 1926; and the much more extensive work of James B. Pritchard, ed., *Ancient Near Eastern Texts Relating to the Old Testament,* Princeton, 1950.

[24] E. A. Speiser, *Ancient Near Eastern Texts,* pp. 60–72.

[25] S. N. Kramer, *Encyclopedia of Literature,* Joseph T. Shipley, ed., vol. I, New York, 1946, p. 2.

Two compositions deal with the destruction of the world and feature the legendary sage Utnapishtim. The first tells of a terrible drought and famine that caused death and destruction, while the second, incorporated in the Gilgamesh Epic, is a Deluge myth. There are two other myths concerned with the underworld, the first of which describes the descent of the goddess Ishtar to the underworld and the consequent withering of all sexual desires on the earth; the second leads up to the appointment of the god Nergal as king of the underworld. Fragments of a third pair of myths sketch the legendary figures Adapa and Etana; the former attempts to explain man's mortality as a result of fatal misunderstanding, whereas the latter is concerned with the quest for the plant of birth and involves a heavenward flight on an eagle's pinion.

The wisdom literature breathes a reflective, critical, and skeptical spirit. A writer reminiscent of Job laments his misfortunes, which seem to multiply in proportion to his righteous deeds, but in the end he is comforted when Marduk comes to his rescue. Largely due to the fact that the extension of royal rights and spiritual opportunities was a trend of Egyptian religion without parallel in Mesopotamia, the thought of the Babylonian individual had a this-worldly orientation. There was little expectation of eternal bliss and, among the sophisticated members of society who developed a cynical outlook on the hereafter, the idea of immortality was all but lost. The hedonistic tendencies of the times notwithstanding, Babylonia saw the systematization of knowledge and the establishment of the concept of order on a scale surpassing anything known in Egypt.

In its legal department, Babylonian literature boasts the Code of Hammurabi, the sixth of eleven kings in the Old Babylonian (Amorite) Dynasty, who ruled from 1728–1686 B.C. The document was put together from what originally were Sumerian enactments.[26] From Sargon (*ca.* 2400 B.C.) of Akkad to Hammurabi, civil disorder and strife had filled the people with anxiety, and they looked for a ruler who would establish justice. Urakagina (*ca.* 2450 B.C.), the last prince of Sumerian Lagash, had already made an attempt in this direction when he undertook to restore the

[26] Theophile J. Meek, *Ancient Near Eastern Texts,* pp. 163–164.

"righteous laws of Ningirsu," in order to mitigate the official corruption of his day and to check the oppression of the poor.[27] And it was in keeping with this legal tradition that the Code of Hammurabi was known then as "the judgments of the righteous." An elaborate system of state law, it preserved traces of earlier custom such as ordeal and the lex talionis. In the customary laws of earlier societies, it represented an enormous advance. All classes, alien and native, were placed under its protection. From the Persian Gulf to the borders of Egypt, a traveler rode in safety imparted by the operation of the Code. Through the early Christian era, the Code survived and subsequently influenced Islamic jurisdiction.

In the sphere of ethics and morality, the Babylonians, despite the Code of Hammurabi, were on much the same level as the Egyptians. Good and evil were recognized as individually and socially effective. But in their moral standards, the gods were not much higher than men.

The exact relation between the Code of Hammurabi and the Hebrew Book of the Covenant [28] is not clear. The diorite stela, which gives the text of the Code, is topped by a bas-relief showing the king in the act of receiving the commission to write the law book from the god of justice, the sun-god Shamash.[29] Likewise the Old Testament Covenant is introduced with the words, "And Jehovah said unto Moses, thus thou shalt say unto the children of Israel . . ."

In the final analysis, the difference between the two claims is a difference between the concept of Shamash and the concept of God. Everyone knew that the Code of Hammurabi incorporated the same old laws.[30] The Hebrew Covenant also might have been influenced, in form and content, by Babylonian, Canaanite, and other foreign elements. But this does not vitiate its distinctive character. Hebrew legislation received the sanction of divine will in that it was accepted as revelation: containing what God ordained and required of man.[31]

[27] Albright, *From the Stone Age to Christianity,* pp. 147–148.
[28] Ex. 20:23–23:19.   [29] Meek, *op. cit.,* p. 163.
[30] Edward Chiera, *They Wrote on Clay,* Chicago, 1938, p. 77.
[31] Millar Burrows, *An Outline of Biblical Theology,* pp. 31-32.

Similarly it is to be conceded that the Babylonian Creation and Deluge myths are paralleled in the Genesis narratives.[32] The Biblical accounts are, however, free from polytheism, gross anthropomorphism, and the other pagan characteristics of non-Hebrew thought. The Genesis account (P) expresses a profound conception of God, creator of the world and man; it proclaims the unity and solidarity of mankind; and it stresses the responsibility of man as child of the Eternal. These elements of revealed truth remain, constituting the core of theistic religion, whereas Babylonian mythology has vanished.[33] Earth-bound and a mere detail in the cosmic structure of the universe, the cults of Babylonia, like the state itself, lacked moral vitality and inspired hardly any true devotion to the gods men feared.

3. *The Sadism and Asceticism of Hittite Religion.* Although Semitic culture set its stamp on Egypt, and in Babylonia it was assimilated to the older heritage of the Sumerians, there was one important segment of the Ancient Orient—Asia Minor or Anatolia —which unquestionably was not Semitic. Between 1900 and 1200 B.C., the Hittite Empire flourished in Anatolia. Next to Egypt and Babylonia, it ranks as the third great empire of Biblical antiquity. Hittite and primitive Indo-European speech seem to be connected by a common descent from a parent Indo-Hittite language.

Two main periods constitute Hittite history, the Old Empire (*ca.* 1900–1650 B.C.) and the New Empire (*ca.* 1450–*ca.* 1200 B.C.). In its opening phase, the Old Empire was contemporaneous with the First Dynasty of Babylon. Indeed, it was the Hittite ruler, Mursilis I, who about 1600 B.C. sent an expeditionary force that put an end to the Babylonian dynasty which Hammurabi had made famous. With the site of Boghazköy as its capital, the New Empire was consolidated by Subbiluliuma, contemporary of the solar monotheist of Egypt, Amenhotep IV (Akhenaton). Aegean invaders, probably Thracians or Phrygians, began to break up the Hittite empire about 1200 B.C. Thereafter the Hittites continued their

---

[32] P narrative, Gen. 1:1–2:4a; J, Gen. 2:4b–25.
[33] See Alexander Heidel, *The Babylonian Genesis,* Chicago, 1951, pp. 139–140.

political state outside the boundaries of Anatolia, with Carchemish as the seat of their government.

The Hittites were the chief cultural link between Babylonia and Europe. Carchemish, on the Upper Euphrates, became, from the twelfth to the ninth century, a Hittite garrison commanding the international route that linked East and West. In their heyday, the Hittites treated on equal terms with Egypt and Babylonia. For several generations they headed a coalition which stemmed the westward expansion of Semitic Babylonia. Defeated repeatedly by the Assyrians in the ninth and eight centuries, the Hittites of Carchemish finally succumbed before Croesus of Lydia in the West shortly prior to the advent of the Persians in the second half of the sixth century B.C.

The Old Testament makes sixty-one references to the Hittites (or children of Heth). Abraham purchased the cave of Machpelah, where his wife Sarah was buried, from Ephron, the Hittite.[34] Esau took Hittite wives [35] and later the Israelites intermarried with the Hittites.[36] David married Bath-Sheba, the wife of Uriah, the Hittite.[37] The Hebrews apparently had a high regard for the military prowess of the Hittites, whom they bracketed with the Egyptians.[38]

Hittite literature deals in the main with religious subjects.[39] Its representations in the cuneiform inscriptions of Khattusas (modern Boghazköy) as well as in the monuments of Cappadocia and North Syria, lead to the conclusion that Hittite religion was independent of, though not uninfluenced by, the religions of neighboring peoples. Strong influences emanating from Babylonia and the Hurri (later Mitanni) sources are in evidence. A particular relation existed, moreover, between Hittite religion and that of the Canaanites. Striking similarities and differences have been noted between the Hittite code of laws (fourteenth century B.C.) and Israelite law.

[34] Gen. 23:10–18.
[35] Gen. 26:34.
[36] Judges 3:5, 6.
[37] 2 Sam. 11:2–27.
[38] 2 Kings 7:6.
[39] On Hittite religion, see Albrecht Götze, "Die religiösen Anschauungen," *Kleinasien: Kulturgeschichte des Alten Orients,* Munich, 1933, pp. 122–160; and his essay in *The Haverford Symposium on Archaeology and the Bible,* Elihu Grant, ed., New Haven, 1938, pp. 136–157.

Together with other instances of Hittite influence upon the early Hebrews, this might lend support to the supposed Hittite origin of the Jewish physical type.[40]

Our knowledge of Hittite religion, then, is based on the thousands of religious texts contained in the royal archives of the Hittite capital at Boghazköy belonging to the New Empire and dating back to the two centuries from *ca.* 1400–1200 B.C. This material illuminates the religious performances and duties of the king. The prayers are royal prayers and, although reflecting the more general religious ideas of the people, they tell next to nothing about the piety of the ordinary man.

It may be safely assumed, however, that the religion disclosed by the written documents was of a highly developed polytheistic nature with a long historic record. The main god was the weather deity, Taru (Tarhunt), corresponding with Hurrian Teshub. His sacred animal symbol was the bull and according to an older conception he was a bull himself.[41]

Exaggerated sexualism and ascetic meditation, in line with the broad sweep of Hinduism and Babylonian religion, highlight the structure of Hittite religious doctrine and practice. That the main goddess, who often preceded her consort, the weather god, in the ceremonial order of the gods, reflects an older religion of matriarchal character is not certain.

In the international treaties to which the Hittites were party, the national gods were invoked as witnesses. Like those of the Canaanites and Aramaeans, the Hittite gods almost invariably appeared standing on the back of animals or seated on a throne borne by animals, but hardly were they ever identified, on such occasions, with animals, as was the case in Egypt.[42]

In addition to its development under the two empires and their sequel in Northern Syria, Hittite religion reflected a proto-Hittite pre-Aryan stage, depicted in idols upon circular plaques of alabaster, and including male and female deities. The most conspicu-

[40] William F. Albright, *Universal Jewish Encyclopedia*, vol. 5, New York, 1941, p. 403.

[41] Hans Gustav Güterbock, *Forgotten Religions*, Vergilius Ferm, ed., New York, 1950, pp. 83–109.

[42] Albright, *From the Stone Age to Christianity*, p. 229.

ous of them was the sun-goddess Arinna, whose name tallied with a similarly called city, and who was known to the Hurrians as Khebat. The sanctuary of Arinna had more than solar significance; it lent itself to syncretic influence and in the classical Hittite age, the weather god, Taru (Teshub), became the male companion of the sun-goddess.

With the coming of the Indo-Europeans, the indigenous deities of Anatolia were both preserved and transformed. Important additions were those who corresponded with Varuna, Indra, Mitra, and Nasatya in the natural polytheism of Aryan India. But the endurance of the old deities may be illustrated by the role of Kubaba (Cybele), represented in the form of a she-lion, who practically inherited the character of Arinna.[43]

An amazing collection of deities, drawn from heterogeneous sources and generally betraying the existence of sky and earth gods, made for a pantheon which represented the relation between gods and men, the former as lords, the latter as slaves. The cults, omina, magic, prayers, hymns, and mortuary rites may be seen within this religious framework.

And in addition to the forces of nature—wind, storm, rain, and wells—the Hittites had come to worship humanized, personalized divinities. The paradox of the orgiastic and ascetic worship of Cybele and Attis shows that the juxtaposition of sadism and meditative self-control was the culmination of Hittite religious perversion. Indeed, this mixture of extravagance and docility was one of the earmarks of a universalism which swept the ancient Orient and eventually spread westward.

In keeping with this wave of religious universalism, reaching its climax in the thirteenth century b.c., the Egyptian gods were freely identified, at that stage, with those of Anatolia. Thus in the public documents, such as the treaty between Rameses II and the Hittite king, Khattusilis (thirteenth century), the chief male deities of Syria and Asia Minor were referred to as Seth (Suteh), the old Egyptian god whose spouse Nephthys was identified with Semitic Anath.

[43] René Dussaud, *Les Religions des Hittites et des Hurrites, des Phoeniciens et des Syriens,* Paris, 1945, p. 341.

The Hittite civilization, product of an extensive intermingling of different races, was epitomized by its religious structure which, however, had its own distinctive cast and essence.[44]

4. *The Baalism of Ancient Syria.* In the cuneiform documents of the Hittites, as in the Nuzi tablets and the Amarna letters, all of the fourteenth-thirteenth century B.C., the early Hebrews were in some way connected with the Apiru (Khabiru), depicted as landless soldiers, sailors, captives, and slaves. The Hebrews, on whom major religious significance centers, are dealt with elsewhere in this book.

Among the neighbors of the Hebrews, and their predecessors in the land, were the Canaanites, Phoenicians, and Aramaeans. Together with Israel, these are the peoples of ancient Syria. Though political and ethnic boundaries might change, the geographic and historical unity of Syria, acknowledged by the Romans, seems fully attested. Syria, along the eastern shores of the Mediterranean and extending far inland, is a land which stretches from the Euphrates westward to the sea, and from the foothills of the Taurus range in the north to the confines of Egypt.

The Canaanites were the pre-Hebraic inhabitants of Palestine and members of an early West Semitic stock domiciled in Syria. Their seafaring kinsmen were the Phoenicians who dwelt in city-states under monarchical government. Sidon was an early Phoenician settlement which in the twelfth century B.C. yielded to Tyre. The great age of Phoenician sea power was between 1200 and 800 B.C., subsequent to the rise of Greece. Wherever the Phoenicians sailed they planted colonies, of which the most important was Carthage. From the seventh pre-Christian century onward, Carthage was engaged in ceaseless commercial conflict with Sicily and the West, and in the third century she confronted the rising power of Rome.

Whether Canaanite, Phoenician, or Aramaean, the Semites of Syria did not produce formidable empires in the shadow of whose royalty unified religions might flourish. Theirs instead was a political order which gave birth to a number of small independent states, torn asunder by mutual jealousies, which continued to guard their

---

[44] See Albrecht Götze's review of Giuseppe Furlani, *La Religione degli Hittiti,* Bologna, 1936, *JAOS,* vol. 58, no. 3, September, 1938, pp. 475–476.

local traditions even when absorbed into the larger imperial systems of the ancient world. To understand their religious life is to probe the nature of many cults and ceremonies, and to discover in these a few salient features representative of the whole.

Yet the subject is not without importance, for here was a basically Semitic culture and population; and Semitic religion has often been compared with its Indo-European sister as one would compare monotheism with polytheism. Yet this need not detain us very long especially since Ernest Renan's proposition with regard to the desert origin of monotheism has already been abandoned. The fact remains that the Semites of Syria, not unlike their polytheist neighbors, had pantheons which show deep roots in the past.

Overshadowed by the imperial religions of Egypt, Babylonia, and the Hittites, the religious voices of Canaan were hushed by the Biblical rebuke administered in no uncertain terms. Actually all the student learned about Canaanite religion was drawn, until the second quarter of the twentieth century, from indirect testimony. At long last, however, in a series of discoveries made at Ras Shamra during 1923–1933, archaeology has provided direct evidence on Canaanite culture as it was in the patriarchal Hebrew age prior to the advent of Israel into the stream of history, with many revelatory glimpses of ancient Syria's religious life.[45]

A mound on the north Syrian coast, Ras Shamra is near modern Latakia and stands practically opposite the jutting promontory of Cyprus. It is the site of ancient Ugarit, a Canaanite seaport which flourished during the latter half of the second millennium B.C.[46] Canaanite religion may be illustrated from the corpus of Ugaritic myths, epics, and legends, particularly the poems about Baal and Anath, the legend of King Keret, and the tale of Aqhat.[47]

The rain and fertility god, Baal, accompanied by Anath, the warrior goddess, takes the lead in the poem bearing their names. According to the story, the lord of earth, Baal, rose from a relatively obscure rank among the gods by dint of his victories over his foes. In his warfare, he received staunch support from Kothar, the

[45] Theodor H. Gaster, "The Religion of the Canaanites," *Forgotten Religions,* pp. 113–143.
[46] See C. H. Gordon, *Ugaritic Manual,* Rome, 1947.
[47] H. L. Ginsberg, *Ancient Near Eastern Texts,* pp. 129–155.

cunning craftsman god, and from his own sister, the ferocious and potent Anath. The basic theme was the shift of authority over the pantheon from the aging god, El, to his son, Baal.[48] Hence the acute crisis involved in the conspiracy of the other gods with or against the rising figure of Baal.

King Keret, the hero of the legend that carries that title, was of divine descent though he ruled a human community, and his wife, the charming Lady Hurriya, was a mortal. While Keret was recuperating from an illness, his eldest son, Yassib, suggested that the father vacate the throne, whereupon the King roundly cursed him.[49]

Of legendary rather than mythological nature, the narrative whose titular hero was Aqhat depicted him as the son of a celebrated personage, Daniel, a man noted for virtue and faithful service of the gods. Presumably an ancient Canaanite sage and saint, Daniel has been identified with the wise man of the same name mentioned by the prophet, Ezekiel.[50] The death of Aqhat, much like that of Baal, brought about a blight upon the fields, and it was also the victim's sister, Paghat in this instance, who rose to wreak vengeance upon his enemies.

Passing on to Phoenician religion, one notes that like that of the Canaanites, prior to the discoveries at Ras Shamra, our knowledge of it was mainly derived from sporadic references. These consisted primarily in data available in the Egyptian texts of the Twelfth and Eighteenth Dynasties, as well as the myths recorded by Philo Byblius on the authority of the Phoenician, Sanchuniathon (*fl. ca.* the seventh century B.C.). Today, it is possible, however, to revise and complete the data of Philo, and it would appear that Phoenician beliefs were based on religious and mythological materials which resemble their Egyptian and Babylonian parallels in distinctness if not in quality and refinement.

The head of the Phoenician-Canaanite pantheon was El (the god) referred to as El Elyon ("the Highest God"), who triumphed over his adversaries and was El Shaddai (god of the mountain), creator, king, sage, and judge. Beside him, as the great active figure in the

---

[48] Julian Obermann, *Ugaritic Mythology,* New Haven, 1948, p. 83.

[49] H. L. Ginsberg, *Encyclopedia of Literature,* Joseph T. Shipley, ed., vol. I, p. 121.

[50] 14:14, 20; 28:3.

cults of ancient Syria was Baal, whose name was a determinative meaning "owner," "lord," regarded by the Canaanites as the god of the north. Baal was identified with Haddu (Hadad), the god of the storm and hurricane, who rode the clouds, caused the lightning, and sent down the rain. In the Ugaritic texts, Baal's appellation was Aleyan (I prevail), and his arch-enemy was Mot ("Death") whom Anath killed in a terrible battle.

As Baal came to be identified with the local cult, he emerged as a popular deity, adored on high places such as the peaks of Lebanon and Mt. Carmel, gaining stature through the performance of special functions and the attainment of new attributes. Every major aspect of religious life might develop its own Baal, and every city its replica of him such as the Melkarth of Tyre. Generally speaking, he was credited with being the male author of fertility in soil and flocks and at proper festivals offerings were presented to him in kind. Despite the fluidity of ancient religious conceptions and functions assigned to the gods, there is no parallel in Near Eastern mythology to the explicit identification among the Phoenicians and Canaanites of the body of Baal with the grain.

Next to Anath, Astarte was the most dominant goddess of fertility. Addressed by her adherents in the plural of majesty Ashtaroth (pl. of Ashtoreth),[51] her name designated cult-centers such as the one at a distance of twenty-one miles east of Lake Galilee, still known as Tell Ashtarah. Consort of El, Astarte (Asherah) was the Elath (goddess) of the cult and was paired with Baal when he succeeded to the headship of the pantheon. Her regular title in the Ras Shamra texts was "Asherath of the sea," the original form presumably having been "she who walks upon the sea," in line with the title of al-Khidr (the green one) of modern Syria: "he who walks in the sea," also a maritime patron.[52]

Adonis was a Phoenician-Canaanite deity who eventually permeated Greek mythology. He was a youth without the royal pedigree and function of Egyptian Osiris. Slain by a wild boar, he was bewailed by his beloved Aphrodite when the gods detained him in

---

[51] Gen. 14:5; 1 Sam. 31:10.
[52] W. F. Albright, *Archaeology and the Religion of Israel,* Baltimore, 1942, pp. 77–78.

Hades. Generally interpreted as a parable on vegetation, its blossom and decay, the myth of Adonis corresponds with that of Babylonian Tammuz. The discovery of agriculture and animal husbandry in the middle Late Stone Age gave the early paganisms of the Near East a new turn signalized in the formation about 6000 B.C. of divine triads, usually based on the father-mother-son relationship. In that light, Adonis, the dying figure, might represent the Phoenician aspects of a myth which fits into a cycle widespread in the ancient Orient.

The history of ancient Syria discloses the coexistence of two striking trends, the one culminating in Baalism, the other in high cultural and religious attainments. In other words, alongside the manifestations of debasement such as the morbid polytheism of the people, the fluidity of divinities, and the dominance of fertility and sacred prostitution, went such impressive accomplishments as the invention of the alphabet on Phoenician soil, the discovery of the Atlantic Ocean, and above all, in the case of the Hebrews, an illuminating response to the call of the Eternal, blossoming forth in a unique ethical monotheism.

The last great racial stock to share in the making of Syria's ancient heritage consisted of the Aramaeans. Inhabiting the plain that extended from the Lebanon range to the Euphrates and beyond, and from the Taurus on the north to Damascus and adjacent lands on the south, the Aramaeans built their states about the time of the Hebrew monarchy.

Towards 1100 B.C., the Aramaeans, whose kinship with the Hebrews the Old Testament confirms,[53] were the target of Assyrian attack. But following the fall of Nineveh (612 B.C.), the Aramaic language became the lingua franca of the lands extending from the Iranian East to the Semitic West, displacing Hebrew and Phoenician. From the Persian Gulf to Cilicia, and from Edessa to Petra and the Nile Valley, Aramaic became the common vernacular.

This Aramaic supremacy was maintained against the heavy inroads of Hellenism until the victory of Islam in the seventh Christian century. As such, Aramaic was the language spoken by Jesus,

[53] See James A. Montgomery, *Arabia and the Bible,* p. 55; Abraham was described as a "fugitive Aramaean" in Deut. 26:5.

his Apostles, and the early Eastern Church. Without it, the expansion of Christianity in the East would have been as humanly impossible as its expansion in the West would have been without Greek.[54]

Damascus, Aleppo, Emesa, and Palmyra were among the cult-centers of Hadad (Adad), the principal male deity of the West Semites, known to the Babylonians also. Palmyra, situated in the desert at the extreme east of Syria, developed peculiar cults of its own. Its temple of Bel remains an imposing structure among the preserved ruins. Baalbek in Eastern Lebanon, city of the sun, known to the Greeks as Heliopolis, was dedicated to the worship of the local Baal with emphasis on his nature as a sun-god.

Rimmon was the name of the deity, Hadad, worshiped at Damascus, of whose devotees were Namaan, the Syrian, and his master.[55] Known in Assyria among the twelve leading deities, Rimmon (Thunderer) had an Akkadian origin if one were to judge by his name. He was adored as lord of fecundity, rain, storm, and lightning, dreaded as destroyer of the crops and scatterer of the harvest.

Aramaean paganism, as portrayed in the early Hebrew writings, had a dynamistic belief in an undefined but nonetheless real blood relationship between the clan and its god. In the early first millennium B.C., the Aramaeans were known to have named their children "sons of Hadad," a custom which was popular among the pagans of Syria and Mesopotamia in early Christian times. Another Aramaean custom consisted in a clan's entry into a contractual relationship with its chosen god.[56] A tribal religion thus appeared among the Aramaeans which was later utilized in the implementation of revelation.

5. *The Abortive Monotheism of Ancient Iran.* The religious history of ancient Iran may be sketched against the background of political development. Three leading dynasties—Achaemenid, Arsacid, and Sassanid—successively occupied the throne of Iran. From the ancient province of Parsa, the Achaemenids under Cyrus

---

[54] Emil G. H. Kraeling, *Aram and Israel,* New York, 1918, p. 139.
[55] 2 Kings 5:18.
[56] Albright, *From the Stone Age to Christianity,* pp. 187–189.

(559–529 B.C.) conquered the Medes of Western Iran and established their dynasty which lasted until the overthrow of Darius III in 330 B.C. by Alexander the Great.

Next came the Parthians who, following the Seleucid supremacy which had arisen in the wake of Alexander, became in 250 B.C. independent in their native province of Parthia, southeast of the Caspian Sea, and beginning about 248 B.C. under Arsaces, founder of their empire, ruled Iran until A.D. 226.

The Sassanids, who succeeded the Parthians, rose to power under Ardashir I (A.D. 226–241). Their rule lasted until the Moslem Arab conquest (641) and was both vigorous and generally beneficial to Iran. The Sassanids restored the religion of Zoroaster to its pristine character and in an epoch of over four hundred years enriched the national heritage.

The early religion of Iran was akin to that of the Rig-Veda and, like the Homeric Greek, it was a naturalistic polytheism. At the head of the pantheon stood Ahura-Mazda; among the chief deities were Mithra, the god of light, and Ardvisura Anahita, the goddess of fertility, "the great stream, the unblemished one."

In the morning twilight of Iranian religious and political history, Spitama Zarathustra (Zoroaster), some time in the seventh-sixth century, preached a new gospel, the general nature of which is made clear in the Gathas of the Avesta.[57] Yet our data for the history of Mazdaism, the proper name of Zoroastrianism, are obscure and conflicting.[58] Member of an Iranian agricultural and cattle-breeding

---

[57] Denoting the sacred writings of Zoroastrianism, the *Avesta* is in five parts:

I. The worship and sacrifice *Yasna,* including the seventeen chapters known as *Gathas* (psalms) of Zoroaster himself, L. H. Mills, *Sacred Books of East,* vol. 31, pp. 1–332; K. S. Guthrie, *The Hymns of Zoroaster,* New York, 1914.

II. *Visparad: Invocation to all the Lords,* Mills, *op. cit.,* pp. 333–364.

III. *Vendidad: Law against the Demons,* J. Darmesteter, *The Zend Avesta, Sacred Books of the East,* vol. 4, New York, 1898.

IV. *Yashts: Worship Hymns,* J. Darmesteter, *Sacred Books of the East,* vol. 23, pp. 21–345.

V. *Khorda Avesta: Little Avesta,* A. H. Bleeck (tr. from Spiegel's German), vol. 3, Hartford, 1884, pp. 1–192.

[58] Hence the highly disputed interpretations of the data by scholars such as A. Christensen, G. Messina, E. Herzfeld, E. Benveniste, and H. S. Nyberg; see Albright, *From the Stone Age to Christianity,* pp. 276 *sqq.*

community in the far northeastern marches of Transoxiana, Zoroaster taught that there was only one supreme being, the good and bright Ahura-Mazda against whom were ranged the evil and dark forces of nature led by Angra-Mainyu (Ahriman). In its details of form and doctrine, Zoroastrianism bears a close resemblance to the Old Testament prophetic tradition.[59] But the only modern heirs of this ancient faith are the Parsis of India who fled Iran during the seventh-century Arab occupation and constitute today a prominent community in the state of Bombay.[60]

The Iranians do not figure in the Biblical table of nations,[61] nor is their Zoroastrian faith specifically mentioned in Scripture. But certain kings of Iran, who were presumably Zoroastrian, are named in the Old Testament.[62] When Jesus was born in Bethlehem of Judea, homage was paid Him by certain wise men from the East,[63] described in the Vulgate version of the Scriptures as Magi and identified in tradition as a religious caste, possibly priests of Zoroastrianism. This is not disproved by the fact that the Greeks attached the epithet Magos to any sorcerer who employed the methods and enchantments of the East.[64] Indeed, the religion of the Magi with its worship of good and evil was selectively shared by Zoroaster and included belief in the advent of a saviour.

The first Indo-European Iranians had, in the second millennium B.C., penetrated the highlands fringing Babylonia on the east in the same way that others of their kinsmen passed through the Khyber into the Punjab and thence into diverse parts of India. The Aryan invaders who brought with them the horse, later utilized to high military advantage by the Assyrians, had had a religion which stood in striking contrast with that of their Semitic neighbors.

With their Aryan cousins of India, the early Iranians shared

[59] R. E. Hume, *The World's Living Religions,* rev. ed., New York, 1946, p. 190.

[60] Consult Irach J. S. Taraporewala, *Religion in the Twentieth Century,* V. Ferm, ed., New York, 1948, pp. 19–43.

[61] Gen. 10.

[62] 2 Chronicles 36:22–23; Ezra 1:1, 8:1; Nehemiah 2:1; Esther 1:3, 10:2; Isaiah 44:28, 45:1; Daniel 9:1, 10:1, 11:1; Haggai 1:1; Zechariah 1:1.

[63] Matt. 2:1.

[64] Acts 13:6 (RV margin), 8:9, respectively, where the Jew Bar-Jesus and Simon of Samaria are each called Magos.

religious affinities including the cult of Mithra (sun-god and dragon-slayer, Indian Indra), fire worship, and belief in a law of destiny superior to gods and men. Varuna, ethical deity in the Vedic religion, was parallel to Ahura-Mazda. Unlike the Hindus, however, the Iranians did not believe in Brahman, the Oversoul to whom all deities were subservient. Finding such a Brahman to be inaccessibly remote, they resorted to a dualistic conception of ultimate reality.

Ahura-Mazda, the supreme being of Zoroastrianism, was conceived of as creator of the world, the Good Principle, and guardian of mankind. His adversary was Ahriman, the Evil Principle and chief spiritual power of darkness. Tradition had it that Ahriman was the offspring of a moment of doubt on the part of Ahura-Mazda, the lord of light and righteousness, who pressed a relentless battle against the arch-enemy and his evil crew. Portrayed as Lord, attended by angels and archangels, Ahura-Mazda, according to his devotees, created the world, electing man as his helper in the struggle for truth, looking to the advent of the good kingdom.

Thus robed in light and righteousness, Ahura-Mazda made his first appearance as one deity among many. It was the singular achievement of Zoroaster that he exalted the name of his Lord and replaced the natural polytheism of Iran with a universal monotheism. In him, as in Ezekiel, the ethical relation of the individual man to his God supplanted the natural cult of gods. In so doing, Zoroaster removed Mithra, god of the old social order, of which the lex talionis was the legal foundation. He launched a new dispensation that brought to the foreground monotheism instead of polytheism, ethics instead of cults, and instead of self-help a law that was no longer founded on the social but rather on the religious concept of good and evil.[65]

And in that part of the Avesta known as the Gathas (hymns), ascribed to Zoroaster himself, Ahura-Mazda is elevated in a magnificent ethical system. The history of Zoroastrianism as a whole, however, shows defection from this lofty conception of divine reality. In its broad sweep, the religion which showed so much promise in the days of its prophet, betrayed a lack of spiritual vigor and its

[65] Ernst Herzfeld, *Zoroaster and His World,* vol. II, Princeton, 1947, p. 487.

ultimate evanescence despite universal claims, suggests the abortive character of Iran's monotheism. The recrudescence of acute dualism, polytheism and syncretism gave rise, as the resurgence of Mithraism and the birth of Manichaeism prove, to sun worship, idolatry, and other forms of deterioration. The modern worshipers of Ahura-Mazda, known as Parsis, number about 130,000, of whom some 100,000 live in India, 20,000 in Iran, whereas the rest are scattered in various other countries.

Mithraism is the religion of the worshipers of Mithra, the Iranian god of the light of the middle zone between heaven and hell, defender of the truth and coadjutor with Ahura-Mazda in the struggle with the powers of darkness. Regarded as a rockborn hero who captured and slew the divine bull, Mithra aided man against the adversities of nature and, translated to heaven, he watched over the faithful until the day of his second coming. Celebrated in grottoes and underground chapels, Mithraism was introduced to Rome in the time of Trajan (A.D. 98–117), although it was known to the Romans as far back as the conquest of Cilicia by Pompey in 67 B.C. As a cult popular among the Roman legionaries during the closing era of paganism, it was a powerful rival of Christianity.

Associated with the cult of Cybele, the worship of Mithra included the rite of taurobolium probably originating in the worship of Anahita, that consisted in the sacrifice of a bull with whose blood the devotees were baptized. Made up of Iranian beliefs, Semitic mythology, and certain elements of the Anatolian nature cults, Mithraism drew its essence from Zoroastrian Mazdaism blended with Babylonian beliefs and practices. Its doom was sealed with the triumph of Christianity under Constantine, and the last attempt to reinstate it, which Julian the Apostate (A.D. 360–363) undertook, proved unsuccessful. But prior to the final disappearance of Mithraism in Iran, under the impact of Islam (A.D. 641), it had another recrudescence under Mani.[66]

Manichaeism was the cult of Mani (*ca.* A.D. 216–*ca.* 276) which combined the ancient worship of Mazda with elements derived from Christianity and Buddhism. Zoroastrian dualism and Christian soteriology, forming the basis of Mani's teaching, were construed

[66] M. N. Dhalla, *The History of Zoroastrianism*, Oxford, 1938, pp. 302–308.

to mean that man's soul, which sprang from the kingdom of light, sought to escape from his body, which represented the kingdom of darkness. Release was to be accomplished through the wisdom imparted by a saviour, who was a docetic Jesus, and must be perfected through renunciation of all material and sensual attachments.

The intention of Mani was to bring the East and the West into closer union through a combined faith, a syncretism, based on the widely accepted creeds of his age. He was put to a cruel death by the Sassanid emperor, Bahram I (A.D. *274–277*), and his doctrine was banned in Iran. Migrating westward and southward, his followers passed through Egypt, North Africa, and thence penetrated Sicily, Spain, and the rest of Europe. In the lands of the West, Manichaeism appeared in the guise of heretical sects such as the Bogomils (beloved of God) in Bulgaria, the Cathari in Italy, while no less a figure than St. Augustine of Hippo was attracted to the Manichaean faith in his youth.[67]

Despite these uncreditable offshoots, Nathan Söderblom [68] described the religion which Zoroaster preached, in the mountains of Bactria, as a "Fight against Evil." Though not predestined to everlasting universality, the voice which the Iranians then heard was clearer and loftier than any that cried in the wildernesses of antiquity's natural faiths. The time was crucial and epoch-making for the cause of religion.

It was a time when Confucius summarized the wisdom of China in reverence toward Heaven and antiquity. His older contemporary, Laotzu, showed the way to quiet goodness and peace of mind. The Buddha, a soul which laid bare the need for deliverance from misery, made his appeal in a great renunciation of worldly possessions and family. From the seemingly inexhaustible resources of Hinduism came the concept of bhakti, devotion to a personal god. Among the Hebrews, the prophets breathed an unquenchable thirst for God, and the communication of the revelation which He gave them made theism an incisive word. Heraclitus, the gloomy solitary of Ephesus, expounded his doctrine and began to speak about the

[67] M. N. Dhalla, *Zoroastrian Civilization,* Oxford, 1922, pp. 339–348.
[68] *The Living God,* London, 1933, p. 167.

logos, which Plato later took up and treated with greater insight.

The Gathas stood alone, among the sacred writings of pagan peoples, in that they disclosed the living picture of a prophet, his surroundings, and the opposition he endured. In a peculiar sense, they deserve comparison with the prophecies of the Old Testament.

The career of Zoroaster demonstrates his unwearied effort to press for a choice between good and evil. To him, Ahura-Mazda was Lord, a supreme being, who rules, rewards, and punishes the living and the dead. Amidst incessant spiritual warfare, Zoroaster remained faithful to his Lord, the All-Wise, attended by beneficent powers and spirits; and the religion of ancient Iran became more luminous because he defined it as action.

The Gathas disclose to us the character of Zoroaster as a man of high purpose, wielding his energies in the face of fearful odds toward the goal of all his striving, namely an encounter with the Lord.

II. RELIGIONS OF CLASSICAL ANTIQUITY

1. *The Enlightened and Personal Henotheism of Crete.* The island of Crete witnessed, in the third millennium B.C., the rise of a rich and variegated civilization, known as Minoan (*ca.* 3000–1100 B.C.) after Minos the law-giver and friend of Zeus according to Greek tradition; in its later stages, this Minoan civilization overlapped with the Mycenaean culture (*ca.* 1100–1000 B.C.) of the Greek mainland.[69]

According to Thucydides,[70] the ancient Greeks ascribed much of their law, art, and religion to Cretan origins. Distinct in type from that of Egypt and Babylonia, Cretan culture attained its height first at the opening of the second millennium, when the Twelfth Dynasty ruled Egypt, and again when the Eighteenth Egyptian Dynasty ruled the East, with a maturity therefore of about six hundred years.

The Cretans were the first known European people to use writing. As Crete declined in culture, Mycenae, home of the Homeric Aga-

---

[69] On Cretan antiquities consult Sir Arthur Evans, *The Palace of Minos,* vols. I–IV, London, 1922–1937, where the word Minoan was first used.

[70] I, 4; cf. Herodotus, I, 171, 173.

memnon, inherited a portion of her sea-power. Recent excavations have brought to light at Knossos, the chief city of ancient Crete, and elsewhere, splendid royal palaces containing treasures of metal work in gold, bronze, and copper, figures of ivory, porcelain, engraved gems, and pottery of rare excellence.

Charred ruins of the Palace of Minos at Knossos tell the story of a devastating avalanche of invaders, irrupting from the European hinterland, which brought the Achaeans and their kinsmen into conflict with the thalassocracy (sea-power) based on Crete. Culminating at about 1400 B.C., this movement, which marked the destruction of Knossos, spelled the conquest of the Aegean world by the barbaric invaders of the north. That is to say, the ancestors of the historic Greeks, speaking an Indo-European language, were on the march. Although darkness followed, the fusion of two streams, that of the ancient Cretans and that of the new invaders, was a preparation for the future culture of classical Greece. Yet the religion of classical Greece was by no means to be a lineal descendant of Minoan worship. The religion of ancient Crete was as different from that of the Olympians as Christianity was from the worship of Odin and Thor.[71]

The essence of Minoan religion was fundamentally akin to the great Oriental faiths, Iranian, Hebraic, Egyptian, and Islamic. It possessed a more spiritual core and was infinitely more profound in its personal quality and intimations than the religion of the early Greeks. The great goddess of the Minoans professed to give the power of immortality to her adherents. She stood close to her worshipers, offering them protection and, although a female deity, she was relatively free from that degradation and ambiguity of sexes characteristic of the Greek mysteries, and partook of a basically monotheistic nature.[72]

There is evidence to show, however, that a plurality of goddesses marred Minoan religion. The Great Goddess herself was projected as Eileithyia, the Snake Goddess, power of fertility, or as the Dove Goddess, the Goddess of Healing, and Patronness of mountains,

---

[71] Toynbee, *A Study of History*, Abridgement, pp. 23–26.

[72] Arthur Evans, *The Earlier Religion of Greece in the Light of Cretan Discoveries*, London, 1931, pp. 37–41.

animals, war, and the sea. It is not clear whether this functional distribution of divine powers was symptomatic of an earlier nature worship or the result of the localizing, humanizing process that stemmed from the concept of divine unity.[73]

The double-axe was the supreme symbol of Cretan religion. Richly ornamented double-axes of thin-sheeted bronze, and miniature axes of different materials, have been found. A male deity, as a counterpoise to the female, has also been encountered. In the absence of official temples, caves and mountain peaks, groves and sacred trees, as well as snakes, doves, and bulls were the chief centers and symbols of demonstration. These, in addition to private chapels and sanctuaries attached to palaces and other mansions, were the substitute abodes of deity. That an enlightened henotheism, with profound mystical significance and personal emphasis was the essence of Minoan religion, no matter what the external mechanics might have been, seems a valid and proper evaluation.

2. *Anthropomorphic Polytheism, Conditioned by Mystery Cults and Tempered by Philosophy: Greece.* The religions of Greece are represented by the Olympian nature worship, backed by the state. Lacking the unfathomable depth of Oriental cults, this religious phenomenon was supplemented and, during the centuries presaging and immediately following the Christian era, replaced by, the Mystery cults: Eleusinian, Dionysian, and Orphic. Offering the Greeks a spiritual vitality not provided in the old Olympian religion, the Mysteries were a revival of ancient and traditional rites suffused with elements drawn from the Minoan cults such as that of the birth and death of the Cretan Zeus. By the time of Alexander the Great, however, the Olympian religion received little more than lip service among the Greeks. In the period of Hellenization which followed Alexander, the several streams of Greek religion—old Olympian, Mystery, and magic, as well as rationalized faith—were commingled with the Oriental cults of Egypt, Syria, Babylon, Anatolia, and Iran. But before this Hellenistic heritage passed into the custody of Rome, two vital forces had entered the stream of

[73] Martin P. Nilsson, *The Minoan-Mycenaean Religion and Its Survival in Greek Religion,* Lund, 1937, is inclined to favor the plurality of goddesses as the basic picture of Minoan religion.

history, Greek reason with the broad sweep of its philosophical illumination of the mind, and Christianity with the fulfillment of divine truth in revelation and in a personal Redeemer.

The foregoing reconstruction of Greek religion has its background in history. The warriors of Indo-European stock who in the latter part of the second millennium B.C. forced their way southward into Thrace and Macedonia, Thessaly and Epirus, eventually marched into central Greece and the Peloponnesus, while at a somewhat later date others of their kinsmen settled in Asia Minor. The fusion of the invading Achaeans, Dorians, and Ionians with the earlier inhabitants of the Aegean world, particularly the so-called Pelasgi of the mainland, produced the Greeks of history.

Although it was obscure and relatively insignificant in the early centuries of the first millennium B.C., the old Greek civilization extended beyond the confines of Greece. It spread round the Black Sea, reached southern Italy, throve home-grown in Asia Minor, and before the dawn of Christianity had already struck firm roots in the ancient Orient.

Hundreds of Greek city-states were to make their appearance throughout the islands and shores of the Mediterranean. An exceptionally large city-state was Athens, extending over the peninsula of Attica. In the age of Pericles (*ca.* 495–429 B.C.), its citizens numbered 30,000, representing a free population of about 250,000, to whom might be added many slaves and resident aliens.[74] Creation of the Greek political genius, the city-state (polis) formed the basis and ideal of Hellenic society.

Commercial colonies were created by 600 B.C., on the shores of the Sea of Marmora and the Black Sea, on the coast of North Africa, round Southern Italy, and the Sicilian coastline, save where Carthaginians had already lodged themselves. The zenith of this Greek civilization was represented by fifth-century Athens which became, in the words of her celebrated statesman, Pericles, "the school of Hellas."

Within three generations of Athenian history, luminaries appeared in a configuration of cultural growth which remains without

[74] W. G. De Burgh, *The Legacy of the Ancient World*, London, 1947, p. 87.

parallel in the annals of culture. There were statesmen such as Pericles and Themistocles; tragic poets such as Aeschylus, Sophocles, and Euripides; and the comic poet, Aristophanes; Phidias and his school of sculptors; the historians, Herodotus and Thucydides; the philosopher, Anaxagoras; Socrates, the greatest of human teachers and founder of the religion of good conscience, and his disciple, the philosopher, Plato.

Under the leadership of Athens, the battlefront of Hellenic freedom held firm. In their defense of freedom, the Athenians twice beheld their city destroyed by the enemy. But the Greco-Persian War (499–478 B.C.), occasioned by the revolt of the Ionian Greeks, who were aided by Athens, ended in Greek victory, and the supremacy of Persia was kept out of Europe. For Athens, the defeat of the Persians at Marathon (491 B.C.) furnished an imperishable memory. The decisive naval victory at Salamis (481 B.C.) over the same foe, marked the rise of Athens to power and the beginning of her rivalry with Sparta.

The short-lived sovereignty of Sparta is of little consequence for the history of religion and culture. The dawn of the fourth century marks a shift of focus northward, toward Macedon. Both Athens and Sparta were thereafter in the background.

The central fact in the history of fourth-century Greece was the emergence of the Macedonian kingdom. The defeat of the mighty Persians in the fifth century had led to the inescapable conclusion: that a trained citizen army loyal to a common cause of freedom was infinitely superior to a colossal array of ill-disciplined levies ordered by an Oriental despot.

With the conquests of Alexander of Macedon,[75] a new chapter in the contest between the East and the West was begun. In the spring of 334 B.C., Alexander crossed the Hellespont, routed the advance guards of the Persians and, in the following year, defeated Darius III at Issus, the northeast corner of the Levant. By June 323, Alexander, who had conquered most of the ancient world, gathered around him at Babylon a great army, ready to invade the Arabian Peninsula but, stricken suddenly by fever, he died at the age of thirty-two.

[75] See C. A. Robinson, Jr., *Alexander the Great*, New York, 1947.

Alexander's eastern conquests were parceled out among his field commanders, who gave rise in particular to the rule of the Ptolemies in Egypt and of the Seleucids in Western Asia. His singular achievement, surpassing all military feats in its impact upon cultural and religious history, was the dissemination of Hellenism over the Eastern world. The two principal affirmations of Hellenism were, first, the equality of men regardless of race and social position; second, the acceptance of the inhabited world as an oecumene, to be regarded by men who have realized the meaning of their sameness, as their city.

The official religion of Greece, with the Olympian gods at its center, was a natural, anthropomorphic polytheism. Besides Zeus, the pantheon included Apollo, Ares, Hermes, Hephaestus, and Poseidon, also generally Dionysus and sometimes Hercules. The goddesses were Aphrodite, Artemis, Athena, Demeter, Hera, and sometimes Hestia. Sharply distinguished from the Chthonian gods whose underworld character was denoted by black or red colors, the Olympian deities had white as their characteristic color, and their temples faced the East; sacrifices to them were shared by the worshipers in a sacrificial meal.

This official religion of ancient Greece had begun in earnest with the Indo-European invaders who introduced the cult of Zeus Pater (Bright Father). But Greek, Helladic, and Cretan, as well as Oriental elements, are represented in the final form which Olympian religion took and which it preserved for a period of two thousand years, beginning about the middle of the second millennium B.C. Lacking an inflexible tradition, sacred scripture, and other-worldly emphasis, it was an official religion in the broadest sense, and membership in it was general, almost automatic.

Nor were the high cults of Zeus, Athena, and Apollo, with all their attributes of virtue and morality, free from a darker side manifest in the animistic practices of the common people. Developed Greek religion, however, being anthropomorphic, made theriolatry (animal worship) a mere phase of polytheism.

Illuminating the structure of this religion are ritual inscriptions, state archives, private dedications, monuments of religious art, and passages in classical literature. Of these, Homer (*ca.* ninth century B.C.), epic poet of Greece, in the *Iliad* and *Odyssey,* is the earliest authority. To the other great epic poet, Hesiod (*fl. ca. 776* B.C.) are ascribed collections of religious and practical maxims, a calendar of lucky and unlucky days comprised in his *Works and Days,* as well as the *Theogony,* giving the origin of the universe and the dynasties of gods. Systematized somewhat under the leadership of Zeus, Homer's pantheon betrayed the already strong anthropomorphic impulse. The nature of the deities was, however, clear-cut and individualized, and despite the banality of many a Homeric passage the utterances imputed an advanced morality to the supreme deity.

The Zeus of Homer thus emerged, in many instances, as a power of righteousness. Not the author of evil, he protected the good and punished the wicked. Although Plato and Euripides might contest the view, vengeance was, nonetheless, the attribute of Homeric divinity even if simultaneously Zeus was god of pity and mercy.

Homer's pantheon had Mount Olympus in northern Thessaly for its home and place of assembly. The relations of the gods, already mentioned, and the functional distribution of offices were a vital religious feature. In addition to Zeus, there were his two brothers, the blue-haired Poseidon and the dusky Hades, who controlled respectively the sea and the underworld of the dead. The queen of heaven was Hera, sister and wife of Zeus. Sons and daughters of Zeus, the other deities of note were either by Hera or some other lesser divinity or mortal maiden who had caught his temporary fancy.

Athena, goddess of craft, intelligence, and skill was the favorite child of Zeus. His noblest son was Apollo, the archer, with power to enlighten, heal, and kill with his shining arrows. Laughing Aphrodite, of distinctly Oriental provenience, was goddess of love and represented sweetness and desire. She and Artemis, the fierce virginal huntress, were inferior in rank though potent in their own rights.[76]

Although he was not regarded as creator of the universe, Zeus was, nonetheless, esteemed progenitor of gods and men. The dark

[76] *The Iliad of Homer,* tr. Samuel Butler, Louise R. Loomis, ed., New York, 1942, p. xv.

background of the underworld was rendered more fearful by the avenging Erinys, bringers of retribution to all who violated the laws of natural piety. Conceived as smoky-haired women, the Erinys, recognized in English usage as Furies following Latin Furiae, were Alecto, Megdera, and Tisiphone, with a milder aspect represented among the Athenians as Samnae and Eumenides.

Apart from Olympian religion and its ramifications in cult, myth, and folk belief, were the Mysteries with their sōteriological tendencies, particularly Orphism, the one and only missionary, universalist religion of ancient Greece. Inculcating belief in an orderly cosmos and a piety based on the essential unity of life and of divine essence, the Mysteries had doctrines of a cosmic nature.[77] Three noteworthy mystery cults, the Dionysian, Eleusinian, and Orphic, gained wide acceptance during the centuries preceding and immediately following the rise of Christianity.

The Dionysian cult projected Dionysus—son of Zeus, together with his wife, Semele, the earthborn daughter of Cadmus, founder of the Greek Thebes—as patron deity. Originating in Thrace, whence it was introduced to Greece, the cult centered in the worship of Dionysus as the incarnation of natural life and vitality, the embodiment of joyous living.[78] As its highest goal, the cult promised union with Dionysus, the god of life and master of death.

The devotees of Dionysus celebrated their rites on suitable mountain tops where in the midst of wild nature, men and women came together dressed in godlike attire. Appearing in flowing garments, and with hair unfettered streaming down their shoulders, the women together with the men worked themselves to a high pitch of excitement. A divine mania, they believed, overtook them as they adored Dionysus to be possessed of him.[79] The final stage in this ceremony of initiation was presumably reached amidst drinking and revelry, when the initiators attacked and dismembered with their own hands an animal, be it goat, fawn, or bull, and partook of the raw flesh reeking with blood.

Sacramental drinking, the eating of raw meat, and ecstatic danc-

[77] Samuel Angus, *The Mystery Religions and Christianity,* New York, 1925, pp. 39 *sqq.*

[78] Erwin Rohde, *Psyche,* tr. W. B. Hillis, New York, 1925, vol. II, p. 285.

[79] Euripides, *Bacchae,* tr. Arthur S. Way, New York, 1912, vol. V, p. 1094.

ing allegedly enabled the devotee to perform miracles. Plato cynically observed, however, that the Bacchic maidens drew milk and honey from rivers when they were under the influence of Dionysus but not when they were in their right minds.[80]

Admitted to the Olympian group, probably in the seventh century, Dionysus, outliving his critics, was placed at the side of Apollo, was worshiped at Delphi, and emerged as the third member of the Eleusinian triad. He was incorporated in the state religion of Athens as the annual spouse of Basilinna and, shorn of his orgiastic rite, became a central figure of Orphic religion. Later, he was merged with other cults and acquired new adherents throughout the Roman Empire.

The Eleusinian cult, centered upon Eleusis, a hamlet fourteen miles west of Athens, ranked among the most ancient of the major Greek Mysteries. The central theme revolved around the story of Demeter and her daughter, Persephone, related in the so-called Homeric hymn to Demeter.

The goddess of fruitful soil, ruler over the fruitfulness of mankind, and guardian of civil life and marriage, Demeter was later identified by the Romans with Ceres. According to the Eleusinian Mystery, when Hades (Pluto) carried away Persephone, Demeter in utter anger and despair made the earth barren until arrangement was made permitting Persephone to return and spend two-thirds of each year with her mother. Probably of Cretan origin, this Eleusinian Mystery, having been incorporated in the Athenian state religion, was celebrated at Agra, a suburb of Athens.

The main Eleusinian rites were held at Eleusis in the month of September, following the planting of seeds. Continuing for nine days, the celebration was concluded with a procession on the fourteenth of the month when the sacred relics of Eleusis were carried to Athens, led by the chief priest, and culminating in the rite of catharsis. Included in the ritual act of purification was the sacrifice of a sucking pig whose blood was sprinkled on the initiates for cleansing.

Dressed in their festal garb, the initiates started back on the nineteenth of the month and their return to Eleusis figured as one of

[80] George Emmanuel Mylonas, *Forgotten Religions,* pp. 176–177.

the most spectacular religious events of the classical world. As they trod the sacred way back to their holy shrine, the pilgrims sang and danced in adoration of Demeter; their emotional outpouring, reaching the point of ecstasy, is reflected in the verse of Aristophanes.[81]

The nature of the initiation, with its peculiar "holy night, clearer than the light of the sun," as the Eleusinian inscriptions describe it, was recalled by Plutarch in his reference to the profound impression which the opening shrine left on the initiates: "He who once enters into philosophy and sees the great light, as when shrines are open to view, is silent and awestruck." [82]

The Orphic Mysteries were based on the interpretation which Orpheus gave to Dionysinian worship. Thus the sacramental feast of raw meat, suggestive of ceremonies which were of great antiquity, and the more refined symbolism of the Eleusinian type were fused in Orphism. But the essence of Orphic religion was to be discovered in that pure life and asceticism through which the initiate achieved identification with the divine nature. A more sedate and contemplative order replaced the orgiastic ecstasy of the Dionysinian devotee, as a means of obtaining immortality. Instructions for the conduct of the soul in the underworld were presumably drawn from the Egyptian *Book of the Dead*. Found in the graves of believers, eight Orphic tablets—seven in Italy, one in Crete—were inscribed in gold and contain some of the basic affirmations of the faith.[83]

The character of the founder, Orpheus, was steeped in mythology. A Thracian poet and musician, whose lyre could enchant beasts and make trees and rocks move, Orpheus was, according to legend, the son of Apollo and Calliope, she that presided over eloquence and heroic poetry and was chief of the nine Muses. Upon the death of his wife, Eurydice, he descended to Hades and so charmed Pluto with his music that he was permitted to take her home pro-

[81] *The Frogs*, tr. Benjamin Bickley Rogers, vol. II, London, 1924, pp. 324 *sqq.*

[82] *De Profectus in Virtute*, p. 10; Mylonas, *op. cit.*, pp. 182–191.

[83] On Orphic literature, see E. Abel, *Orphica*, Leipzig, 1885; O. Kern, *Orphicorum Fragmenta*, Berlin, 1922; T. Taylor, *The Mystical Hymns of Orpheus*, London, 1896.

vided he did not look back. But through the anxiety of love, he broke his pledge, and Eurydice, who was following in his trail, vanished among the shades. In his deep sorrow Orpheus withdrew to the hills, where a troop of Thracian bassarids (nymphs) tore him limb from limb.

Orphism taught that purification from original impurity through reincarnation and the acceptance of divine essence was the final aim of religion. A syncretism, it was compounded out of Dionysinian Mystery and Minoan elements, particularly the story of the life and death of the Cretan Zeus. Together with the other Mystery cults, Orphism provided Hellenic society in the classical age with a spiritual sustenance which the worship of the Olympians sorely needed.

It is difficult to explain the long persistence of Olympian religion among a people endowed, as were the Greeks, with so much artistry and intelligence. Yet, although the affairs of the gods and goddesses filled many a page in the classical Greek literature, mythology was by no means the true religion of the people. They frequently laughed it to scorn even while they continued to esteem religious essence.[84]

At its very core, Greek religion was invariably a worship of nature, of the fertile soil and good earth. It was their gratitude for all that nature bestowed upon them that led the Greeks to idealize the forces and elements of mother earth. Their cult became more sincere and profound as they related it to the intricacies of urban life. Where religion was welded with patriotism, it gave them new insights and greater understanding of the complexities of existence. But when civic life began to decline, the traditional religions also showed signs of atrophy. In the course of time their religious consciousness was dulled, and it was open to the inroads of many sordid beliefs and rites as well as the intrusion of Oriental cults.

When Christianity was born, the ancient beliefs, smoldering in the cities, were still vibrant in rural Greece. Undoubtedly the city population remained religious but not along the lines bequeathed to them by their ancestors. Christianity won the battle of Greece by

[84] Cf. W. K. C. Guthrie, *The Greeks and Their Gods,* London, 1950, pp. 294–295.

conveying its message in koine, popular Greek, based on the refined Attic. Its heavenly verities were keyed against the claims of
other Oriental rivals and in the face of the decadent Olympian religion and the Mysteries, to that self-same philosophical heritage
which the masses had failed to grasp but which the Apostles and
Church Fathers could wield to such high advantage.[85]

3. *The Grafting of Greek and Oriental Religions upon a Functional Polydaemonism: Rome.* Italy entered the stream of history in
the eighth pre-Christian century. Preceding the rise of Rome, the
Etruscan civilization, centered upon Etruria, comprised at the
height of its power the Italian territory lying between the Arno
and the Tiber and extending inland to the Apennines. Of an unknown origin, the Etruscans seem to have come from that part of
Asia Minor which lies between Syria and the Hellespont, and to
have represented a mixed stock with traces of the Alpine. Largely
due to Latin bias and especially since the rise of the Roman Republic (*ca.* 509–31 B.C.), the importance of Etruscan religion and culture has been minimized.[86]

The Roman Empire came into being in 27 B.C. when Octavius
was made Augustus Caesar. Divided into East and West under
Diocletian, who ascended the imperial throne in A.D. 284, the Empire did not actually split into the Western and Eastern (or
Byzantine) Roman Empire till after the death of Theodosius the
Great in A.D. 395. The Western Empire came to an end in A.D. 476,
whereas the Eastern lasted until the Turkish conquest of Constantinople in A.D. 1453.

Etruscan religion showed concern with the hereafter and held
out faith in personal immortality. But the future life was in jeopardy, since the controlling spirits, whose beneficence was uncertain, had to be constantly appeased. Arranged in hierarchical order,
the deities gave precedence to a triad comprising Tinia, Uni, and
Minerva. While the principal deities gave protection to the Etruscan cities, lesser gods and spirits served the common needs of the
people.

[85] Paul Elmer More, *Christ the Word: The Greek Tradition from the
Death of Socrates to the Council of Chalcedon,* Princeton, 1927, p. 298.

[86] Cf. Tenney Frank, *A History of Rome,* New York, 1923; Franz Altheim,
A History of Roman Religion, tr. Harold Mattingly, London, 1938.

In honoring their gods, the Etruscans made blood sacrifices and other simpler oblations; highly developed divination assumed the proportions of a sacred art. In fact, the rise of the Roman Republic may be explained as a response to the challenge of the Greek and Etruscan efficiency. Faced with the powerful forces of Greek culture and Etruscan influence, the Romans of their own free will chose to adopt Hellenic civilization, much as Japan in her modern history adopted that of the West, and raised themselves to a new level of order and subsequent ascendancy.[87]

The primitive religion of the Romans knew no mythical histories of the gods. It had no pantheon and conception of the underworld, nor epic poets like Homer and Hesiod.[88] Impersonal in their character, the spirits (numina) were powers of the unseen realm and of the fields. And until they had learned from the Greeks and Etruscans to visualize their deities as personal, the Romans contented themselves with a primitive, functional understanding of the divine beings.

At home and on the farm, they turned to Saturnus for sowing, to Ceres for growth of the grain, to Consus for harvesting, and to Flora for the blossoms of the fields. Regnant over all, was Jupiter who brought sunshine and rain and was the sky-father.[89] The organized state religion assigned priests (flamines) to the chief deities. These, in addition to Jupiter, included Mars and Quirinus, the two war gods, as well as Janus and Vesta, the last deities invoked at the ceremonies, who were respectively the keeper of the door and the guardian of the vestal virgins in the temple.

To the extent that it resisted Greek and Etruscan influences and kept itself intact throughout Roman history, this religion was a polydaemonism; [90] that is, its divine powers were not construed as real gods but rather as particular manifestations of mana.[91] These divine powers were numina inasmuch as they had numen, the mysterious dynamic of mana.

[87] Toynbee, *A Study of History*, Abridgement, p. 251.

[88] Carl Clemen, ed., *Religions of the World: Their Nature and History*, New York, 1931, p. 204.

[89] John B. Noss, *Man's Religions*, New York, 1949, pp. 80–94.

[90] John Murphy, *The Origins and History of Religions*, Manchester, 1949, pp. 220–236.

[91] H. J. Rose, *Primitive Culture in Italy*, London, 1926, p. 44.

Such an interpretation may be substantiated from the spiritual life of the family, the heart of Roman religion and the source of that *pietas* which was the most genuinely religious element in the ancient faith of the people. Four principal powers dominated the family religion: Vesta, the spirit of the hearth-fire; the Penates, spirits of the household stores, and Lares, the protecting spirits of farm and field; Genius, at first possibly the spirit of the clan, was identified with the head of the house; and the spirits of the dead members of the family and of ancestors.

Obviously, therefore, the Romans would seek to adopt Greek and Oriental religious forms if only as a means to enhance their spiritual stature and add a new dimension to their faith. During the sixth century B.C., they imported the famous *Sibylline Books*, a collection of oracles ascribed to the sibyl (prophetess) of Cumae (a Greek colony in Campania, Italy) and reputedly purchased by Tarquin the Proud, the seventh and last legendary king of Rome. Purporting to set forth the coming history of Rome and the world, these Books were carefully preserved and frequently consulted until destroyed by the fire that was set in the Capitol in 82 B.C. A later collection intended to replace the original text was assembled in Sicily, Greece, and Asia Minor and retained until ordered burned by a general of Emperor Honorius about A.D. 400.

Religious importations from the Orient included Magna Mater (Cybele), introduced on the advice of the Sibylline oracles. The Mystery religion of Bacchus, Ma of Cappadocia, Adonis of Syria, Isis and Osiris (Serapis) of Egypt, Mithra of Iran were all brought into Rome. The pattern of introducing alien cults and deities was sustained by a penchant for the esoteric, mysterious, and exotic; it also grew out of a deep-seated hope in immortality which the state religion had failed to satisfy as had the skeptical priests and hardened politicians.

The official edict of the Roman Senate (42 B.C.) that proclaimed Julius Caesar a god and caused shrines to be dedicated to his worship, the demand of Caligula (A.D. 37–41), Nero (A.D. 54–68), and Domitian (A.D. 81–96) that they be worshiped during their reigns had deep significance. It meant that amidst the deadly chaos of sect and creed, the empty clangor of mystery and cult, the crying need of the Roman Empire rose for a basic spiritual unity to order the clashing conceptions of man, society, and nature.

A military anarchy upset the Empire in the second third of the third Christian century. Only under Aurelian (A.D. 270–275) was an attempt made to find a religious solution to the internal unrest. At the head of the Roman pantheon, he placed Sol Invictus (the sun), a foreign deity which he hoped might conciliate the centrifugal forces of his realm. But the time for the restoration of paganism had gone and despite persecution and temporary retreat Christianity forged ahead. The two main obstacles which held back the Gospel message were the Roman aristocracy, jealous of its ancient powers, and the provincial folk, obsessed with their traditional beliefs. The conversion of these two social strata took time and involved the Church in protracted missionary effort, testing the very essence of her faith and commitment to Jesus Christ. That despite the aridity of polydaemonism and alien religions, Rome possessed a sense of justice unknown by any other people, before or after, suggests the ubiquity of divine grace no matter what the bankruptcy of culture and the futility of paganism may be.

III. The Old Religions of Northern Europe

1. *Religious Crudity and Simplicity: The Celts.* Like the overwhelming majority of the peoples of modern Europe, the Celts were Indo-European. About the twentieth pre-Christian century, the time of their first appearance, they inhabited the regions of central Europe, particularly the valleys of the Rhine, Rhone, Danube, and Elbe. Both intelligent and industrious, they moved out of their original habitat and proceeded into many lands in their westward and southward migrations.

About 600 B.C. they crossed the Alps and occupied the valley of the Po where they upset the Etruscan domination. A century later, they crossed the Rhone and pushed their conquests into Spain where they fused with the Iberian population. About 400 B.C. they launched a new assault upon Italy, conquering and setting fire to Rome in 390 B.C. In the course of the third century B.C., Celtic invaders traversed the Balkans and founded in central Asia Minor the country of Galatia which bore their name.

These farreaching exploits were not, however, a sign of Celtic strength; the invaders tended to coalesce with other peoples and in time lost their identity. In the Roman Empire, Gaul was the name attached to Celtic France. Celtic racial and cultural affinities have survived among the Bretons, Scots, Welsh, and Irish, although by race and national traditions Ireland is the most peculiarly Celtic country of modern Europe.

It is difficult to assess the religion of the Celts in its pure forms of beliefs and institutions.[92] Their early representatives did not know writing and in a relatively short time merged with other races; their extraordinary individualism militated against the formation of centralized states; their tribal jealousies, for instance, facilitated the task of Julius Caesar who contrived to establish the suzerainty of Rome over Gaul by the simple strategy of setting one clan against another.

Each segment of the Celtic stock apparently had its own gods, religious practices, and institutions. For this, our principal sources are the Greco-Roman authors and the inscriptions which reproduce the names of deities. There are, besides, the national legends and epics of Ireland and Gaul which tell of saints whose hallowed memories lifted them to the rank of popular heroes. These materials are not altogether trustworthy, however, for it has been established that they were subjected to literary embellishments at the hands of later commentators.

Julius Caesar [93] described the religion of Gaul at his time: "Among the gods, they most worship Mercury. There are numerous images of him; they declare him the inventor of all arts, the guide for every road and journey, and they deem him to have the greatest influence for all money-making and traffic. After him they set Apollo, Mars, Jupiter, and Minerva. Of these deities they have almost the same idea as all other nations: Apollo drives away diseases, Minerva supplies the first principles of arts and crafts, Jupiter holds the empire of heaven, Mars controls wars."

Other than the deities thus far enumerated, which were dressed

[92] T. D. Kendrick, *The Druids,* London, 1928, gives all classical references in the original and with translation.

[93] *De bello gallico,* VI, 17: *The Gallic War,* tr. H. J. Edwards, New York, 1917, p. 341.

in local garb and carried Celtic names, there were the specialized, more indigenous divinities which had no Roman counterpart. That zoömorphism was rife may be fully illustrated by the existence of a three-headed and horned deity who beneficently extended his power over nature and humanity; male and female bears, the wild boar, and the horse frequently paired with the goddess Epona, protectress of stables, were often represented. In the epic literature of Ireland, Lug (Lugh) was the god of light, a sun deity, who stood for genius and was possibly the peer of Gallic Mercury. In all likelihood, the Celtic gods resembled those of other Indo-European peoples in that they ruled the natural phenomena, and men looked to them for help and favor.

Simplicity and barbarism characterized the Celtic cult. It was not until the sixth century of our era that St. Samson demolished the cult of stones in Great Britain as St. Martin, toward the close of the fourth century, had abolished the cult of the trees in Gaul. On the authority of Julius Caesar, Tacitus, and others, human sacrifice was common. The consultation of oracles held sway, and the media of divination included the crow and eagle in Gaul, the hare in Breton communities. The cult of the dead showed that there was a deep concern with universal immortality and transmigration. Disposal of the mortal remains was both by interment and incineration as the dolmens of the Bretons, which date back to neolithic times, prove. But Celtic eschatology tended to be vague and laid emphasis on the joy and renewed youthfulness to be experienced beyond, presumably on an ocean island of bliss, rather than on the conception of judgment, reward, and eternal justice.[94]

An institution peculiar to many of the Celts was Druidism, the system of religion, philosophy, and instruction, consisting of pre-Celtic and Celtic beliefs including faith in the immortality of the soul. Witnessed by the testimony of Julius Caesar as well as the Spanish-born Roman poet, Lucan (A.D. 39–65) and the Roman naturalist and author, the Elder Pliny (A.D. 23–79), Druidism was common to Gaul, Britain, and Ireland, where its ceremonies—at least in Gaul—involved human sacrifice at the hands of the priests known as druids. The druid was a natural philosopher who pro-

[94] L. Gougaud, *Les Chrétientés Celtiques,* Paris, 1911, pp. 12, 16–17, 25.

fessed to know the courses of the stars, acted as judge and arbiter in disputes and as teacher of the Gaulish nobles. In the Irish and Welsh sagas, the druids appear as conjurers and not as priests or philosophers, but research on druidism being inconclusive our knowledge of it is far from precise.

Whether in Gaul or across the Channel, Celtic religion did not differ in essence from that of other peoples at the same level of civilization. Their worship was addressed to crude deities which presided over the world of natural forces. Practicing a barbaric cult, they were not above sorcery and magic. Not long ago, Ernest Renan drew an idyllic picture of the Celts. But one needs to overlook a vast deal of crudity and ignore a multiplicity of sinister aspects of Celtic religion before he is able to attribute to them, in good conscience, above other peoples, a naturally Christian soul.[95]

2. *Cold Impersonalism, Alertness, and Nihilism: Germanic Religion.* As it is here used, the word Germanic refers to those peoples of Indo-European race who settled in the lands comprising modern Germany and the Scandinavian countries. Our knowledge of these peoples, who came into historical notice about the fourth pre-Christian century, is largely derived from Greek and Italian sources. Of the Greek sources, the geographer, Strabo (*ca.* 63 B.C.–*ca.* A.D. 21) deserves mention. Other than Julius Caesar and the Elder Pliny, the Roman authorities included the historian Tacitus (*ca.* A.D. 55–*ca.* 117) and Ammianus Marcellinus (*ca.* 330–*ca.* 395) as well as the fifth-sixth century statesman-historian, Cassiodorus. Important data were also given by the early French historian, St. Gregory of Tours (*ca.* 538–593), the English monk and ecclesiastical historian known as the Venerable Bede (673–735), and the Lombard historian, Paul the Deacon, who flourished in the eighth century. The meagerness of internal evidence was due to the long duration of the barbaric stage and the loss of many older traditions, since the Germanic peoples did not begin to write till about A.D. 800.

It is to be noted, furthermore, that even though Germanic religion is here viewed in its totality, its expression among the several groupings was not uniform. For despite the measurable degree of similitude in belief and rite, wide divergences were by no means

[95] G. Bardy, *Les Religions non-Chrétiennes,* pp. 173–184.

lacking. With this important consideration in mind, we might include in a general outline of Germanic religion the names of leading and secondary deities, the nature of the cult, and conceptions of moral life.

The Latin writers who made mention of the Germanic pantheon left the impression that it was almost identical with the Greco-Roman Olympian religion. Now, then, a certain identity of religious essence undoubtedly existed between the Germanic religion, on the one hand, and the classical on the other. Divinization of the forces of nature—such as light, sky, and fertility—was a common procedure in worship. Yet each of the two racial stocks conceived its deities along lines compatible with the principles of ecology, that is, the mental relations between organisms and their environment. How could the somber and cold regions of the North, where the Germanic peoples dwelt, inspire the same enthusiasm for the light which illumined Hellas?

It has too frequently been assumed that Tiu, the Teutonic god of sky and war, was identical with his counterpart among the several Indo-European peoples, particularly Zeus of the Greeks and Jupiter of the Romans. Tiu was not, however, the unchallenged god of the Germanic peoples.

Tacitus informs us that Tiu was regarded as chief god among the Semnones, a subtribe of the ancient Suevians who were exceedingly proud of their origins. But it ought to be remembered that during the Roman epoch, Tiu had become among the Scandinavians a god of war, the son of Odin, and that he thus was regarded as the Germanic Mars.

A ceremony was enacted on the bank of the river Spree at a forest dedicated to Tiu. The celebrants gathered in groups of delegates at fixed times and stood close to the forest; and they sacrificed a human victim. Into the forest no one entered unless he was bound as a sign of dependence upon the divine power. If one happened to stumble and fall, he was not permitted to arise but could only withdraw from the forest by rolling out. It was there that the supreme deity resided and thence, they believed, the nation came.[96]

[96] A. Bros and O. Habert, "Celtes, Germains, Slaves," J. Bricout, *Où En Est l'Histoire des Religions?* Paris, 1911, vol. I, pp. 411–412.

It is clear, however, that the cult of Tiu was superseded by that of Woden, better known as Odin, the god of wind and tempest who instilled fear in men. Attended by two ravens, Hugin and Munin, who reported to him the happenings of the universe, Woden-Odin was lord of battle. At Valhalla, his royal hall, he entertained those slain in battle and there he held court as the two awful and beautiful Valkyries ministered to him. God of wisdom and science, he gave one eye in order to be able to drink of the fountain of wisdom controlled by Mimir. Odin was also master of the arts, inventor of the runic characters, and protector of the crafts in a manner reminiscent of Roman Mercury.

In Norway and Iceland, Thor (Donar), god of thunder, was widely worshiped as deity of strength, helper in war, defender of the people; he validated contracts and marriages, warded off demonic influences, and healed from disease. Thor also was conceived as the vigor of youth, his hair and beard were red (the color of lightning), and he rode a goat-drawn chariot, armed with a magic hammer. The Romans equated him with Jupiter but since the latter had other functions, the analogy cannot be taken literally. At any rate, Thor ended as a benevolent deity, was not only a destroyer but a god of fertility as well, master of the vivifying storm and, in his reformed nature, he fought against evil, crushing the wicked with his iron hammer.

Alongside these mighty gods stood female deities of whom the most eminent was Freya, goddess of love and beauty. She was particularly popular in North Germany and Scandinavia, becoming a celebrity of folk religion and legend.

Aside from these, and other borrowed deities, the Germanic peoples feared a host of evil powers which were opposed, however, by Balder, personal enemy of Loki, the god of dark night and somber winter. A medley of extraordinary and mysterious personages— spirits of the dead, elves, spirits of oppression, and demons—gave rise to sorcery and exorcism and peopled the unseen world.

The priests occupied an important position which, as Tacitus observed, won them the obedience which men owe to God only. Even after the conversion of Germany to Christianity, the priests continued to exercise a formidable influence. Although not constituting a special caste, they were controlled by the state and their primary function was to offer sacrifice and to officiate at the ceremonies. They had charge of the consultation of deities, a task which they performed through strange methods such as observation of the neighing of horses, the flight of birds, the cauldrons containing sacrificial meat, and the intestines of enemies. The priests also had oversight in the enforcement of laws and thereby gained prestige with the kings.

Since the sacred abodes of deities were mainly in forests, temples were rare. The victims of sacrifice were mainly men—although domestic animals, horses, cows, pigs, and lesser forms of libation were also offered—and the institution lasted till the Christian conquest. Fire and water were held to be sacred, and the survival of the soul was an important belief.

Even in lifetime, the soul was believed to depart from the body during sleep, taking the form of a snake or mouse. Ideas concerning the hereafter were confused but, regardless of degradation, the moral life was marked by an esteem of womanhood, the prevalence of monogamy save among the chieftains; and despite ferocity, irritability, and quick discouragement, the Germanic character showed attachment to family life and friendliness toward guests. As among most ancients, the moral life was not related to religion.

Internal evidence of a highly illuminating character is available in the Eddas, both prose and poetic, providing a true picture of the old Norse religion in its relation to the main body of Germanic paganism.[97] The poetic Edda is a collection of earnest, profound religious poetry excelling the more artificial, skeptical review of the same material which the prose Edda offers. Yet the poetic Edda itself, much like Homer and the early dramas of Aeschylus, eludes the comprehension of modern man whose world is no longer peopled by similarly immanent pagan gods.

The complete theology of the Germanic peoples, even as it finds fairly lucid expression in the Eddas, is far from easy to grasp.

[97] Murray Fowler, *Forgotten Religions,* pp. 237–250. See *The Poetic Edda,* tr. Henry Adams Bellows, Princeton, 1936; *The Prose Edda,* tr. Arthur Gilchrist Brodeur, Oxford, 1929.

Breathing a cold impersonalism, it defies interpretation, and any attempt to read Christian ethics into its myth of Balder will do violence to its essence as well as to Christian ethics. The most impressive quality of this theology is a tense alertness everywhere, a conception of the gods who preserve themselves by constant vigil and wakefulness, and the idea that the universe is caught in a perilous balance between life and death, growth and decay, order and chaos. All this and the pervading notion that all things that are—men, animals, rocks, and birds—are doomed to an eventual and inexorable nihilism which in its turn will give rise to a new cycle of birth, death, and recreation, such seem to be the core of Germanic belief in ultimate reality.

3. *Slavic Religious Primitivism.* The Slavic or Slavonic-speaking peoples are known to us from Latin, German, and Danish chronicles, from Byzantine and Arabic sources as well as from their own, rather late, folklore and native literature.[98] To this last category belongs that earliest Russian chronicle composed by Nestor (*ca.* A.D. 1056–*ca.* 1114), the celebrated monk of the Pechusky cloister of Kiev. Disregarding the question of the work's reliability, it ought to be noted that its compilation was made in the period that followed the conversion of Russia to Christianity in A.D. 988 under the leadership of Prince Vladimir (980–1015), who had once set up pagan idols in his country but later accepted the new faith and became a devout saint.

The word Slav (slave) conjures up the first entry of people who belonged to this branch of the Indo-European family as the enslaved captives of the Asiatic conquerors known as Avars. From the sixth to the ninth century, the Avars sought to settle the Slavs, whom they held in servitude, in the land, forming a vast circle around Hungary, which they had wrested from the wreckage of the Roman Empire.

Despite the inauspicious circumstances attendant upon their first appearance in European history, the Slavs had a culture and religion associated with the Vedic, Iranian, Greek, Latin, Celtic, and Germanic peoples, and their primitive paganism is best understood within the conspectus of the Indo-European heritage. Long after the glory of Rome was ended, and soon after Constantinople had

[98] C. H. Meyer, *Fontes Historiae Religionis Slavicae,* Berlin, 1931.

fallen to the Turks, Philotheus, the Russian monk, proclaimed that "Two Romes had fallen and gone, the Western and the Eastern; destiny has determined for Moscow the position of the Third Rome; there will never be a fourth." [99]

Slavic paganism was the religion of small, unintegrated communities, impatient of authority though frequently achieving the power of unity under foreign yoke. The Slavic idea of God was represented by the word Bogu, probably borrowed from Iranian Baga. The thunderer, Perun, was their chief deity and with him was identified Svarog (god of heaven), Perkun of the Lithuanians, and Thor of the Scandinavians. Other deities included the sons of Svarog, Dazbag the sun, Chors, and Viles, the god of cattle. Another leading deity was Svantovit, worshiped among the Slavs who inhabited the regions along the Elbe, and the center of whose worship was on the island of Rügen in the Baltic Sea.

The central religious ceremony was sacrifice and libation in which the priests professed to ward off the demonic influences by the sprinkling of blood, followed by orgiastic celebrations and oracular practices. Authorities agree that Slavic primitive religion gave a place to belief in the immortality of the soul without, however, manifesting any clear conception of the hereafter. The soul was said to go to a place somewhere at the end of the world, a paradise (raj), and its tedious journey thither required a meticulous store of physical provisions and objects. The soul of the ancestor apparently became a sort of home-god (Domovoj) who watched over the family. Certain primitive celebrations in connection with the solstice and equinox have survived in festivals of the Russian Church.

[99] Joseph L. Hromadka, *Great Religions of the Modern World*, p. 286.

CHAPTER V

ETHNOCENTRIC RELIGION: SHINTO

As THE ethnic religion of the Japanese people, Shinto was marked by reverence for the spirits of the imperial ancestors, the great national figures of the past, and a variety of nature deities. Thus inherent in race, Shinto (the way of the gods) was subsequently influenced by Buddhism, which penetrated the island empire during the sixth Christian century. Wedded together, these two religions were not actually separated until 1871 when a law to that effect was promulgated.

In its ordinary expression at shrine and temple, Shinto with its peculiarities of rite and ceremony was not, however, regarded until the surrender of Japan to the United Nations in August, 1945, as a religion, but rather as a form of patriotic commitment. Hence the now-defunct requirement of the Japanese government that all nationals, including Buddhists and Christians, should participate in the Shinto cult as a sign of patriotic loyalty. On the other hand, Sectarian Shinto, which owed its origin to the initiative of individual founders, emerged in a variety of denominational forms and was legally recognized as a religion albeit within the general Shinto framework.

Few are the documents which illuminate Japanese history prior to the Buddhist infiltration. Having devised a system of writing that was of Chinese origin and reached the archipelago about A.D. 405 by way of Korea, the Japanese produced a number of annals dating from the eighth century. Included among these were some ancient myths, a genealogy of kings of whom the earliest did not reign prior to the Roman Emperor Tiberius (42 B.C.–A.D. 37), and a miscellany of quasi-historical texts.

Compiled during an age of excessive Buddhist enthusiasm, these literary materials failed to give Shinto its proper setting in the national history and shed but little light on its religious significance. For the rest, it may be observed that the cursory passages of Chinese authors who referred to Shinto and the results of seventy years of archaeological research in the field of Japanese prehistory, have not as yet been conclusively coördinated.[1]

Nor are we in a better position to define the precise making of Japan's ethnic structure. There seems to have been no conspicuous influx of foreign races. The primitive Ainu, belonging to a Caucasian stock, formerly occupied most of the archipelago but are now confined to part of Hokkaido (Yezo) and Karafuto (Sakhalin) in the North Pacific. Radically different from the rest of the population, the Ainu have a religion of their own, inculcating belief in supreme beings (*kamui*) to whom offerings (*inao*) are made.

Without the benefit of priests and temples, and traditionally excluding women from participation in religious observances, the Ainu are today in a state of regression. Their worship is of a domestic type, the northeast of the residence serving as a direction of devotional orientation, whereas a window, from which nothing is thrown out and no one looks upon the outside world, is designated as a place of holiness. The bear plays a role as sacred animal, and it is made the core of an elaborate sacrificial ceremony involving the eating of its burnt flesh at a common meal.

Of a mixed racial constitution, the original forbears of the historic Japanese founded their first state, centered upon the island of Yamato, several centuries after the hypothetical 660 B.C. of the native sources. They had to fight for every foot of land against the staunch Ainu resistance.[2] Presumably they had come into being as a result of the fusion of several stocks who, in addition to certain undetermined elements, included Korean, Oriental Siberian (Manchu) immigrants as well as Formosan and Malayan settlers.

Whereas direct cultural contact between prehistoric Japan, on the one hand, and China of the literate Chou Dynasty (*ca.* 1027 B.C.– 256 B.C.), on the other, is not attested, evidence of a linguistic and anthropological character points to strong ties with Korea. Equally

[1] Jean Buhot, *Histoire Générale des Religions,* edited by Maxime Gorce and Raoul Mortier, Paris, 1947, p. 467.

[2] Kenneth Scott Latourette, *The History of Japan,* New York, 1947, p. 12.

established is the testimony from the fields of phonetics and ethnography which supports the early connections of Japan with the Malayans and Polynesians to the south.

No successful foreign invader had vanquished Japan throughout its recorded history until World War II. Kublai Khan's armadas of A.D. 1274 and 1281 did not penetrate beyond the coast of landing. It is likewise true that Japanese intervention in the affairs of the mainland was not much greater. In consequence of this isolation, Japan's culture shows remarkable continuity, the rise and fall of political regimes being conspicuously less than elsewhere. Until A.D. 1400, the nearest country, Korea, which was itself marginal to China, served as the main filter through which foreign cultural influences permeated the Japanese islands.

The more notable swells in the continuity of Japanese civilization may be reckoned as five. First, the Nara and Early Heian era (*ca.* A.D. 700–900) when the classics of Old Shinto were compiled. They were the *Kojiki* (Record of Ancient Matters) in A.D. 712; the *Nihongi* (Chronicles of Japan) in 720; the *Izumo Fudoki* (Topography of the Province of Izumo, containing some mythology) in 733; the *Kogoshui* (repetition of material in *Kojiki* and *Nihongi*) in 807; the *Manyoshi* (Collection of One Thousand Leaves) in 750–900; and the *Engi Shiki* (Rituals of Engi) in 923.[3]

Second, the Kamakura period (*ca.* 1192–1233) when the warrior for the first time dominated the court aristocracy and the exaltation of the military circles was introduced. Third, the Ashikaga age (1337–1533), whose closing stage was coincidental with the advent of European influence, was a period of luxury, public extravagance, overbreeding, and decline in the spirit of loyalty and devotion. Fourth, the Tokugawa Shogunate (1603–1868) under which peace and security facilitated the growth of industry and trade. Along with the rise of large cities, Japan saw the advent of a wealthy class of commoners, the educated plebeians, at about the same time when the European bourgeoisie sprang into being. Fifth, the Meiji Era (1868–1912) which witnessed the introduction of a constitution,

[3] Robert O. Ballou, *Shinto: The Unconquered Enemy*, New York, 1945, pp. 25, 32.

an elected Diet, universal conscription instead of service by a military class, and a heavy accent on plebeinanization.[4]

I. ANCIENT SHINTO

In a summary and rather nebulous fashion, the *Kojiki* and *Nihongi* depict the ancient epoch, citing details which develop greater volume as one moves toward historic times. The scene of this early religious activity is laid in the western half of Japan, where three centers of cultic and mythological tradition are distinguishable. These centers are Hyuga in the far south, Izumo opposite Korea, and the plain of Yamato south of Lake Biwa, where Jimmu Tenno, having arrived from Hyuga, took his legendary stand in the face of his foes. With his companions, he amassed the weapons necessary for warfare and consequently bequeathed, according to mythology, to his descendants the task of spreading their dominion over the entire archipelago.

The intricacies of ancient Shinto are but sketchily intimated in the annals, which were more concerned with the official history of the ruling dynasty. It is clear, however, that Hyuga was conceived as the original home of the maritime deities, the place where the gods settled after they had created the islands.[5] Izumo was home of the cult devoted to Suso-no-wo, the storm-god. Yamato boasted its own cult of the sun, personified in the goddess Amaterasu. The submission to Amaterasu of the deified descendant of Suso-no-wo was not only the signal of the vassalage of Izumo to Yamato but also of the rise of the sun-goddess to national preëminence.

1. *Shinto Mythology.* Naïve and incoherent, this mythology leaves the impression of a nightmare and is frequently tedious. The eminent Japanese scholar and theologian of Shinto, Hirata Atsutane (1776–1843), recognized that the deities of the first six generations were hollow personalities and arbitrarily invented. The first was Ameno-Minaka-Nushi-no-Kami (The Divine Ruler of the August Center of Heaven).[6] The sixth deity, Musubi-no-Kami (The

---

[4] A. L. Kroeber, *Configurations of Culture Growth,* Berkeley, 1944, pp. 673–680.

[5] N. Matsumoto, *Essai sur la Mythologie Japonaise,* Paris, 1928.

[6] D. C. Holtom, *The National Faith of Japan,* London, 1938, pp. 43, 50, 182.

Divine-Producing-Wondrous-God) [7] was elevated to this rank among the numerous divine beings because he formed the embryo, the fruits of vegetation, and otherwise gave the spark of life and growth.

Designating all Shinto deities, the word *kami*, too readily equated with *kami* (on high), is more likely identical with Ainu and Eskimo *kamui*, that is, sacred, divine. In the seventh generation, the divine couple Izanagi (sky-father) and Izanami (sky-mother), of uncertain etymology, formed Japan on the summit of the globe; standing on the bridge of heaven, they shone forth as the greatest creation deities. In modern times, both among Christian apologists and Japanese scholars, an attempt has been made to read a primitive monotheism, complete with monist and trinitarian intimations, into the original conception of deity represented by the significance of *kami* to the early adherents of Shinto.[8]

2. The Cult. Primitive Shinto saw no fundamental relation between the conception of deity and ritual purity, nor between religion as such and divination. The three categories of deity, ritual, and divination were nonetheless grouped under the general heading of the supernatural.

Burial of the dead was preceded by a period of mourning that lasted ten or more days; while members of the family gave themselves to weeping and lamentation, their friends danced and provided doleful music. Upon other occasions bones were burned in order to determine by divination whether a day was auspicious for the performance of a given deed. Before setting out on a journey, a traveler chose someone known as an abstainer who undertook to abstain from combing his hair, washing, partaking of food and the practices of normal life; this abstainer was rewarded if the journey proved successful, but if it failed he was held guilty for any mishap and incurred a heavy penalty. Dating back to remote antiquity, the nature of Shinto divination was not unlike the parallel usages of the Chinese under the Shang Dynasty (*ca.* 1766–*ca.* 1122 B.C.).

---

[7] *Kojiki*, tr. Basil Hall Chamberlain, ed. W. G. Aston, Kobe, 1938, p. 17.
[8] D. C. Holtom, *Modern Japan and Shinto Nationalism*, Chicago, 1943, pp. 112–122.

Other than the hereditary corporation of diviners (*urabe*), there were the sarume (sorcerers) who delivered oracles through spiritism.[9]

Rated as the principal causes of impurity were sickness, death, and every kind of blood effusion. Special huts and shanties were set aside for the isolation of expectant mothers about to be delivered, for the consummation of marriages, and the separation of the dying. Communal homes for women were built at Kyushu and certain rites revolved about children whereby a boy's utterances were regarded as oracular. Attached to some temples were the Miko, young dancers who as the priestesses of Shinto were deemed competent when they attained the age of seven to pronounce oracles. Sacred prostitution was practiced from the earliest times. A custom that was not abolished until the fourteenth century was for a young imperial princess to be sent, upon each new accession to the throne, to a temple where she spent many years as inmate. The chief priest of Shinto was the Mikado himself, who allegedly held the office in perpetuity, ever since the inception of the cult under the apocryphal Jimmu Tenno.

Although human sacrifice has not been explicitly attested, sacrificers formed a prominent corporation. As the oldest and most important of the festivals were connected with agriculture, the ordinary offerings consisted of food, rice, green vegetables, as well as of fish, birds, trophies of the hunt, and occasionally horses and farm implements. The horse played an important though obscure role in Shinto sacrifice, and each temple was provided with a stable. Genchi Kato,[10] the twentieth-century Japanese authority on Shinto, could not affirm whether these sacrificial offerings were really of a votive character or merely an expression of wealth and prosperity.

Phallic ceremonies formed an aspect of ancient Shinto ritual and have survived until the present time. Connected with the great parents, particularly the mother-deity Izanami, phallicism had its own temples on Mt. Tsukuba in Ibaraki Prefecture. Of a worldwide significance, the phallic rites had parallels in the worship of the

[9] W. G. Aston, *Shinto: The Way of the Gods,* London, 1905, pp. 112, 203.
[10] *A Study of Shinto, the Religion of the Japanese Nation,* Tokyo, 1926.

Greek Aphrodite, Egyptian Isis and Osiris, and the great earth-mother of the Yoruba on the west coast of Africa.[11]

3. *The Ethical Structure.* Involved in the principle of ritual purity was the paradoxical negation of elementary human charity. To illustrate this one needs to remember that since disease and the flow of blood were considered marks of impurity, a stranger who suddenly took ill or was wounded almost automatically became subject to social hostility and ostracism. Mitigating the harshness of this custom, however, was a redemptive procedure whereby the unfortunate victim was permitted to escape upon the payment of an indemnity.

The word *tsumi*, ordinarily rendered as meaning guilt, designated all that was displeasing to the gods, and the conscious shunning of such misdeeds by the Shintoist was called *imi* (avoidance).[12] The eighteenth-century scholar Motoori Norinaga explained that *tsumi* comprised three distinct types, namely uncleanness, sin or crime, and calamity.

Obscurity in ethical ideas stemmed from the fact that the difference between ceremonial impurity and moral guilt was not clearly defined in ancient Shinto. Thus guilt included all forms of ritual impurity that were held to be abhorrent to the gods, as well as antisocial conduct, acts harmful to agriculture, general wickedness, and incest. Abstinence (*imi*) was the only device held to be effective in combating *tsumi*. It is obvious, therefore, that apart from the influences of Confucianism and Buddhism the suitability of Shinto ethics to advanced culture would have been highly doubtful.

II. MEDIEVAL SYNCRETISM

1. *The Influences of Confucianism, Taoism, and Buddhism.* Although Confucianism was by no means strange to the aristocratic Japanese, since it formed the core of his education, it met a formidable rival in Buddhism. In order to preserve its identity, Confucianism resorted to the technique of grafting its essence upon Shinto. The dreadful events of the period 1181–1221 when the Emperor, his family, and partisans were subjected to humiliation

[11] Holtom, *The National Faith of Japan,* pp. 119–120.
[12] W. G. Aston, *Shinto: The Way of the Gods,* pp. 247–248.

and personal injury at the hands of ruthless warriors from the Eastern provinces, shocked the orthodox Shintoists.[13] For to them the Emperor was not merely a monarch with divine rights but actually a living deity.

Coming to the rescue, the Confucianists invoked in behalf of Japan's ruling dynasty the same principle which China had long recognized as applicable to her own sovereigns, namely that Heaven ordains the punishment of those who lack virtue, that is, the corrupters of the Emperor's government and their accomplices. As far back as the eighth century, Confucianism and Shinto had been in intimate association. Yet the ethical emphasis that grew out of their intimacy had not been engendered by Shinto, which managed to contribute no more than the stock of primitive values rooted in the national soul.

Wherever a luminous religious aspect emerged in Japan, it was possible to trace its origin to some external source. In the fourth Christian century, Shinto defended itself against the cult of the polar star, on the grounds that it was of foreign extraction. Ancient Shinto paid little attention to astral religion save that of the sun, and to a lesser degree the moon. As in the sixth century and the modern era, its primary understanding of religion was steeped in the sullen, often ferocious, aspects of an ethnocentrism which found expression in excessive nationalism.

Like Confucianism, Taoism was known to the elite; but the Japanese soul, taught to cherish the rough and ready Shinto ritual, did not relish the more poetic and refined essence of Taoism. The Taoist motif embodied in P'ong-lai-chan—an island of idyllic bliss and immortality—figured nonetheless in the lacquered art of seventh-century paintings. Giving an exposition of yin-yang, the Taoist masters enjoyed a temporary popularity which won them a status comparable to that of medical doctors. They soon lost their prestige in the country, largely through an obsession with magic and a propensity to disseminate the elements of Chinese superstition.

During the Kamakura period, these Taoist soothsayers found themselves in conflict with the staunch Buddhist reformers. In sum,

[13] Genchi Kato, *op. cit.,* pp. 190–196.

Taoism never succeeded in penetrating the depth of Japan's religious life. During the five centuries (ninth to the fourteenth) of Shinto's stagnancy and passivity, Buddhism discovered in Japan a most inviting field for the development of art, thought, and morality.[14]

Having reached Korea in the second half of the fourth century, Buddhism made its way in A.D. 552 from the southern Korean province of Kudara into Japan. Although it did not meet with immediate approval, the Indian faith was adopted in Yamato, aided by the turn of internal politics. The enlightened and valorous Shotoku Taishi (573–622), who had become regent, recommended in his edict of 604 that all subjects observe concord, noble faith, and religious reverence. His appreciation of the superiority of Buddhism over the national religion enhanced the reputation of the former and consequently, for the first time in their history, the Japanese began to think and speak in terms of the moral law.

Despite the piety of Shotoku and his consort, the Empress Suiko, the new religion was not always sufficiently understood. The Japanese were inclined to equate their Shinto rites with the recitation of Buddhist sutras and generally ignored the wide disparity between the two doctrines. This rather blind syncretism may be understood within the framework of Far Eastern religious accommodation and toleration, which stands in marked contrast to the Near Eastern Semitic spirit of uncompromising rigidity. That Buddhism continued to attract converts, however, was borne out by the fact that in 624 it claimed 816 monks, 569 religious teachers, 46 monasteries, and that its followers among the two sexes were not fewer than 5000.

Accompanying the advance of Buddhism was the stock of Confucianist ideas, perpetuated through the study of the Chinese classics, which proved congenial to the agnostic Japanese mind. Characterized, despite its remarkable agility and brilliance, as slow in the adoption of cultural meaning, the Japanese mentality began to undergo amazing changes. Everywhere were evident the signs of new tempo and greater facility of movement from the old pattern to the new. Princes were wont, in principle at least, to abandon the

[14] Buhot, *op. cit.,* p. 490.

usual extravagance of the funerary rites; Empress Jito (abdicated A.D. 697) expressed her desire that when death came she be incinerated like a nun. The inhuman practices of an archaic paganism were allowed to lapse into disuse. Even in matters such as kindness to animals, Buddhism in the years 730 to 741 effected a change whereby the burden of a horse was reduced from 200 to 150 pounds.

In the wake of Buddhism new religions, philosophies, preachers, and technicians entered Japan. After the middle of the seventh century, Japan established new relations with China and thus reaped the harvest of the latter country's intercourse with India. Though they themselves did not go beyond the confines of China, the Japanese were nevertheless eager to absorb the ideas, rites, and artistic expressions of Indian Buddhism.

Except in the conservative northwest, which remained relatively hostile to foreign influences, new Buddhist temples seemed to mushroom everywhere. Erected in 681, the temple of Yakushiji was transferred in 718 to a site in the new capital, Nara, and its ornaments included the highly attractive little bronze statues of pure T'ang design. There are indications that the religious art of Japan acquired in this era a greater degree of vitality and refinement than anything hitherto known. Even among the Ainu, subdued shortly before in the east if not in the north, the beneficent law of Buddhism had won many supporters who flocked into the orders. In the meantime, Buddhism kept an eye on the political and legislative scene and lost no opportunity to worm itself into the country and effect alliances with the ruling class.

2. *Ryobu.* A rescript issued in 722 declared that the religion of the land and the imported Buddhist doctrine served the same lofty purpose. The attempt to fuse the two mighty faiths culminated in Ryobu (dual), a system worked out by the priests of the Shingon Buddhist sect.[15] The duality involved consisted in an emphasis on the two phases of reality as expounded in Shingon metaphysics, namely matter and mind, male and female—that is, the dynamic and potential aspects of perceptive reality. Ryobu Shinto is Shinto interpreted and understood in the light of these two categories.

[15] Holtom, *The National Faith of Japan*, pp. 36–38.

Although it was of a much earlier inception, Ryobu developed its classical form in the first half of the thirteenth century during the Kamakura period,[16] and attained its high authority in the Japanese Middle Ages. Rendered more profound and ethical, Shinto may be said to have benefited immensely from this union with Buddhism. And in thus absorbing Shinto, Buddhism had brought to its task a broad experience garnered in the course of its long pilgrimage across Asia where it had coördinated the folklore and mythologies of the many peoples encountered.[17] A new note was thereby struck in the religious history of Japan. For in embracing the deities and demons, saints, goblins, and thought forms of India, China, Iran, and other lands, Shingon Buddhism had sought to interpret them as manifestations of the one and same Buddha.

Threatened with absorption into the highly assimilative Buddhist matrix, the response of Shinto took the characteristic form of nationalist self-assertiveness. Entrenchment in the folkways and time-honored ceremonies was its chief defense against the onrush of Buddhist currents. And for the recovery of its peculiar religious motifs, Shinto relied upon new schools of doctrine which were set up in opposition to Ryobu.

3. *The Seventeenth-Century Revival of Shinto.* Fed by the streams that flowed from antiquity, the revival of Shinto which proceeded under the Tokugawa Shogunate during the seventeenth century was Japan's reaffirmation of her national heritage in the face of aggressive Buddhism. Whether as the Urabe priesthood at their Kasuga shrine in Nara, or the Watari priesthood identified with the Outer shrine at Ise, the representatives of the national cult had successfully preserved its identity despite the steady encroachment of rival religions. Even when the absorption of Shinto into Buddhism seemed like a foregone conclusion, these champions of the old national faith strove to preserve the believers' enthusiasm. In typical Shinto style, they contended that the Japanese kami were in reality the originals after whom the Buddhist deities were fashioned.[18] Above all, they urged upon their people the necessity of

[16] For native sources on the Kamakura period see Chitoshi Yanaga, *JAOS,* vol. 59, no. 1, March, 1939, pp. 38–55.

[17] Masaharu Anesaki, *History of Japanese Religion,* London, 1930, p. 125.

[18] John B. Noss, *Man's Religions,* pp. 415–416.

return to the deification of the Emperor and stressed the unique role of Amaterasu.

The revival was called into being by the fulminations against heresy voiced by Kada Azumamaro (1669–1736),[19] a native of Kyoto. He was possessed of the firm conviction that the revival of the nation demanded restoration of the true way of the gods, that is, recovery of the classical Yamato speech and religion as well as the recapture of the true vigor of the nation through the study of Japanese philology. The most powerful nationalistic movement was sponsored by the Fukko school, whose aim was the revival of antiquity with all of its ostensible treasures of wisdom and learning geared to an emperor-centered nationalism.

Three frontline scholars laid the intellectual and religious foundation for this resurrection of the Japanese past. They were Motoori Norinaga and Hirata Atsutane—both already cited—and Kamo-no-Mabuchi (1697–1769) who discovered the golden age of an allegedly glorious mythology to which he ascribed the qualities of simplicity and stability. In that remote era, ruler and subject were said to have lived in reverence toward the great deity Amaterasu-Omikami, achieving true greatness through punctilious conformity with the way of the gods.

III. Modern Shinto

An upsurge of patriotic devotion to the Emperor swept away the Shogunate and initiated the restoration of 1868. But before this happened a long period of political, cultural, and religious incubation was necessary.

1. *The Tokugawa Epoch (1603–1868)*. The religious spirit of Japan had lost much of its vigor during the violence and anarchy that marked the Ashikaga regime. Even where the priests had won the merit of saving culture, they had failed in setting an example of virtue and brought little satisfaction to the spiritual needs of the people.

Zen Buddhism, which had stepped in to fill the breach, was less a religion and more a philosophy, an attitude of egotistical though cultured individualism. The Tendai sect which exercised an enor-

[19] Holtom, *The National Faith of Japan*, p. 44.

mous influence upon all Japanese Buddhism took exception from the very beginning to Zen, which actually showed signs of increasing departure from the beaten path of Buddhism. Toward the close of the Ashikaga period, neo-Confucianism, as it was reinterpreted by the skeptical and metaphysical Chu Hsi, attracted numerous Japanese intellectuals.

Having ceased to exercise spiritual power, Buddhism likewise lost its grip in the political domain. Oda Nobunaga (1534–1582)— the feudal chieftain of obscure antecedents who in 1568 had overcome his principal rivals and emerged as the most powerful man in Japan [20]—did not think that he could pacify the empire without setting fire to the Buddhist monasteries. By this action he gave implicit support to the Jesuit missionaries who had suffered immeasurably through the connivance of the Buddhist monks.

The changes wrought by the first Tokugawa rulers did not alter the already prevalent suspicion of Buddhism. Indeed, they lent support to the merchant class which had sprung into being in the Kamakura epoch and had no record of coöperation with the Buddhists. To be sure, the Shoguns might occasionally choose their counsellors from among the Buddhist priests. But more often they recruited their advisors from the ranks of the Confucianist scholars who throughout the seventeenth century constituted the majority of the country's intellectuals.

The dictator, Nobunaga, and his successor, Hideyoshi (1537–1598), had cultivated Shinto as the traditional religion linked to the imperial institution through which they proposed to govern. A third dictator, Iyeyasu (1543–1616), who initiated the Tokugawa Shogunate which endured till the restoration (1868), was deified upon his death as the Toshodaigongen (East-shining-great-Divine-Hero), and his tomb at Nikko became an object of worship.[21] His successors also had the privilege of apotheosis and, insofar as the state budget permitted, were immortalized in sumptuous mausoleums.

Edo, the future Tokyo, was originally a little hamlet, and its

[20] G. B. Sansom, *The Western World and Japan,* New York, 1950, pp. 108, 126.

[21] Genchi Kato, *op. cit.,* p. 51.

castle served as headquarters of the Tokugawa Shogunate. The Edo government adopted the policy of prohibiting the importation of certain Chinese books in its Edict of Kanei (1630) as part of the attempt to close Japan to contact with the rest of the world. A quarter century later, however, Yoshimune's love of learning caused the Government to adopt less stringent measures toward scientific works, a policy which was maintained till the latter half of the nineteenth century.[22]

Meanwhile, the old symbols of Shinto were the subject of arbitrary interpretations. Yamago Soko, a distinguished seventeenth-century Confucianist and professor of military science,[23] was one of the luminaries of Tokugawa times. Taking his point of departure from Chinese ethics, he criticized as immoral the sacrifice of human beings to the River-god, allegedly practiced in the reign of Emperor Nintoku (A.D. 313–399) ;[24] he instituted a new ethic embodied in the code of chivalry which became the pseudo-religion known as Bushido (the way of the warrior). Bushido was subsequently exploited by the militarists of Japan and by the custodians of the national classics, who sought to exalt the memory of the ancient heroes and, as foes of the Shogunate, prepared the ground for the restoration of the Emperor in 1868.

All these trends fitted into the outlook and philosophy of the literate classes. But they also had repercussions, through romance and folk tale, in the more lowly strata of society. In general, however, Shinto, as it was known among the masses, did not radically change. The common man humbly brought his offerings to the kami, consulted the mediums for oracles, and certain fanatics continued to push their concern for ritual purity to the extent of going out to bathe in midwinter beneath the ice-cold cascades of Mt. Ontoke.

It would be vain to search the depths of Shinto for those universal values which distinguish the great religions. One ought to recognize, nevertheless, that Shinto preserved a profound quality which belongs to the soul of old Japan, a characteristically pure aesthetic expressed in an imposing though humble simplicity.[25] At

[22] Shio Sakanishi, *JAOS*, vol. 57, no. 3, September, 1937, pp. 290–303.
[23] Sansom, *op. cit.*, p. 270.
[24] Genchi Kato, *op. cit.*, p. 125.
[25] Jean Buhot, *op. cit.*, p. 507.

its core, this cult represented a communion with nature along lines which were often lacking in the most archaic cultures of the West. Even the crude purity of ritual possessed a congeniality of its own; it was the mother of that most meticulous devotion to the family and homestead, to the national hero and homeland, which distinguished the pre-industrial Japanese.

2. *The Restoration (1868)*. A disquieting feature of Shinto consists in that it preserves in the more or less dormant state an enormous potential for fanaticism. The eminent statesman, Mori Arinori (1847–1889),[26] who was minister of education, once pushed aside with the tip of his cane a curtain at the entrance to a sanctuary at Ise; a fanatic who saw him commit this alleged insult, did nothing at the time but within a year assassinated the statesman. The assassin was, of course, condemned and executed but his coreligionists regarded him as a saint.

When the threat of United States warships at last forced Japan to abandon her isolation (1852–1868) and to inaugurate a new order, no particular religion was recognized by the State. But in 1884, Shinto was invested with a special status on the assumption that no state can ignore her traditional public rites. Thus, the temple ministers, or some of them at least, became officials of the Government. The cause of religion was thereby dealt a mortal blow.

Jinja (state or shrine) Shinto came to the foreground as the central theme of intensive propaganda, and the national press began to highlight state ceremonies such as imperial funerals and military expeditions. Concurrently there was written into the educational system the doctrine of *kokutai shinron* (new thesis on national polity) which was a critique of the national concepts of the function of the state, calculated to inspire the people with loyalty to the Emperor, excessive patriotism, and faith in the greatness of Japan.

As a consequence, the divine ultimate reality which the cult imposed on the worshiper was the Emperor. Otherwise, it may be said that as a royal personage, Emperor Meiji (1868–1912) was a truly illustrious sovereign, a monarch of great wisdom and valor. Not only the occupant of the throne but all members of the Imperial line were the recipients of veneration in a manner that was fre-

[26] Sansom, *op. cit.*, p. 459.

quently scornful of historical facts. Those in power had obviously made up their minds, and it was clear that in their desperate attempt to whip up patriotic passion they would stop at nothing, not even the promulgation of outrageous falsehoods. Thus, the celebrated Mitsui family—of worldwide industrialist fame—dedicated the Akina shrine on the Kamo River in Kyoto to their ancestors who had died in the Buddhist faith but were now, after the lapse of many years, canonized as Shinto saints.[27]

Of the thirteen independent bodies of Sectarian Shinto, fully one-half had sprung into being since the Tokugawa came to power.[28] Some of these sects had an ethical emphasis, others revolved about peculiar rites, and others still claimed a vague sort of monotheism. One sect, Tenri Kyo, founded by a woman who lived about a century ago, has been styled the Christian Science Church of modern Japan,[29] claiming at one time a membership of five million. In reality, however, all Shinto teaching is inherent in those primitive elements embedded in the mythology which is jealously guarded and carefully interpreted in line with the national consciousness.

3. *The Impact of Christianity.* The quarter of a million Christians of Evangelical affiliation are considerably more persuaded of the truth of their faith than were their forefathers of the Meiji era (1868–1912) who saw in Christianity, above all else, the secret of the West's material superiority. Nor are we entitled to forget, in examining the nature of Japanese Christianity, the fact that a foreign religion incites not only suspicion and dislike in a given country but also curiosity, wonder, and a measurable degree of support.

For even in the West, there are those who at times imagine that they might make better Moslems, Buddhists, Theosophists, or Vedantists than Christians. Be that as it may, the movement toward federation was real among the churches of Japan if only as a necessary step toward freedom from foreign control. It would be prudent for us to ignore at present the serious question as to the kind of

[27] Genchi Kato, *op. cit.*, p. 52.
[28] Holtom, *The National Faith of Japan*, p. 267.
[29] *Ibid.*, p. 69.

Christianity that might develop if the nationalization of the Church in any country became absolute.

Passing to the more positive aspect, we must note the rise of independent movements within Japanese Christianity, even amidst the most adverse conditions of nationalist and intellectual consolidation that took place during the Meiji era. In line with the national temper, some of these movements were highly fanatical. But others bore the impress of creative power such as that wielded by Toyohiko Kagawa. Won through the devoted love of missionaries to courageous, altruistic living for the underprivileged, Kagawa without propounding any theories put the Gospel into practice. He gave himself first to the lowest dregs of the port area of Kobe and then enlarged the sphere of his ministry to include groups in both the cities and rural districts.

With his labor unions and coöperatives, Kagawa attracted the attention of the world. By his efforts to improve the lot of the poor and suffering, he set Protestant Christianity in a light which outshone that of Roman Catholicism and Eastern Orthodoxy and made for the winning of many converts. In him the world saw the rise of a true Christian who represented the universalist character of the Church and brought warmth and vitality to countless followers of Jesus Christ in both East and West. Though imprisoned more than once by a Japanese government that suspected his agitation and deemed him dangerous, Kagawa was later commissioned when earthquake struck Tokyo to rebuild the city, with particular regard to better living conditions for the poor.[30]

It would be idle to defend the theory that the Japanese are either less or more religious than other peoples. That an eclectic predisposition enables them to absorb what they regard as worthy and noble in other doctrines seems to be an established fact. Even if at times their behavior follows patterns that strongly suggest their strangeness to the spirit of the West, they are not, however, different in the domain of feeling. Love, the greatest of all religious virtues, is not alien to them.

The riddle of Japan may be explained in part from what we

[30] Kenneth Scott Latourette, *Missions Tomorrow,* New York, 1936, pp. 19, 21, 198, 209.

know about its standards of social behavior. The thoroughly planned quality of Japanese behavior is a well-defined part of the social structure, whose institutions seek to keep everything under control.[31] Thus the Japanese feel that society must be orchestrated in order to avoid discord between the various personalities involved. Individuals owe their first obligation to superiors, rather than to each other or eternal truth. The family rather than the individual is the basic social unit, and personal abnegation is the primary theme.

The Emperor heads the social ladder and acts as supreme Father of the whole nation. All power and authority in the nation are inherent in him. Next come the members of the Imperial Court nobility, the remote cousins of the Emperor. But partly due to their isolation, these royal personages have been supplanted in modern times by the military aristocracy, particularly those of Samurai ancestry (feudal lords who held the power of life and death over the commoners), the wealthy, the cultured, the high officials of the state, and the landowners. Jealous of their ruling power, these elements of society, despite official declarations of equality, tend to despise other groups, especially the Eta (outcasts of menial standing) and the immigrant Okinawans and Koreans.

As regards the purely religious aspect of Japanese life, three reflections might be in order. First, having demonstrated its utter bankruptcy during the period of Japan's imperialist experiment, Buddhism will seek to rehabilitate itself in the humiliated empire. Second, though discredited and abolished by Imperial edict, State Shinto will continue to nourish, in some form, the fundamentally ethnocentric yearning of the people. Third, as the religion of the conquerors, Evangelical Christianity will attract many who seek to safeguard their personal interests. The impact of Christianity upon Japan, though the complexities of the situation and the hiddenness of divine purpose permit no forecast of the future, will so far as human instrumentalities are concerned depend upon the purity of faith and clarity of witness among those who preach by word and deed.

[31] Frederick S. Hulse, "A Sketch of Japanese Society," *JAOS,* vol. 66, no. 3, July–September, 1946, pp. 219–229.

CHAPTER VI

THE BIBLICAL INTERPRETATION
OF LIVING RELIGIONS

THE CLARITY of the Scriptural voice with regard to the living religions is frequently offset by the hollow incoherence that marks the thought even of believers who treat the subject. As in other aspects of the Christian religion, the Bible provides the Church with its supreme authority on the living religions. Viewed as a literary foundation, the Bible is the holy ground upon which the entire citadel of pertinent thought is laid.

This is true if only because the great religions of antiquity figured among the chief living religions of the Bible world. The Scriptural disclosures regarding them retain their cogency as a positive interpretation of the world's great religions today.

Whether in Prophet, Gospel, Epistle, or any other part of Holy Writ, the cogency and relevance of the Biblical record in relation to the living religions derive from the unique character of Scripture and the divine, redemptive purpose that inspires the whole. There is a distinctively Biblical spirit and outlook blending forces and motifs which in some other religious system might represent spiritual aridity and darkness.

The Bible creates a regenerative outlook which combines the condemnation of evil with compassion toward the evil-doer. Its novelty includes the particular and the universal, the immanent and the transcendent, the temporal and the eternal. Nowhere else are the unity, personality, love, and holiness of God proclaimed on so high a level and deliberately poised to heal man's infirmity and to usher the humble seeker into a living faith in the Eternal.

In its total impact upon the other religions, the Bible shines through in a forthright interpretative vein. This is made vivid in a perfect harmony which rises to a new order of simplicity, sincerity, sympathy, and communicability, adding fresh evidence for the divine origin and inimitable artistry of Scripture.

I. THE BIBLICAL CONCEPTION OF GENTILE RELIGION

1. *The Nature of Gentile Religion.* The Bible refers to the Hebrews as the Chosen People of God whose religion was the outcome of special revelation and stood in sharp contrast to the other religions of the world. Nations other than the Hebrew were described as Gentile. Of Latin derivation, the term Gentile corresponded with the late Hebrew *goi*, a synonym of *nokri*, that is, a stranger. But *goi*, and its plural *goyim*, originally meant, in the Old Testament, nation, and was applied to Hebrews and non-Hebrews alike.

The Hebrews, as offspring of Abraham, Isaac, and Jacob, were chosen for a purpose. "I will also give thee for a light to the Gentiles, that thou mayest be my salvation unto the end of the earth." [1] The Kingdom of Peace, the final restoration of the faithful, and the establishment of the true religion shall include Hebrew and Gentile.

". . . the mountain of the Lord's house shall be established on the tops of the mountains, and shall be exalted above the hills; and all nations shall flow unto it. And many peoples shall go and say, come ye, and let us go up to the mountain of the Lord, to the house of the God of Jacob." [2]

Jewish writers have frequently emphasized, moreover, that the strict laws which were enacted to prevent the corruption of manners and of the holy faith were neither intended to humiliate the Gentiles nor to brand them as inferior.

Exclusiveness and the spirit of hostility toward the Gentiles were an ever-present danger to the Hebrew community. The Gentiles were often despised as heathen and idolatrous. But this antipathy toward aliens has been exaggerated by some expounders of Biblical religion. Whereas the idolatry of the Canaanites, for example, was

[1] Isa. 49:6.
[2] Isa. 2:2–3; see also Amos 9:12; Zech. 9:7.

passionately denounced, intermarriage with the Gentile peoples has been widely attested.[3]

The Law conferred upon the alien Gentile a status which assured protection. The Old Testament records the cases of many Gentile persons who figured as the recipients of high honor and were distinguished exemplars of fidelity. Considerable light is shed on the subject by the illustrious careers of Ruth, Eliezer, and Job. In second Isaiah the salvation of God is offered to all men regardless of birth and former religious affiliation.

"Neither let the foreigner, that hath joined himself to the Lord, speak, saying the Lord will surely separate me from his people; neither let the eunuch say, Behold I am a dry tree. . . . Also the foreigners that join themselves to the Lord, to minister unto him, and to love the name of the Lord, to be his servants . . . , even them will I bring to my holy mountain, and make them joyful in my house of prayer . . . for my house shall be called the house of prayer for all peoples." [4]

Nor does the Bible date the beginning of holy history from the call of Abraham and the rise of Israel. At the very beginning of the Biblical drama, there is the unity of mankind. Mention has already been made of the support which the early chapters of Genesis give to the existence of a general revelation.[5] In a penetrating passage, John [6] alludes to the piety of Abel. "For this is the message, which ye heard from the beginning, that ye should love one another: not as Cain was of the evil one and slew his brother. And wherefore slew he him? Because his works were evil and his brother's righteous."

In subsequent generations when apostasy became rampant, men like Noah and Enoch were still to be found among the Gentiles.[7] They were righteous men and worshiped the true God. The Flood was the direct judgment of the Eternal visited upon a humanity that had perpetuated corruption and given itself to vanity. But the life of Noah and of his household was spared.

As Adam had been blessed when he was created, so now at the dawn of a new era Noah was bidden to be fruitful. The principles

---

[3] Ruth 1:4; 2 Sam. 3:3; 1 Kings 7:14.
[4] Isa. 56:3–7.   [5] See above, pp. 27–28.
[6] 1 John 3:12; cf. Gen. 4:1–5.   [7] Gen. 6:9.

of an early universal religion are detectable in the careers of Abel, Enoch, Noah, and their unnumbered peers. In projecting the so-called Laws of the children of Noah,[8] the Old Testament offers the conception of a general revelation common among the Gentiles. For, despite the wickedness and idolatry of the Gentiles, the faithful few preserved a body of the truth, enshrined in a natural religion which differed not in kind, only in degree, from the fuller ethical and spiritual structure made known to Israel.

2. *Recognition of Non-Hebraic Monotheism.* The Old Testament writers recognized distinct forms of monotheism in the alien religions known to them. While spiritual truth was predicated upon the divine self-revelation of the Eternal, it did not preclude interlinkings with the extra-Biblical world and a measure of overlapping with the other religions, on the grounds that the Creator had always informed history.

To be sure, Hebraic monotheism was sharpened and progressively clarified in the Abrahamitic and Mosaic tradition, but the operation of God's purpose to illumine mankind long preceded the age of Abraham. Even after the Covenant with Israel came into force, there were notable cases of Gentile faith and true religion. An ultimate universalistic intent was signified in these intimations of the truth apart from and parallel to the spiritual experience of Israel.

Foremost among these cases was the type of living religion whose monotheism the Scripture depicted through the figure of Melchizedek.[9] The writer of the Epistle to the Hebrews recognized the priestly order of Melchizedek as one of supernatural inception. Although not a Hebrew himself, Melchizedek was "without father, without mother, without genealogy, having neither beginning of days, nor end of life, but made like unto the Son of God, abideth a priest continually." [10] In fact, as High Priest, Christ is not only the successor of the Levitical priesthood; prior to Levi and superior to him, the high priestly office of Christ is "after the order of Melchizedek." [11]

---

[8] Gen. 9:1–29.
[9] Gerhardus Vos, *Biblical Theology,* Grand Rapids, 1948, pp. 91, 163.
[10] Heb. 7:3.   [11] Heb. 5:6, 10.

A contemporary of Abraham, Melchizedek was king of Salem (later Jerusalem) and priest of the Most High God.[12] When Abraham defeated the coalition of chieftains ranged against him, Melchizedek went out to welcome him, offered him the hospitality of bread and wine, and received his tithes. In paying him tithes, Abraham acknowledged Melchizedek as priest of the Eternal. He furthermore acknowledged El Elyon, whom Melchizedek worshiped, as identical with the true God and thus conceded that they both shared a common faith.

When Jerusalem became capital city of David, the Psalmist in an apt comparison recalled the former spiritual glory of the city under the righteous Melchizedek. David was hailed "a priest for ever after the order of Melchizedek." [13] In this Biblical conception of the possible validity of Gentile faith, a major theme is set forth which Peter, standing at the sunrise epoch of Christianity, reiterated in the memorable words, "Of a truth I perceive that God is no respecter of persons: but in every nation he that feareth him, and worketh righteousness, is acceptable to him." [14]

That the Old Testament recognized the vitality of faith among certain adherents of alien religions is further confirmed in the role and character of Jethro, a priest of Midian. Jethro became father-in-law of Moses and a formidable champion of the true religion.

The way this happened is told in a story with romantic overtones. Finding himself at a well where Jethro's daughters drew water for their flocks, Moses had an opportunity to defend them against the intruding shepherds. Moses thus won an introduction to Jethro's family, leading to his marriage with Zipporah, one of the charming daughters.[15]

Far more significant, however, to religious history was the position accorded Jethro in the Book of Exodus. He appears as the ranking counsellor of Moses, and his leadership was fully acknowledged during the formal inauguration of the worship of God among the early Hebrews.

"Now Jethro, the priest of Midian, Moses' father-in-law, heard of all that God had done for Moses and for Israel his people. And

---

[12] Gen. 14:18 *sqq.*
[13] Ps. 10:4.
[14] Acts 10:34–35.
[15] Ex. 2:16–22.

Jethro . . . came unto Moses into the wilderness where he was encamped, at the mount of God. . . . And Moses went out to meet his father-in-law, and did obeisance and kissed him. . . . And Jethro said Blessed be the Lord, who hath delivered thee out of the hand of the Egyptians. . . . Now I know that the Lord is greater than all the gods. And Jethro . . . took a burnt-offering and sacrificed for God: and Aaron came and all the elders of Israel to eat bread with Moses' father-in-law before God." [16]

Jethro was also credited with being the one who recommended, when he saw that Moses was wearing himself out with the details of government, the appointment of deputy judges to deal with the smaller matters, whereas weighty and more difficult issues were to be brought to the attention of Moses himself.

That Moses had actually learned the worship of God from his Midianite (Kenite) father-in-law, whose sheep he tended on Horeb (the mountain of God) where the Eternal first spoke to him, is a distinct possibility though disputed among the scholars. For our purpose, the unmistakable fact which the Bible underscores is that Jethro—a Midianite spokesman of some living non-Hebraic religion—was styled Reuel [17] which being rendered means "God is his friend." He exercised a decisive influence over the worship and legal administration of the nascent Israelite community and was held in honor among the Hebrew authorities.

II. The Biblical Understanding of the Ancient Oriental Religions

Political, ethnic, cultural, geographic, as well as religious considerations conspired to distort the true picture of Israel's neighbors which the Bible projected.

1. *The Canaanites.* Of considerable importance among these neighbors were the Canaanites whom the Hebrews partly displaced in the Land of Promise. Bracketed with the Hittites, Amorites, Perizites, Hivites, and Jebusites, [18] the Canaanites do not figure in the table of nations [19] as Semites, but are identified with the offspring of Ham, that is, are designated as immigrants who came

---

[16] Ex. 18:1–12.   [17] Ex. 2:18.
[18] Ex. 3:8; Deut. 7:1.   [19] Gen. 10:6–20.

from the south (Negroes, Ethiopians), or are equated with other members of the Indo-European family such as the Hittites, Mitanni, and Hurrians, who had penetrated Syria-Palestine from the north.

A generally-employed geographic expression, Canaan therefore denoted in the realm of religion and ethnology almost everything that the Hebrews were not expected to be. With its many gods and idols, the religion of the Canaanites was roundly denounced in Scripture as the antithesis of the holy faith.

Having escaped the Egyptian bondage, the Hebrews entered the Holy Land by way of the wilderness. In comparison with the desert, they found the land of Canaan viable, a country "flowing with milk and honey." [20] As followers of a nature-worship, the Canaanites were deservedly condemned. Fear was expressed lest by associating with them, the People of God might fall prey to the same pagan influence. Hence the imprecation, "Cursed be Canaan; a servant of servants shall he be unto his brethren." [21]

The Hebrews were, nevertheless, spellbound by the glamour of the more advanced Canaanite civilization. They fell upon riches which they had not amassed and appropriated property which was not their own.[22] Even more seductive was the temptation to forget the Lord who brought them forth out of the land of Egypt, out of the house of bondage. Hence the warning: "Ye shall not go after other gods, of the gods of the peoples round about you . . . lest the anger of the Lord thy God be kindled against thee, and he destroy thee from off the face of the earth." [23]

At temple and shrine the ornate nature-worship of the Canaanites gave rise to a public immorality which drew forceful prophetic rebuke. Equally if not more abhorrent were the sins of the Hebrews themselves who were guilty of complicity in the selfsame glorification of sex and public prostitution current among their neighbors.[24]

In the evaluation of Canaanite religion nothing is more misleading than the tendency to stress Gentile infidelity and ignore Israel's flagrant disobedience. Actually, paganism among the Hebrews was more culpable than its Canaanite counterpart, not less.

---

[20] Ex. 3:8; Deut. 11:9.
[22] Cf. Deut. 6:11.
[24] Jer. 2:20.
[21] Gen. 9:25.
[23] Deut. 6:12–15.

The Scriptures leave little doubt that the true worship of God was seldom uniformly observed in Israel. From King Solomon whose "wisdom excelled the wisdom of all the East," that is, who was enamored of Gentile and other intellectual attainments,[25] and from the law-givers who borrowed the legal and monarchical patterns of Canaanite government in the face of Samuel's solemn warning,[26] to King Ahab under whom Israel weakened to Canaanite religion, which credited Baal with guardianship over field and flock, until the decisive victory of Elijah over the devotees of Baal on Mt. Carmel,[27] the record is clear. It is marked by interaction between Hebrew and Canaanite, with punishment meted out to the reprobate on either side.

2. *The Religion of Egypt.* Abraham, Joseph, and Moses knew Egypt at first hand, and the Hebrews ever since have had a vivid recollection of Egyptian cultural and religious institutions. During the Captivity they had established a living contact with the structure and detail of Egyptian beliefs. The close proximity between Canaan and Egypt must have deepened an already existing similarity in particular customs and folkways. The Old Testament was explicit, however, in its denunciation of Egyptian idolatry, the worship of stellar and animal forms, magic, sorcery, and the polytheistic cults. Nebuchadnezzar of Babylon would be sent to break the pillars (obelisks) of Bethshemesh (Heliopolis), house of the god Ra, and the temples of the Egyptian gods will be burnt with fire.[28]

Despite a degree of theistic essence beneath the profligacy of Egyptian cults and the transient monotheistic order of Akhenaton, the people were held in the bondage of idolatry and the pharaohs continued to be symbols of pride and oppression. Deified as Horus, the pharaoh stood between mortals and gods and was justly deprecated in the Bible, his hollow religion being despised.

Egypt's blasphemous arrogance was punished. She had been instrumental in the destruction of both Israel (721 B.C.) and Judah (587 B.C.), having used the petty Hebrew states to further foreign policy and lay her bid for greater international power. Ezekiel,[29]

---

[25] 1 Kings 4:30–31. [26] 1 Sam. 8:4–22.
[27] 1 Kings 17–18. [28] Jer. 43:8–13.
[29] 29:1–16.

who announced her impending doom and the twilight of her gods, specified that her agony would last until she should have learned that the Lord is God, whereupon she would be restored.

This spiritual decadence notwithstanding, Egypt exhibited from her remotest history a remarkable knowledge of personal religion and ethical standards. Among the commendable elements of her religious process were insights regarding human conduct, sin, justification, immortality, and the existence and power of the Divine Being.[30] Apart from the condemnation of her perversion, the Biblical attitude toward Egypt was conciliatory and constructive. As in the case of the Hebrews themselves, God will punish then restore. "The Lord will smite Egypt, smiting and healing; and they shall return unto the Lord, and he will be entreated of them, and will heal them." [31]

In their finest expression, the insights of Egyptian religion were a dilution of general revelation. The fleeting monotheism of Akhenaton was a vision of God obscured by the official act of a pharaoh who elevated Aton to the rank of the Almighty. Yet Egypt and Assyria, along with Israel, will be made a blessing. "Blessed be Egypt, my people, and Assyria the work of my hands, and Israel mine inheritance." [32]

3. *Mesopotamian Religion.* The Old Testament also discloses an intimate knowledge of Mesopotamian religious customs and culture. The eponymous figure of Hebrew history, Abraham, was born in a Sumerian city, Ur of the Chaldees.[33] But the bond between Israel and Mesopotamia went beyond the reality of a common origin. Shinar, the alluvial plain where Babel, Erech, and Akkad arose,[34] was understood in the Hebraic tradition to be a country ruled by Amraphel in the time of Abraham.[35]

Presumably neither Semitic nor Indo-European, the Sumerians, whose language was of the agglutinative type represented in our time by Turkish, Hungarian, and Finnish, founded Mesopotamian culture and religion. They endowed Mesopotamia with a peculiar

---

[30] Henry S. Gehman, ed., *The Westminster Dictionary of the Bible,* Philadelphia, 1944, p. 152.

[31] Isa. 19:22.   [32] Isa. 19:24.

[33] Gen. 11:28, 31; 15:17; Neh. 9:7.   [34] Gen. 10:10; 11:2; Dan. 1:2.

[35] Gen. 14:1, 9.

continuity which for three millennia outlived the vicissitudes of political and ethnic upheavals.[36]

The Old Testament reflected this long and impressive religious tradition of Mesopotamia. Babylon (Babel), the city whose name symbolized human pride and the ruin that inevitably follows it, was the setting of that Tower upon which the unity of mankind was broken, where greed and the confusion of tongues bore their fruit in utter disruption.[37] The Tigris and Euphrates, sources of Mesopotamian fertility, are two rivers of Eden,[38] a garden near the head of the Persian Gulf conceived as the scene of man's primitive age.

Historic and personal contact with the religion of Mesopotamia equipped the Biblical writers to draw upon a rich heritage and to employ it as a vehicle for divine revelation. In the pre-exilic period, relations between the Hebrews and the Valley of the Two Rivers were not always cordial; but the Babylonian Exile brought the seed of Abraham back to their ancestral homeland, and an intimate knowledge of Babylonia was acquired.

In the measures taken to insure the purity of the seed of Abraham, one is likely to surmise the occurrence of many intermarriages. Undoubtedly dating back to the time of Moses if not earlier, the content of the Torah went through many redactions but, like the Prophets and Writings, did not assume final form till later. It was only after the bitter experience of the Babylonian Captivity and the subsequent unfolding of Jewish history that the Old Testament canon was permanently established in the second Christian century.

In its interpretation of Mesopotamian religion, the Old Testament is direct and incisive. The essentials of religion are set forth in a manner showing penetrating insight into divine truth. Armed with an inspired pedagogy, the Biblical author utilized the Mesopotamian religious format, which fitted into a common Semitic history, in order to communicate the message of an ethical monotheism. Whether it did or did not reflect the Mesopotamian cosmogonies, the Biblical hexameron (six days of creation) did not

[36] S. N. Kramer, *Sumerian Mythology*, Philadelphia, 1944, p. vii.
[37] Gen. 11:9.   [38] Gen. 2:8–17.

teach legend and mythology and was a deliberate refutation of magic.

In a series of utterances, the Old Testament, appropriating the symbols and patterns of Semitic thought, depicted the depth of human tragedy in Mesopotamia and simultaneously provided an answer to the insatiable longing of ancient man for God. A sound interpretation of man and history was thus offered in the story of the Fall. Steeped in metaphor, vision, and parable, the teaching on original sin is an indestructible valuation of man's nature and destiny.

Where ancient geographical knowledge was drawn upon, such as the references to the Tigris and Euphrates, the theology set forth loses nothing of its relevance, even for those versed in modern geology and topography. Couched as they are in Mesopotamian terminology, the accounts of the Flood and of the Tower of Babel convey, nevertheless, a moral and spiritual message distinctive in its emphasis on the heinousness of sin and the holiness of the Creator.

Although here and there corresponding with Mesopotamian religious culture, the Bible even in its legal aspect bears the stamp of the Eternal. Judged by spiritual norms, the Code of Hammurabi lagged behind the Torah. Whereas legal refinements were not the province of Hebrew Law, its inimitable consciousness of divine righteousness and its uncompromising assault against rottenness make it unique.

III. The Bible and Ancient Iran

Less directly related to Palestine than Mesopotamia, Iran occupied, particularly after the Babylonian Captivity, an eminent position in the Biblical view of religious history. At the height of its power, the Persian Empire extended from India to the Arabian Peninsula and beyond.[39] In 721 B.C. Sargon II of Assyria deported 27,290 Israelites of whom some were transplanted to Iran, where they conceivably effected a juncture with Zoroastrianism.

1. *The Religious Role of Iran.* Cyrus, the Zoroastrian king of

[39] Esther 1:1; 10:1; 2 Chron. 36:20; Dan. 8:20; 10:13–20; 11:2; 1 Macc. 6:1; 2 Macc. 1:19.

Iran, conquered Babylon in 539 B.C. and approved the return of the Jewish exiles to Palestine. Having thus served Israel in the discharge of her role as purveyor of the true religion, he was called the Anointed,[40] a title which the Old Testament applies to God and the New Testament reserves for the Saviour. Elsewhere he is described as "my shepherd," an epithet which the Scriptures also limit to the Eternal.[41]

Some authorities have deemed the religion of Zoroaster the source of key Biblical concepts such as those of Satan, angels, demons, the Son of Man, the Messiah as saviour and deliverer, the doctrine of the resurrection, divine judgment, and even the theistic conception of God. The immensity of such claims for the religion of Iran, if they were proven to be sound, might upset the foundation upon which, in the cultural and historic domain, the basic teachings of the Bible rest. While a few scholars saw an early contact between Israel and Iran, permitting the transmission of Hebrew ideas to Persia, others maintained that the original fount of the conceptions concerned was none other than the Avesta, the sacred text of ancient Iran.

Both of these assumptions are extremely doubtful. Careful analysis of the Biblical material for which an Iranian parallel has been proposed, leads to the conclusion that prior to the last two centuries B.C., Persia exercised little influence upon Judaism. Where borrowings from Persia are reasonably well substantiated, it is almost invariably a matter of the sharpening of already accepted Hebrew concepts and views.[42]

2. *A Critique of Iranian Religion.* It has already been noted [43] that the lofty doctrine embodied in the *Gathas* never quite overcame the natural polytheism and dualism of Iranian religion. Whereas Zoroastrianism, at its highest level, deferred the victory of Ahura-Mazda over the hosts of evil until the hereafter, Biblical religion affirms that the Adversary, in the beginning, now, and always, is subject to the sovereignty of God. If certain Zoroastrian ideas had left an impress on any Hebrews who returned from Babylonia dur-

---

[40] Isa. 44:25; 45:16, 20.   [41] Isa. 44:28; Ps. 23:1; John 10:14.
[42] Albright, *From the Stone Age to Christianity*, p. 280.
[43] See above, pp. 90, 92–93.

ing the reign of Cyrus, such an impress was subservient to their faith in the eternal God whose Kingdom was not only other-worldly but also began here on earth.[44]

Where Judaism bore the imprint of Iranian concepts of demons, only Apocryphal books such as that of Enoch were involved. Satan, it must be recalled, was the chief opponent of God and man at the very beginning of the Biblical record. As seducer of Adam and Eve, he figured in Hebrew religious thought long before relations with Persia were established. Nor is it true that angels, whom the New Testament portrays as great spiritual personalities with specific missions, are identical with the Holy Spentas of a decadent Zoroastrianism which were manifestly construed as divinities in their own right.[45]

In their inconsistency, eventual decadence, and dissolution, the religious texts of ancient Iran provide no more than a fragile basis for the sublime doctrine of redemption. Nor would a Biblical interpretation of ancient Iranian faith be adequate if it did not deal with the oft-repeated view that Zoroastrianism offers a prototype of Jesus. All that needs to be said in this connection is that the Iranian tradition which told of a giant, created by Ahura-Mazda, who died at the age of thirty from a narcotic administered by the creator himself, scarcely deserves to serve as a prototype for the person and work of Jesus. For the Eternal who created man in His own image gave the world in Christ, whom He crowned with glory and honor, the means of rescue from all infirmity and thereby restored in His creatures the consciousness of holiness, love, and immortality.

IV. The Biblical Approach to the Greco-Roman Heritage

Although Greece was known to the Old Testament writers as a country at the end of the earth,[46] it came at an early date within the geographical purview of the Hebrews who recognized it as Javan (Ionia).[47] But direct intercourse between Israel and Greece did not develop till after the conquest of Alexander the Great, who

---

[44] M. J. Lagrange, *Le Judaisme Avant Jésus-Christ,* Paris, 1931, p. 405.

[45] Irach J. S. Taraporewala, *Religion in the Twentieth Century,* Vergilius Ferm, ed., New York, 1948, p. 23.

[46] Isa. 66:19; Ezek. 27:13; Joel 3:6.

[47] Gen. 10:4–5.

granted the Jews many privileges. According to Josephus,[48] when Jaddua, the high priest, went out to meet the conqueror, he fell at his feet in worship of the God of Israel.

Following the death of Alexander, Greek language and culture became naturalized in Palestine and other parts of the Near East, persisting through the Roman period initiated by Pompey the Great who invaded the Holy Land in 63 B.C. Antiochus Epiphanes (175–163 B.C.), eighth ruler of the Seleucid Dynasty which governed Syria after the Macedonian, had fostered the ascendancy of Hellenism in the Bible world. He robbed the Temple, set up the statue of Jupiter in the Holy of Holies, commanded the sacrifice of swine, forbade circumcision, and destroyed all copies of the Scriptures that fell into his hands. Having revolted against these measures, the Jews, led by Judas Maccabee, in 165 B.C. won a signal victory over their Syro-Greek foes, and the Temple was duly purified.

1. *Revulsion against Hellenism.* In its attitude toward the aggressive character of Hellenistic culture, the Bible is stoutly represented by the pertinent passages of the Book of Daniel which described Antiochus Epiphanes as the "little horn." [49] As an apocalyptic writer, Daniel brought his people the hope of deliverance from the Greek tyranny and the restoration of their religious freedom.

The true meaning of the Biblical interpretation of Greek idolatry is that the prophetic truth and the vitality of faith in God are not shaken when blasphemous acts such as the erection of an idolatrous altar in the Temple, take place.[50] Neither to Daniel, nor to his New Testament successor John, were the political events of their times in themselves a matter of ultimate concern. These were merely singled out as examples of what disobedience and antagonism toward God will entail.

Hellenistic culture was patently the enemy of the worship of the one true God practiced by Israel.[51] Yet the sequence of events gave birth to an altogether unexpected result. When monotheism triumphed over Hellenistic idolatry, the Jews looked for a Messiah who would make the Law supreme among the nations. The most

---

[48] *Antiquities*, XI, 8, 5.   [49] Dan. 7 :8.
[50] 1 Macc. 1 :54.
[51] A. J. Festugière, *L'Idéal Religieux des Grecs et L'Évangile*, Paris, 1933. p. 9.

crucial event in the history of religion is that the Messiah appeared in the person of Jesus Christ who was not recognized, however, by the Jews themselves but by Gentile Greeks. That the Greeks thus became a parable of the entire Gentile world, Paul explained on Mars Hill.[52] They sought after God but were unable to know Him despite their art, culture, and philosophical thought. Yet God was ready to overlook the times of ignorance and received as His own all who came in repentance and faith in the Risen Lord.

Peter, therefore, defended Gentile Christianity, recalling that he had been guided to accept the Gentile household of Cornelius.[53] Indeed, an Apostolic Council recognized as Christians in good standing all such Gentiles as believed the Gospel message. The Church was thus rooted in Europe and Ephesus. Symbolic of the new status which Christianity conferred upon the Gentiles was Paul's choice of Timothy, child of a Jewish-Greek marriage, as a chief disciple.[54] Paul and Silas now turned to the evangelization of the West.

2. *Greek Culture and Philosophy.* As Christianity stood on the threshold of Europe, with the glories of its Occidental conquests in the dim unknown, the rich heritage of Greece loomed on the horizon. Palestine, which had given the Christian his Law, Prophets, and Saviour, now confronted Greece which was about to endow the Church with a firm foundation in reason, order, equilibrium, symmetry, and a taste for creative ideas coupled with a repugnance for obscurantism. Mirrored in the Gospel of John, the essence of Greek ideas could only bring out the absolute independence of the New Testament religion. A just and proper evaluation of Athens and Jerusalem was thus set forth in the light of revealed truth.

Heraclitus (*fl. ca.* 500 B.C.) had spoken of the logos in the sense of word, maxim, doctrine, constitution, or reason. Vaguely discerning the idea of universal law, Heraclitus failed to envision the logos as the Word that became flesh. Thus the Gospel of St. John had for its central theme the substitution of a supernatural revelation for the gropings of the human mind. "In the beginning was the Word, and the Word was with God, and the Word was God.

---

[52] Acts 17:22–31.   [53] Acts 10:34.
[54] Acts 16:1.

. . . In him was life, and the life was the light of men. And the light shineth in the darkness; and the darkness apprehended it not. . . . And the Word became flesh, and dwelt among us and we beheld his glory, glory as of the only begotten from the Father, full of grace and truth." [55]

Stoic philosophy seized upon the logos idea bequeathed by Heraclitus. Following in the wake of Socrates, Plato, and Aristotle, and their disciples, the Stoics created a moral integration of life and culture and laid the Greco-Roman world in their debt. But the Word, exemplar of the world, a divine Light who through the Cross and the Resurrection brought man redemption and virtue, was a Christian concept of living reality and ultimate truth completely free from dependence upon Greek thought. It was and is a concept that led beyond the realm of pure thought into the arena of action motivated by faith in the living God and evidenced by the holy, selfless witness of the saints who follow Christ.

The Portico (or Porch) of Stoic Zeno (*fl. ca.* 336–264 B.C.) may be said to have surpassed in moral discernment the Academy of Plato and the Lyceum of Aristotle. Where the philosophers had bungled life with their interminable dialectic and speculation, the Stoics brought to their labors a gravity and a charm, reminiscent of the tragic poet Aeschylus (525–456 B.C.) and compatible with the religious perception that dominated their utterances. Yet Stoicism was essentially a pure pantheism, its logos nothing more than the rational principle of the mind.[56]

Socrates (469–399 B.C.), founder of the religion of good conscience,[57] abandoned physics for ethics and began to formulate concepts. Belief in reason was not the only component of his faith since he belonged to religion as much as to morality and philosophy. The secret of his religion was the certainty that the power which he experienced, namely the friendly guidance of Providence, was the central power of life. He regarded the mysterious inner voice, which he knew to be common and natural, as divine instruction. Yet though he did not stiffen into a tragic heroism, or a Stoic resig-

[55] John 1:1–14.
[56] Gustave Bardy, *Père Lagrange and the Scriptures,* tr. Richard T. Murphy, Milwaukee, 1946, pp. 101–102.
[57] Nathan Söderblom, *The Living God,* London, 1933, pp. 234–263.

nation, we read in Plato's *Apology* that in contemplating the tragedy of life, Socrates said that "For a good man there is no evil whether he live or die."

Plato (*ca.* 427–347) was the ranking religious thinker of Greece, and no student of his *Dialogues* misses the spell of his style and ideals. His mystical religion, rational theology, and dialectic possessed an irresistibility which the *Banquet* (or *Symposium*) particularly demonstrates in its vivid and powerful exposition of the idea of the beautiful. Yet this atmosphere of beauty was a mixture of exalted and debased ingredients, choking the soul in a cloud of polytheism. In his rational theology and dialectic emerged the characteristically Greek notion which upheld the primacy of the intellect. Therefore, the logos could be no more than an idea, a perfect essence, with all the pervasive color which a master logician could instill. The inescapable conclusion was that mental discipline was the height of all attainments and that moral perfection was little more than gnosis.[58]

Aristotle (384–322 B.C.) held the attention of Christian thinkers from the thirteenth century onwards, largely through the influence of Thomas Aquinas. But his cold logic evoked less curiosity among the churchmen than the supple and flowing dialectic of Plato, who seemed to hold many a Christian thinker enthralled especially during the formative part of ecclesiastical history. Aristotle's contribution to religious thought was climaxed in his proof for the existence of God, the First Mover.

"This First Mover is unique, eternal, incorporeal, indivisible—most pure act, that is, not simply intelligence but the thought which thinks itself and in its thought finds its beatitude." [59] Yet the Pure Act which Aristotle proposed fell short of the Christian faith because it presumed to unlock the mystery of the Eternal in terms of a distant, inaccessible Being. Like his teacher, Plato, Aristotle was a powerless observer of the traditional cults and official religion of Greece; both failed to reach down to the level of the average person.

[58] James H. Dunham, *The Religion of the Philosophers,* Philadelphia, 1947, pp. 10–39.
[59] Aristotle, *Metaphysics,* XII, 7: 1072b, 28.

Plato and Aristotle affirmed the existence of the transcendent God, along with whom stood other corporeal or incorporeal divinities. Their theological structure was, therefore, deficient at the core. Actually, the Academicians took refuge in Stoicism, and the Peripatetics devoted themselves to science. Both the Stoics and the Epicureans lacked real concern for the First Mover and questioned Plato's idea of a bodiless God.

The times were opportune for the rise of Christianity, and Biblical religion was gradually successful in converting the Gentile soul. The Greek heritage was admissible once it rid itself of the gods and goddesses which, though they had lost their status with the people, were still enshrined in the mythology, literature, and art of the Greco-Roman world, imperceptibly fortified by a patriotic and individualistic consciousness.[60]

The triumph of Biblical religion was predicated upon a complete response to the Eternal's call as it was conveyed in the Gospel and apprehended through the categories of the Christianized Greek thought. When during the reign of Nero, Paul argued for his life before King Agrippa and the Roman procurator, Festus, he elicited from the former the retort, "With but little persuasion, thou wouldst fain make me a Christian," and the latter, having first accused Paul of madness with too much learning, concluded at last that the Apostle was innocent and should be released had he not appealed his case to Caesar.[61]

[60] Martin Perrson Nilsson, *Greek Piety,* tr. H. J. Ross, Oxford, 1948, p. 187.
[61] Acts 26:24–32.

CHAPTER VII

REFLECTIVE GENIUS, TRAINING IN WISDOM, AND PRACTICE OF THE OCCULT: HINDUISM

Hᴵɴᴅᴜɪsᴍ denotes the socio-religious beliefs and practices of the Hindus, a community of the more than 350 million inhabitants of the Republic of India. Noted in particular for its emphasis upon divine immanence and a graded social structure, Hinduism goes back to about 1500 B.C., ranking as the oldest among the great religions of the modern world.

The roots of Hinduism go even deeper than the Aryan tradition established by the invaders who drifted into the heart-shaped peninsula in the half millennium from 2000 B.C. to 1500 B.C. Excavations at Harapa and Mohenjo Daro prompted Sir John Marshall to describe the existence in India of an archaeological civilization thoroughly independent and individual in its making.[1] Highly developed and articulate, this Indus culture reached far back in prehistory and was comparable with the cultures of the Nile and Tigris-Euphrates valleys.

Other than the Dravidians, whose Indian origin is open to question, the Indus civilization included another flat-nosed, dark-skinned race. Later demoted to the rank of *dasas* (slaves), the early progenitors of this stock together with other aborigines, as well as the Dravidians and Aryans, are the makers of Hinduism.

Six classes of literary works, composed in Sanskrit, constitute the sacred writings of Hinduism.[2] They are (1) the *Vedas* (books of knowledge), written presumably prior to the first pre-Christian

---

[1] S. Radhakrishnan, *Legacy of India*, G. T. Garratt, ed., London, 1937.
[2] Robert Ernest Hume, *The World's Living Religions*, New York, 1946, pp. 20–22.

millennium, which include the *Rig-veda* (psalms)[3] and the *Atharva-veda* (charms);[4] (2) the *Brahmanas*[5] (priestlies), composed in the period 1000-800 B.C., which mark the change from the simple nature-worship of the Vedic religion to ceremonial worship with its animal sacrifices and priest control; (3) the *Upanishads*[6] (séances), dated about 800 to 600 B.C., which are the speculations of forest sages, breathing the spirit of troubled inquiry into the problem of reality, the individual soul, and the world soul behind all phenomena; (4) the *Law of Manu,*[7] from about 250 B.C., which is the most impressive code of the faith, offering an interpretation of religion in terms of ethical and moral values; (5) the *Bhagavad-gita*[8] (song celestial), the New Testament of Hinduism; and (6) the Epics and Puranas (ancient tales) including two masterpieces, the *Mahabharata* and the *Ramayana,*[9] wherein much of folk Hinduism was crystallized.

In its classical development, Hinduism found room for all kinds of discordant and seemingly contradictory beliefs, ranging from animism and polytheism to pantheism, monism, and even theism. An inward intuitiveness marked off the domain of *dharma* (religious law) as the law and destiny which shape the believer's end.[10] And corresponding with the six classes of sacred texts, there appeared a number of religious concepts and cults representing the impact of Hinduism upon India and the world of religion.

Included among these is caste, a peculiarly Hindu phenomenon inherent in a system of social stratification born out of the significance attached to *varna* (color) and *jati* (birth). While the Vedic deities have vanished, Hinduism in its popular phase betrays the influence of primitive worship and the dread of unseen powers.

[3] R. T. H. Griffith, *Hymns of the Rig-veda,* 2 vols., Benares, 1896.

[4] Whitney and Lanman, *Harvard Oriental Series,* 1905.

[5] J. Eggeling, *Satapatha Brahmana,* 5 vols., Sacred Books of the East (hereafter abbreviated *SBE*), New York, 1882–1900; A. B. Keith, *Harvard Oriental Series,* 1920.

[6] F. Max Müller, *SBE,* vols. I and XV, New York, 1879; R. E. Hume, *The Thirteen Principal Upanishads,* Oxford, 1934.

[7] G. Buhler, *SBE,* vol. XXV, New York, 1886.

[8] Edited Franklin Edgerton, 2 vols., Cambridge, Mass., 1944; S. Radhakrishnan, New York, 1948.

[9] R. C. Dutt, *The Ramayana and Mahabharata,* Everyman's Library.

[10] John Clark Archer, *Great Religions of the Modern World,* p. 51.

Hindu ritual was next to caste in the importance which it assumed, involving a sacerdotalism depicted in a Brahman priesthood and stated sacrifice. *Karma* (deed, action) revolved about a religion of works with belief in transmigration as an integral part.

With the rise of Hindu philosophy, Brahman emerged as a Supreme Being, absolute, eternal, impersonal, and neuter. Through the practice of mental discipline, union (*yoga*) between the world soul (*atman*) and the universal soul (*Brahman*) was sought. On a theistic and lofty level, devotion (*bhakti*) toward a personal deity was introduced. In Krishna, the adorable god of the Bhagavadgita, a theistic motif asserted itself.

The soil of Hinduism is strewn with fallen rebels, reformers, and interpreters. In the sixth century B.C., Mahavira and Gotama founded, respectively, Jainism and Buddhism. The former religion persists in a small Indian community, and the latter, assimilated to the parent Hindu faith, has had a gigantic growth in East Asia.[11] About the beginning of the twelfth Christian century, Ramanuja initiated a qualified non-duality which conceived of a personal Supreme Being. Under the impact of Islam, Nanak (1469–1538) preached the existence of one God and in the attempt to reconcile Hinduism and Islam founded Sikhism.

Tulsi Das (1532–1623) propounded a theism based on the Ramayana. But the most admirable interpretation of Hinduism was the Vedanta, a monist-pantheist system grounded in the Upanishads. Its leading light was Shankara (*ca.* A.D. 788–850), philosopher, mystic, and commentator on the Bhagavadgita. The bright character of Hinduism shines forth in the Vedanta and bhakti faith. The most profound insights arising from a soteriology involve a critique of sin, sanctity, and redemption unlike Christianity in that it is mediated through speculation and undue emphasis on the validity of good works.

Release from *samsara* (enchainment to the endless round of existences) is the chief end of salvation. That, rather than emphasis on human depravity and the need for sanctification through divine initiative, is the main axis of Hinduism. Such is the essence of a faith which in the person of Gandhi (assassinated in 1948)

[11] See below, pp. 199–218.

challenged the materialism of the West and today continues to reaffirm its ancient standards in modern form.

Fed by both the intellectual and popular streams, Hinduism gave birth to a conglomerate of folk beliefs and rites. Its two major divisions, the Vishnuite and Shivite, enjoin the adoration of Vishnu (creator) and Shiva (destroyer), giving rise to some sixty subsects. Outwardly committed to some personal deity, folk religion may have its expression, on the one hand, in a bhakti salvation by faith and, on the other, in Vallacharyas which practices sensual and other crudities of worship such as the veneration of Kali, black goddess of death.

Within the pale of folk religion are sects which idealize human and animal figures as well as the male and female sex organs. Idolatry and high religious insights combine to form the Hindu religious structure. Along with sublime Vedic verities are excessive dietary laws, rituals of bathing and cleanliness, worship at sacred shrine and festival, offerings for the dead, and myriad marks of primitive animism.

I. THE ETHOS OF HINDUISM

The ethos of a people is their character in its intellectual, ethical, and social expression as distinguished from emotional behavior. That Hinduism represents a peculiar ethos may be seen from a close scrutiny of its philosophical, social, and religious norms.

1. *The Philosophical Structure.* Hindu philosophy occupies an original and permanent position in the history of thought. The Rig-veda is older than the Old Testament and the Upanishads antedate Plato.[12] Extreme veneration of teachers and of traditions, worn out through exhaustion and inbreeding, accounts for the arrested development of this philosophy. Yet Vedanta philosophy has not ceased to exert a worldwide influence, and Hindu thought, like the banyan tree, is capable of spreading in several directions.

The originality of this philosophy partly derives from the fact that it does not fit into any of the purely natural or supernatural patterns. Essentially a generic idealism, it culminates in an intellec-

[12] George P. Conger, *Philosophy—East and West,* C. A. Moore, ed., Princeton, 1944, pp. 12–23.

tual monism woven out of Indian experience and contemplation. Its procedure, not unlike geometry, ordinarily began with a proposition such as that the sum of the angles of a triangle is equal to two right angles. To be acceptable as an axiom, the proposition must be verified in order to show, by actual measurement, that the 180 degrees of the three angles is equivalent to two right angles. Proof of a geometric proposition is said to be a parable of the realization of transcendental truth through Yoga union with the universal spirit.[13] All Hindu philosophies share a common purpose, namely the extinction of sorrow by the acquisition of knowledge regarding the true nature of things, that is, freedom from the bondage of ignorance.

Thus the philosophical significance of salvation comes through searching self-analysis. Toward that goal, the six schools of philosophy known as the *Sad Darsanas* (six insights) offered an interpretation of ultimate Reality and the essence of existence. They comprised (1) the science of logical proofs (*Nyaya*); (2) knowledge of the nature of reality (*Vaisesika*); (3) a harmony of the philosophy of the Vedas through reason and a systematic account of cosmic evolution, that is, a comprehensive view of the universe (*Samkhya,* the oldest school); (4) union of the individual spirit with the universal (*Yoga*); (5) examination of the Vedas in order to arrive at a correct knowledge of ritual and the texts (*mamsa*); and (6) the end of the Veda, the summary of all knowledge (*Vedanta*).

The six schools grew out of the Upanishads as supreme authority and were cast in the sutra style of concise aphorism. Inherent in the eternal cycle of nature, their central assumptions were, in effect, that in the process of regeneration, the soul, life, and death, must be regarded as phases of a single cycle; and that dharma, the moral law of the universe, accounts for the eternal cycle of nature and the destiny of the human soul. The schools agreed, therefore, that knowledge is the goal of freedom and that yoga is the means for the attainment of final liberation.

2. *The Social Structure.* Although recent legislation has somewhat altered the picture, the social structure of Hinduism has his-

[13] Theos Bernard, *Hindu Philosophy,* New York, 1947, p. 3 and *passim.*

torically consisted in the joint family, village community, and caste system.[14]

Consanguinity in the male line of descent, the residuary of an early stage of society, was the basic principle of coherence in the joint family. Males descended from a common ancestor, or sons adopted through an artificial kinship, formed the collectivistic institution inherent in the joint family. A kind of domestic commune, the Hindu joint family had a counterpart in the French provincial and Russian types. It held land and cattle in common and although its continuance was subject to the consent of members, a rigid authoritarianism, hallowed by religious tradition, prevailed in private and public affairs and ruled out free competition. Due to a number of factors, including Western influence and internal pressures, the joint family, even of the exceptional matriarchal variety known in Malabar, has been in a state of disintegration during the last century and may no longer be regarded as an inviolable institution.

The small village is the typical community where six out of seven Hindus spend most of their lifetime.[15] A small segment of petty landlords, normally claiming twice-born status, dominate the life of the community. Below them are the cultivators, ordinarily associated with the fourth caste of *sudras* (toilers), outcastes, exterior castes, fifths (*panchamas*), untouchables, and depressed classes who figure at the bottom of the economic scale. Actually, all gradations of the village community depend upon the *Brahmans* (priestly caste) and some others such as the agricultural and aggressive gentry.

The emergence of the caste system has been traced back to the isolation of Indian society in prehistoric times;[16] but the origin of caste is a controversial issue among specialists. It is likely that the institution owes its earliest forms to the mores of the Austronesian neighbors of India on the East. From Australia to Assam, endogamy (marriage within the group) was evidently an institution going

[14] L. S. S. O'Malley, ed., *Modern India and the West,* Oxford, 1941, pp. 2, 381–386.
[15] Daniel and Alice Thorner, *Most of the World,* Ralph Linton, ed., New York, 1949, pp. 563–569.
[16] J. H. Hutton, *Caste in India,* Cambridge, 1946, pp. 164–166.

back to Paleolithic and later Neolithic times; it guaranteed social solidarity, through interbreeding, and social avoidance, even while permitting economic exchange with foreign elements. If so, the endogamous society of the Austronesian region might well have been the original pattern of Hindu caste.[17]

3. *The Religious Structure.* As regards religion, the ethos of Hinduism may be analyzed under three categories, namely conception of the truth, standard institutions, and sacraments.[18]

It has already been noted that the Hindu conceives dharma as the truth which shapes and sustains human destiny. It is at once the norm that sustains the universe and the principle which endows things with being. For the modern Hindus, dharma (from the root *dhr,* to uphold, sustain, nourish) is the whole duty of man in relation to life; its basic aim is the realization of dignity which is the abode of the Supreme Being (Brahman). Its sources are believed to be the Vedas, the tradition of those who know it, the conduct of virtuous men, and individual conscience. Since its rules are mutable, legislative enactments such as those that abolished caste, untouchability, and widows' disabilities, acquire the binding force of dharma.

Standard religious institutions include the temples, image worship, rituals, sacrifice, dietary regulations, fasts, ancestor-worship, and cow protection. Next to caste, the temple with its image worship is the foremost visible institution. While meditation and worship are the peculiar means by which the mind reaches out to purity and communion with the Infinite, in Hinduism symbols take on special significance as an agency of worship. In fact, Hindu apologists justify idolatry on the grounds that the symbol does not subject the Infinite to the finite but simply allows the worshiper to look beyond the object that stands before him. They maintain that the symbols, gods, and goddesses of Hinduism can become transparent of divine reality.

There are four sacraments: birth, initiation, marriage, and the funeral. With the exception of initiation, these apply in various degrees to all Hindus. Applicable to the three upper castes only, the sacrament of initiation is prefaced by a prayer addressed to

[17] Ralph Linton, *JAOS,* vol. 68, no. 2, April-June 1948, pp. 125–126.
[18] S. Radhakrishnan, *Religion and Society,* London, 1947, pp. 101–138.

Savitar (the sun) : "The excellent glory of the Quickening Sun, the god, may we attain ; may he stimulate our devotions." [19] But this has been interpreted for the modern Hindu to mean, "We meditate on the effulgent glory of the divine light. May he inspire our understanding." [20]

II. Evidences of General Revelation

The ascetic ideal, faith in the Unseen, and other distinctively Hindu characteristics confirm the reality of God's general revelation. These evidences are embedded in the cultural, social, and religious complex of Hinduism and may be observed at close range in the intellectual, spiritual, and practical domains.

1. *The Intellectual Assets.* In the basic concept of revelation, the institution of priesthood and sacrifice, the unrivaled position of sacred science, the way of perfection and saintliness, Hinduism, despite perversion, bears testimony to general revelation. Shankara, the greatest philosopher of classical Hinduism, affirmed the authority of revelation :

"The authority of the Vedas . . . , just as the light of the sun is the direct means of our knowledge of form and color ; . . . depends on an extraneous basis and is mediated by a chain of teachers and traditions." [21]

To him revelation was the truth of supreme intuition established by the authority of the sacred texts.[22]

In the Bhagavadgita,[23] Lord Krishna, the incarnate personal deity, declared, "But thou canst not behold Me with this (human) eye of yours ; I will bestow on thee the supernatural eye. Behold My divine power." The implication is that no one can have a vision of Brahman save by divine grace. The spontaneity and directness of experiencing the Divine is thus not part of human knowledge but of revelation. Vedanta philosophy, which developed from the revealed teachings of the Upanishads, upholds the latter in the affirma-

---

[19] *Rig-veda* III : 62, 10.
[20] Radhakrishnan, *op. cit.,* p. 135.
[21] *Vedanta Sutra,* tr. G. Thibaut, SBE, vol. 34, p. 295.
[22] Christopher Dawson, *Religion and Culture,* New York, 1948, pp. 42–43, *passim.*
[23] Tr. Radhakrishnan, p. 271.

tion that the soul (*atman*) itself is revealed to the elect by the Creator's grace.[24]

2. *Spiritual Validity.* Rudolf Otto,[25] one of the most discerning Western interpreters of Hinduism, found in the early Vedic hymns evidence of man's consciousness of sanctity.[26] He cited Krishna's transformation as an example of the numinous, the *mysterium tremendum,* in religion. He considered this transformation a moving theophany, worthy of comparison with the great experience of the Eternal depicted at the close of the Book of Job where the transcendent God speaks. "Here today, behold the whole universe, moving and unmoving, and whatever else thou desirest to see, O Arjuna, all unified in my body." [27]

Hinduism surpasses nearly all living non-Christian religions in its vital spiritual expression represented by the doctrine of *bhakti* (grace). Not unlike Christianity, the bhakti faith provides a way of salvation. Hindu soteriology, denoted by the words *mukti* (release) and *moksha* (deliverance), can scarcely be interpreted save within the framework of salvation.[28] But the contrast between Christianity and Hinduism sharpens to a fine edge along the three cardinal lines of holiness, sin, and redemption.

Whereas Hinduism proposes to lead the devotee from the unreal to the real, from darkness to light, and from death to transmigration, Christianity receives the words of revelation seriously. "Sanctify yourselves, therefore, and be ye holy; for I am the Lord your God." [29] That is, the believer is to be holy because God himself is holy.

Christianity is salvation because the power of the holy God, made known in Christ, redeems man from sin; the Hindu word for sin, *klesa,* refers, however, to the trouble which the enchained soul (*atman*) suffers through the endless cycle of *samsara.* The mysti-

[24] R. E. Hume, *The Thirteen Principal Upanishads,* pp. 349–350, 376.

[25] *Gottheit und Gottheiten der Arier,* Giessen, 1932, pp. 1–15, 65, 82.

[26] Robert F. Davidson, *Rudolf Otto's Interpretation of Religion,* pp. 99, 111, 117.

[27] *Bhagavadgita,* ch. XI, 7.

[28] Rudolf Otto, *Die Gnadenreligion Indiens und das Christentum,* Gotha, 1930; tr. *India's Religion of Grace and Christianity,* New York, 1930, pp. 13–18.

[29] Lev. 20 :7.

cism of Shankara, based on the Upanishads and the Bhagavadgita, spells self-evaluation, whereas that of a Christian mystic, such as Meister Eckhardt, means communion with the living God, the Lord who calls the individual by name and restores in Christ the integrity of immortal souls.

Salvation in its Hindu import amounts to the identity of atman with Brahman, freedom from the burden of good works in the sea of oneness with the Infinite. The greater maturity of Christianity in this respect is shown in the meaning of its redemptive message. In the last analysis, the difference is between salvation which, in the case of Hinduism, is escape and deliverance through annihilation; and a salvation, in the case of Christianity, which is deliverance from sin by means of a redemptive, creative intercourse with the Eternal who in Christ transforms man both now and forever.[30]

3. *Practical Outcome.* Apart from the evidences of general revelation, which are brought out in the Hindu concepts of truth, grace, and the Eternal, there is the practical side wherein this highly developed religion needs to be tested on the basis of its cumulative impact on life and articulate results. The real issue here hinges on the very essence of all religion, that is, the meaning of being and existence.

The problem of being comes to the forefront in the conflict between the traditional Hindu view which was one of world- and life-negation, on the one hand, and the more recent and rather liberal view, on the other, namely that of world- and life-affirmation.[31] From magical mysticism and the practice of the occult, a heightened sense of pessimism and otherworldliness was acquired, and it gradually led to a flight from reality which relieved the mind from the necessity of trying all things on the anvil of pragmatic objectivity. But when Hindus finally awakened to the light of modern times, the pendulum swung to the other extreme of world- and life-affirmation.

Whether life negating or affirming, however, the longing for God remains central in the Hindu conception of being. The futility of

[30] Sten Rodhe, *Deliver Us from Evil,* Lund, 1946, *passim.*
[31] Albert Schweitzer, *Indian Thought and Its Development,* tr. Mrs. C. E. B. Russell, London, 1936, pp. 252–265.

this longing is largely due to the failure of Hinduism to recognize God as a forgiving and saving Father. Contributing to this failure are three defects in the Hindu outlook: [32] The concept of the soul as autonomous from personality, marching through many incarnations and actually detached from the actions of the person temporarily associated with it; the lack of positive certitude that God is holy and that union with Him is predicated upon repentance; and the fact that union with ultimate Reality tends to become a mechanical process rooted in formal or mental exercise, instead of faith, and therefore unfit as a proper response to the call of the Eternal.

That in Jesus Christ, God reconciled man to Himself remains a strange message to most Hindus. For, despite the concern of their great and ancient culture with the status of man, the perennial issues involved in human infirmity and disorder have not as yet evoked the unqualified obedience of faith in God among the exponents of Hindu religious thought.

III. Modern Resurgence of Hinduism

1. *The Response to Western Influence.* In his famous and delightful *Minute on Education* (1835), which decided the issue whether English, Sanskrit, or Arabic was to be the medium of higher education in India, Lord Macaulay (1800–1859) affirmed his conviction that Oriental education tends not to accelerate the progress of the truth but to delay the death of expiring errors. Although he had no desire to see the British Government support the cause of missions, Macaulay knew that the impact of Western education would actually promote the cause of Christianity.[33]

The Sepoy Mutiny (1857–1858) was a revolt against British authority in India, the cumulative revulsion of a people shaken by the annexation policy and the rapid introduction of Western standards. The greatest issue involved was the establishment of the prin-

[32] Sabapathy Kulandran, *The Message and Silence of the American Pulpit,* Boston, 1949, pp. 131–132.
[33] C. S. Milford, *The Triumph of God,* Max Warren, ed., London, 1948, pp. 276 *sqq.*

ciple of equality before the law, a blow to the conception of a society frozen in its castes and types.[34]

That the Mutiny failed meant that in its secular and religious aspects, the Western impact upon Hinduism in the second half of the nineteenth century was bound to be greater than it was in the first. Western influence became a spur to Hindu culture and religious thought.

2. *New Hindu Defenses.* In setting up her defenses against the Western assault, India gave birth to a number of movements and leaders.

The Brahmo Samaj (society of God) was Hinduism's first religious response to the Western impact. Founded at Calcutta in 1824, it owed its inception to Ram Mohan Roy (1772–1833), Brahman in caste, who became the first great Hindu reformer of modern times. He admitted his debt to contemporary missionaries such as Carey, Marshman, and Duff.[35] Thanks to his knowledge of Indian as well as British literature, Roy was able to mediate between his own culture and that of the West. His book, *The Precepts of Jesus, the Guide to Peace and Happiness,* discloses a keen appreciation of Christian ethics, although he undervalued the meaning and exercise of prayer. Despite his contempt for idolatry, he clung tenaciously to the Vedic hymns and sought along deistic, not theistic, lines to restore Hindu worship to its pristine purity.

Brahmo Samaj was a throwback to natural religion. The tenets of this faith were summed up in six propositions: (1) God is a personal being; (2) He was never incarnate; (3) He hears and answers prayer; (4) He is to be worshiped in spirit; (5) He forgives those who repent and cease from sin; and (6) He is known through nature and intuition.

Debendranath Tagore (1817–1905) developed Brahmo Samaj along more strictly Hindu lines and repudiated Christian influence. Keshab Chandra Sen (1834–1884) was strongly attracted to Christian mysticism before he evolved belief in himself as the divinely appointed interpreter of "the new dispensation." In the long run,

---

[34] L. S. S. O'Malley, *op. cit.,* p. 75.
[35] Harvey De Witt Griswold, *Insights into Modern Hinduism,* New York, 1934, pp. 36 *sqq.*

Brahmo Samaj could not compete with the other rival movements which propagated a creed suffused with religious, racial, and political motivation.

Chief among these was the Arya Samaj (Aryan Assembly), a native reform church of the Vedic religion founded by Dayananda Sarasvati (1824–1883), a Brahman. The sect taught that there are three external substances, God, spirit, and matter, and that the hymns of the Vedas are the only inspired scriptures. Its practical ends were the promotion of education, reform of the caste system, and the abolition of child marriage. Sarasvati owed less to Christian influence than any other leading, nineteenth-century Indian reformer. Yet under his guidance, the principles of Western education were favored.

Also characteristic of the new defenses created by the Hindu resurgence were the movements initiated by Ramakrishna and Vivekenanda. Ramakrishna (1834–1886), illiterate saint of Bengal, was a mystic on the order of St. Theresa, who owed much to the Christian mystics as well as the Hindu saints. He owed less, however, to rationalism and Western secularism; the popular biographical accounts of his career were undoubtedly brought into conformity with aspects of the Gospel stories. His best known disciple, Swami Vivekenanda (1862–1902), the Apostle of Hinduism to the West, was actually the product of a Christian missionary college.

In the Western world, Vivekenanda proclaimed that the East excels in spirituality largely because of Hindu catholicity. According to him, Hinduism was the greatest religion by virtue of its tolerance, absorptive capacity, and spiritual depth. In the United States, Vivekenanda founded at San Francisco the Ramakrishna Mission which taught the worship of Ramakrishna as god-man in line with Krishna, Buddha, and Christ.[36]

The Theosophical Society carried the exaltation of Hinduism a step further through antagonism to Christianity. Organized in India by the Russian, Elena Petrovna Blavatsky (1831–1891) and the English Annie Besant (1847–1933), Theosophy was a protest against any exotic religion. Abroad, it adopted the slogan,

[36] Swami Satprakashananda, *Religion in the Twentieth Century,* Vergilius Ferm, ed., New York, 1948, pp. 411–412.

"There is no religion higher than the truth." Jiddu Krishnamurti, who began as a teacher of Theosophy in Europe and America, established in 1929 his own independent religion based upon a hazy pragmatism which apparently had little connection with the views of Hindu saints.

Rabindranath Tagore (1861–1941), son of the founder of Brahmo Samaj, was a poet, dramatist, novelist, and Nobel Prize winner for literature (1913). Together with Gandhi, Nehru, and Radhakrishnan, Tagore ranks among the foremost intellectual figures reared by modern Hinduism. A rationalist and humanitarian, he had not, however, made a careful study of Christian thought. His world outlook was expressed in *Saddhana* (Fulfillment), lectures delivered at Harvard, and in his *Gitanjali* (song offerings), short devotional verses in Bengali. In his *Religion of Man,* the infinite ideal is a divine humanity which suggests the identity of Tagore's thought with Ramanuja rather than with Shankara.[37]

3. *Hindu Apologetic: Universalism.* The unequaled prophet of modern Hinduism is Mahatma Gandhi, whereas its apologist and political giant, respectively, are Sarvepalli Radhakrishnan and Jawaharlal Nehru.

Mohandas Gandhi (1869–1948) occupied in the second quarter of the twentieth century the center of the stage in India. The title Mahatma (great-souled) had a distinctly religious connotation. Though Western in culture, Gandhi was convinced of the spiritual superiority of Hinduism over Western materialism, and that was the heart of his apologetic. He proclaimed, therefore, that India needed to unlearn much of what she had acquired from the West and work out her salvation within a primitive simplicity of her own. Whereas others might idealize the past, Gandhi contended that India must actually go back to it.

Gandhi's utopia was free from the props of industrial civilization. His popularity with the masses was in large measure due to the fact that he sounded a new note, namely the return of Rama Raj, the golden age of Hinduism, clothed in religious and moral garb; and that as a saint he was invested with the halo which

---

[37] J. N. Farquhar, *Modern Religious Movements in India,* New York, 1915, pp. 385–386.

aroused national feeling and stirred up dormant passions.[38] According to his own confession of faith, the New Testament awakened him to the value and rightness of passive resistance. The Sermon on the Mount, particularly the words of our Lord, "Resist not him that is evil," [39] left a profound impression on his soul.[40] The Bhagavadgita heightened this conviction and Tolstoy's *The Kingdom of God Is Within You* gave his theory of passivity its permanent form.

He was not a Christian.[41] His Hindu apologetic is a widely accepted perfectionism alive to the realities of the political and social order. His humility, espousal of the underprivileged, and pacifism had a prodigious influence upon India and the world. Taken all in all, his life, ideas, and personal examples are resplendent, though vague, and dealt a mortal blow to secularism despite the diffuse character of his universalism.

Sir Sarvepalli Radhakrishnan (1888–   ), illustrious Hindu scholar, thinker, and interpreter, has enlarged through his many writings the scope of Hinduism and glorified its universalism by reading into it meaning derived from other sources, particularly Christian. That he has at times done violence to the Christian vocabulary by freely adapting it to Hindu use was presumably justified by him on the grounds that he offered a new interpretation of his own heritage in the light of the wider truth.

Mr. Jawaharlal Nehru (1889–   ) minced no words in his *Autobiography* (1936) in expressing horror at the spectacle of organized religion. But in the *Rediscovery of India* (1944), this hostility was somewhat modified, and after he became Prime Minister his attitude was softened still more. With his newfound interest in Hindu culture and his great international prestige, Mr. Nehru undoubtedly wields an influence which might determine the direction that the new universalism and apologetic of Hinduism, propounded by the country's sages and men of vision, is likely to take.

---

[38] L. S. S. O'Malley, *op. cit.,* pp. 97–98.   [39] Matt. 5:39.

[40] J. J. Doke, *M. K. Gandhi: An Indian Patriot in South Africa,* London, 1909, p. 84.

[41] C. F. Andrews, *Mahatma Gandhi: His Own Story,* New York, 1930, p. 163. M. K. Gandhi, *Autobiography: The Story of My Experiments with Truth,* Washington, 1948, pp. 170–171.

IV. CHRISTIANITY AND HINDUISM

The relation of Christianity to Hinduism is essentially that of the Gospel to a religion inherent in reflective genius, training in wisdom, and the practice of the occult. That many Christians have erred in their approach to and evaluation of this religion may be conceded. The early missionaries faced a Hinduism that was passing through a period of disintegration and decomposition. Idolatry was dominant, cruel customs and obscene rites were rife, and the nobler virtues of this faith were concealed behind a veil of ignorance.[42]

On his own part, the Hindu even when sympathetic toward Christianity, drew the line between the Western Christ of the missionary and what appeared to him to be the true character of the Oriental Christ. In the mind of many an intelligent Hindu, the Western Christ was foreign to the genius of India, laid down a series of dogmatic assertions about plenary inspiration, and considered everything false that did not originate in the Western, European, Greco-Roman, and modern imperialist tradition. Such a Christ was tolerated only because He carried with Him the cultural and military prestige of a conquering race.

The Oriental Christ, on the other hand, was revered as the possessor of a well-defined spiritual role in history. The Hindu agreed, within this category, that Christ is unique in comparison with ordinary men. Yet the Hindu maintained that there have been and will be numerous incarnations of God. While forcefully rejecting the view of those Christian radicals who regard all men as equally divine—Christ no more than anyone else—the Hindu simultaneously accepts many special revelations in the form of divine incarnations.[43]

Christianity goes beyond both the so-called Western and the so-called Oriental Christ. The true Christ of the Gospel, the Son of God and the Son of Man, chooses to enter the stream of culture yet refuses to be equated either with a projection of culture or with

---

[42] Sydney Cave, *Christianity and Some Living Religions of the East*, London, 1929, p. 17.

[43] Swami Akhilananda, *Hindu View of Christ*, New York, 1949, p. 43.

any illusory incarnation of man's religion. In the Hindu tradition, Christ longs to be interpreted, without syncretism, through the categories of India's patterns of thought. Likewise in the West, He sets the true standards of culture; He is glorified through the metaphors and available channels of intellectual communication without ever associating Himself with the worldliness and imperfections of the Occident.

The Gospel stands in absolute contradistinction to the religious universalism of Gandhi and Radhakrishnan.[44] They emphasize the similarity of all religions, that all faiths lead to the same God and that there can be no meeting-ground among the followers of different religions who adopt different historical events as the basis of their faith; on the other hand, the Gospel is not eclectic, derives its message from the living, self-revealing God, and proclaims Jesus Christ as Lord Incarnate, a historical Saviour and through His Resurrection an everlasting contemporary. For Christianity, redemptive history thus centers in a Person and in the crucial facts of His life and ministry. This faith is vindicated in the witness of humble men. Christianity maintains that to conceive the truth of God in any other way save that which He provides is to make an idol of God and hence to facilitate the liquidation of the whole structure of holiness and true religion.[45]

It is indisputable that there has been an earnest search for the truth in Hinduism through the ages. The experiences and ideals of the Bhaktas, the genuinely spiritual portions of the Vedic literature, the practice of devout Hindus, their higher types of thought and humility of life, are often worthy means of glorifying the Saviour. A. J. Appasamy,[46] the son of a convert from Hinduism, reflected upon his father's practice of yoga regularly despite his otherwise staunch Anglicanism. He reflected, furthermore, upon the incident that in 1920 Sadhu Sundar Singh, the Christian preacher and convert from Sikhism who mysteriously disappeared in 1929, had given all who knew him in the West the impression of a rugged Christian though characteristically Indian in mien and soul. At last, Appasamy

[44] Rajah B. Manikan, *World Faith in Action*, Charles Tudor Leber, ed., New York, 1951, p. 249.

[45] John McKenzie, *Two Religions*, London, 1950, p. 91.

[46] *The Gospel and India's Heritage*, London, 1942.

came to the conclusion that all the riches of devotion and prayer, treasured in Hinduism, should be offered up to Christ.

The relation of Christianity to Hinduism, with its implied opposition between a theistic, redemptive universalism, on the one hand, and an indeterminate, dehumanizing, rationalist universalism, on the other, offers in miniature form the basic problem which arises when the Gospel is preached among the nations. This opposition and the problem involved are not bound to end in deadlock. The elements of a solution are provided in the valiant and ready response of the Church to consecrated, living witness undergirded throughout by the grace of God and the guidance of the Holy Spirit.

CHAPTER VIII

THE RELIGION OF HUMANISM: CONFUCIANISM

CONFUCIANISM is the second largest religious system in the world. The Chinese continue to be Confucianists with a leaning toward Taoism and Buddhism. Yet the religio-cultural heritage of China is in full dissolution. Obscured by the cult of nature and the heavy demands of war, revolution, and Communism, the rudimentary monotheism of China has been relegated to oblivion.

I. THE HISTORICAL BACKGROUND OF CONFUCIANISM

Until the founder of Confucianism was divinized, this religion had been an ethical system primarily concerned with social and political affairs, a this-worldly structure of public and private morality strictly silent on matters of divine worship.[1] Despite its unecclesiastical character, however, Confucianism did not long preserve its detachment from that inborn religious longing which moves men to the worship of a person. As the foremost figure in China's annals and expounder of the state religion, Confucius steadily gained in stature and was eventually elevated to the highest rank of veneration. The dignity and prestige attached to his name guaranteed the triumph of his school in both official and popular circles.

Although it received the support of the state, Confucianism owed its primary debt to the scholars whose training in the classics had inspired their devotion to the seer who dominated the entire scene of national culture. In the temples, erected in every provincial seat of administration and in the capital city, Peking, the place of honor was accorded to the tablet, or statue, of Confucius; and ranged

[1] Crawford Howell Toy, *Introduction to the History of Religion*, Cambridge, 1948, p. 543.

on either side were other tablets inscribed to the leading school-men, the disciples and interpreters of Confucianism.

The examinations required of candidates for public office pre-supposed knowledge of the Confucianist classics. The entire educa-tional system was geared to what the Master and his successors had taught. Basically ethical in content, education laid emphasis on major themes such as the family, ancestors, and filial piety, its ideal being the principle of moderation in social behavior. Ceremonies, visits to shrines, the philosophy of naturalism, social equilibrium, and adjustment to social pressure were calculated to engender a pattern of life that hampered progress and frowned upon inno-vation.[2]

1. *Confucius and the Classics.* Confucius (551–479 B.C.) was born in the state of Lu, now known as the Province of Shantung.[3] China was under the Chou Dynasty (1122–250 B.C.) whose reign was longer than any other known to history save that of the royal house of Japan. Benefactors of China's culture, certain strong Chou monarchs had contributed to the growth of literature and thought. In fact, the literary language perfected under the Chou differs no more from modern classical Chinese than does Chaucer's English from that of the twentieth century.[4]

A reformer and a teacher, Confucius was a genius in statecraft and in philosophy. He presumably believed in a ruling Providence, yet his reticence on the subject of supernatural was proverbial. His years of service under the Prince of Lu endowed him with the sagacity of a political scientist and the insights of a government official.

A story is told to account for the abrupt interruption of his political career. A troupe of eighty beautiful girls and thirty horses were brought one day to the palace as a present to the Prince. Disturbed by the incident and alarmed lest evil entrench itself in high places, Confucius, careful not to act precipitately, bided his

---

[2] Kenneth Scott Latourette, *A Short History of the Far East,* New York, 1947, p. 166.

[3] On the case for Confucius as a forerunner of democracy, and the impact of Confucianism upon Western thought, see H. G. Creel, *Confucius: The Man and the Myth,* New York, 1949.

[4] Latourette, *The Development of China,* Boston, 1937, p. 21.

time in the vain hope that the ruler would repent. However, when the carnal frailty of the Prince became evident, Confucius shook the dust of the wicked palace from his feet.[5]

Modern research has shown this story to be a later fabrication. The withdrawal of the Sage from public office resulted from the pursuance of a forthright policy. Acting as a reformer, he had sought to reduce the power of the great clans. Although he succeeded, through diplomacy and persuasion, in inducing the dismantling of their city-castles in the state of Lu, his position was thereby seriously endangered, forcing his voluntary departure.[6]

He traveled in the country looking for some ruler who might accept his services and heed his counsel. His wanderings lasted thirteen years and produced no tangible result. Having now attained the age of sixty-eight, he realized that he was no longer fit for public office. He therefore settled in his native Lu, determined to devote his last years to literary pursuits. He composed his only original work, *Spring and Autumn,* a dry chronicle of his home state.

Confucius was more creative, however, than the West realizes. He was the first to lay emphasis on the conception of the "superior man" as a moral person rather than one who was socially prominent. He was not, as is popularly supposed, an ardent exponent of filial piety, the institution which subsequently became a permanent feature of Chinese civilization.[7]

Utilizing earlier materials, he laid the groundwork of the classics which were to constitute the standard literary heritage of China. Taken together, they comprise the Four Books and the Five Canons. The Four Books are the *Analects,*[8] sayings of Confucius and his disciples ; the *Doctrine of the Mean* and the *Great Learning,*[9] two short treatises on ethical culture compiled by successors of

---

[5] Millar Burrows, *Founders of Great Religions,* New York, 1931, p. 38.

[6] Homer H. Dubs, "The Political Career of Confucius," *JAOS,* vol. 66, no. 4, October-December, 1946, pp. 273-282.

[7] E. R. Hughes, *Chinese Philosophy in Classical Times,* London, 1941, pp. 24-30.

[8] Tr. W. C. Soothill, Shanghai, 1910 ; also, tr. Arthur Waley, London, 1925.

[9] Tr. E. R. Hughes, London, 1942.

Confucius; and the *Book of Mencius*,[10] comprising the teaching of that philosopher.

The Five Canons include, in addition to Confucius' own history of Lu, the oracular *Changes* and the *History,* a compilation of the historical records of the past; the *Odes,* a collection of songs and ballads current at the time; and the *Rites,* a collection of rules describing the common ceremonies of China.[11]

2. *Unification of China, Rise of the Han Dynasty.* The closing period of the Chou, known as that of the Contending States (403–221 B.C.), saw the dignity of the Emperor reduced to a mere shadow. Out of the seemingly endless strife emerged the state of Ch'in (221–207 B.C.) in northwest China and its strong ruler, Shih Huang. The name of China is actually derived from the Ch'in which Shih Huang made famous among the peoples of Asia.[12]

Shih Huang is credited with the completion of the Great Wall, mightiest defense line in the world till the nineteenth century, stretching along the northern boundaries of the Eighteen Provinces. In order to promote progress, Shih Huang sought to break the dead hand of the past by setting fire to the then existing literature of China. He denounced the Confucianist tradition and favored Taoism which with certain modifications descended from his day. Despite this narrow outlook, however, his reign was marked by the reduction of the many styles of writing into one and, above all, by the establishment of unity in the empire.[13]

The Han Dynasty (202 B.C.–A.D. 220) enjoyed a four-century duration, interrupted by an interval of divided authority during the first quarter of the first Christian century. In preference to the old legalistic conception of arbitrary and absolute sovereignty, Han Kao-Tsu (202–195 B.C.), founder of the Han, adopted the Confucian conception, namely that government should be founded on justice.

The early Han rulers established the power of the Emperor, sup-

[10] Tr. L. A. Lyall, London, 1932.
[11] The Five Canons, tr. James Legge, *The Chinese Classics,* Oxford, 2nd ed., 7 vols., 1893–1895.
[12] L. Carrington Goodrich, *A Short History of the Chinese People,* New York, 1943, p. 34.
[13] Derk Bodde, *China's First Unifier,* London, 1938.

ported by a graded bureaucracy. Civil servants, trained in Confucianism, were frequently recruited from among the maternal relatives of the monarch because of their complete dependence upon his favor. The institution of inspection which later became the Censorate was organized, and the authority of the Emperor was construed as a mandate of Heaven.

Han China was open to foreign influences, detected in the art, trade, and industry of the period. In exchange for the Chinese silk, worn by the ladies of the Near East and the Greco-Roman world, the vine was introduced from the lands of the Eastern Mediterranean. In glasswork, the art of China also betrayed Near Eastern inspiration.

Parallels between the history of Han China and of the Greco-Roman world have been noted. The imperial system of the Han and that of Rome were contemporary. Confucius and his disciples were broadly the contemporaries of Plato and Aristotle, together with their immediate heirs and predecessors. Shih Huang, China's first unifier, lived only a century after Alexander the Great. A similar sequence marked these two ranking civilizations of the East and West, namely an age of philosophers, a warrior state empire, and finally disintegration.[14]

3. *Introduction of Buddhism, Rise of the Tang Dynasty.* The fall of the Han broke up the Empire into the Three Kingdoms (A.D. 220–265). Meanwhile, the Buddhist leaven permeated the social, intellectual, and religious consciousness of China.

The world of appearances, to which the Confucianist thinkers were committed, had left a void in the spiritual life of the Chinese which Buddhism, with its profound insights and mystical overtones, offered to fill.[15] Buddhism offered the prospects of nirvana in some Western Paradise. Borrowing from the Buddhist teachers their monastic emphasis, Taoism began to revive its claim to a mystical interpretation of existence and its promise of immortality. Nor were the Confucianist scholars themselves immune to Buddhist influence if one were to judge by the increasing temples, tablets, and

[14] John King Fairbank, *The United States and China,* Cambridge, 1949, pp. 62, 94.

[15] C. P. Fitzgerald, *China: A Short Cultural History,* London, 1935, p. 261.

images dedicated to Confucius. That Buddhism pushed back the cultural frontiers of China is evidenced by the Indian elements introduced, as well as a variety of Greek art observable in the Central Asiatic iconography which it brought into the country.

Four centuries of political disunion closed when the Tang Dynasty (A.D. 618–906) initiated the golden age of Chinese history celebrated in art, literature, and philosophy. The territorial expansion and material prosperity of the Tang ushered in the most brilliant Chinese culture.

Buddhism attained the apex of its development in the Empire; in 740 the capital alone had sixty-four monasteries and twenty-seven nunneries. [16] Tai Tsung (d. 649) was the ruler who provided the vision and dynamic that directed the dynasty in its creative course and splendid achievements. China then could vie with the Arab empire based on Damascus, and later, Baghdad; compared with its power, the empire of Charlemagne was indeed petty and backward.[17] Confucianists continued to control the affairs of the state and jealously guarded their cultural ascendancy.

In 630 Tai Tsung decreed that all districts in the Empire should build temples to Confucius, and in 647 he proclaimed the Temple of Confucius at the capital a hall of fame for eminent scholars and officials.[18] Yet his fanatical espousal of the Confucianist cause did not last. The edicts which suppressed Buddhist orders and banned the admission of Manichaean teachers from Persia were soon relaxed and religious freedom was restored.

Perhaps due to remorse and personal bereavement, but more likely as the sign of growth in wisdom and statesmanship, Tai Tsung opened the country to representatives of other faiths. In 635 he welcomed a Nestorian bishop and, three years later, issued an edict of toleration toward Christianity. The heart of the message which the Nestorian missionaries brought from their home base in the Near East was the life of Our Lord, particularly the Sermon on the Mount, the Passion, and the Resurrection.[19]

[16] A. K. Reischauer, *Great Religions of the Modern World*, p. 123.
[17] Latourette, *A Short History of the Far East*, p. 121.
[18] Lewis Hodous, *Great Religions of the Modern World*, p. 11.
[19] John Foster, *The Church of the T'ang Dynasty*, London, 1939, pp. 31 *sqq.*

4. *The Mongol Challenge to Native Rule: The Manchus.* An interregnum of a half century separated the Tang from the Sung Dynasty (A.D. 960–1279), which failed to maintain the high imperial power of the former regime.

Chu Hsi (1130–1200), recognized as the greatest neo-Confucianist scholar, flourished during this age.[20] He favored a patriarchal government and regarded the Emperor as a saint, the father-mother of the people. The divine in the universe was reduced to the psychic principle *Li* and the material principle *Chi.* A materialist thinker, Chu Hsi endorsed the latent agnosticism of the Confucianist school. In contrast to Buddhism's losing battle, Confucianism's reassertion of its power was largely due to the interpretation of Chu Hsi which enabled it to retain its hegemony for about seven more centuries.

The military ineptitude of the Sung paved the way for the Mongol invaders. Under the determined efforts of Genghis Khan, and his successors (*ca.* 1162–1227), the hordes of central Asia overran not only China but North India and Russia, and sacked Baghdad in their westward thrust toward Poland and Hungary.

In 1215, the memorable year of Magna Carta, the Mongols laid the foundation of their capital city on the site of Peking. Kublai Khan (*ca.* 1216–1294) became Emperor of China and founded the Yuan Dynasty (1279–1368).

A native dynasty, the Ming (1368–1644), restored Chinese sovereignty in part of the Empire. During the Ming period, Europeans began to cast covetous eyes on the Far East. The Portuguese led the way, followed by the Spaniards. The Venetian traveler, Marco Polo (1254–1323), had set out to find Cathay and the storied court of the Great Khan.

In the sixteenth century, the Dutch sent mariners to the East Indies. Still later, came the English explorers and traders. In the wake of all these, came Christian missionaries. The Jesuits, exponents of the Counter-Reformation, sent their representatives to the Americas as well as to the Far East. St. Francis Xavier died (1552) on an island within sight of the Chinese coast.

Akin to the Mongols and Tartars, the Manchus (1644–1911)

[20] Chu Hsi, *The Philosophy of Human Nature,* tr. J. P. Bruce, London, 1922.

came out of Manchuria and overpowered the tottering Ming, but the frightful carnage attendant upon their rise was followed by stability. Having organized a mighty state, the Manchus adopted Chinese culture, gave honor to Confucius, recognized Taoism and Buddhism, and encouraged a literary revival.

Until decadence overtook their state, culminating in the Nationalist restoration of 1911, the Manchus had managed to govern China with a measure of efficiency. Two of their monarchs truly deserved to rank with the country's most enlightened rulers.

The Manchus discovered that despite their great resources and administrative gifts, their weakness on the sea could prove disastrous. The growth of Western influence within their borders was bound to create grave concern, and friction between the Chinese and the Europeans began to mount.

In 1784, the first American vessel reached the shore of China. The object of Western policy was to wrest from China better terms for trade. These terms were correctly interpreted by the Chinese as a violation of their national sovereignty. The reaction of the Manchu rulers was vigorous, as may be seen from the ruthlessness with which Christian missionaries, especially the Jesuits, were treated. In the outcome, Manchu power declined in direct proportion to the increase of Western influence.

That in their hour of weakness the Manchu rulers still thought in Confucian terms, taking refuge in an ancient system of human relations which held no meaning to Westerners, was part of the tragedy that hastened their demise. For example Chi Ying, the Imperial Clansman who negotiated the treaties of 1842–1844 with the British government, opening China to Western commercial exploitation, thought he could best serve his country by treating the adversary within the framework of the Confucian friend-friend relationship. Despising the British as "uncivilized barbarians," he nevertheless resorted to the traditional device of appeasement and sought to win the personal favor of the hard-headed British emissary instead of taking into serious consideration the policies and ultimate objectives of a realistic Western power.[21]

[21] J. K. Fairbank, "The Manchu Appeasement Policy of 1843," *JAOS,* vol. 59, no. 4, December, 1939, pp. 469–484.

The political revolution which dislodged the Manchus was part of that tidal wave which swept China when the Industrial Revolution had finally caught up with the Far East. Every aspect of China's culture was thereby affected.

Traditionally linked to the monarchy, Confucianism was naturally shaken to its roots. The passing of the old bureaucracy and of the examination system, based on the classics, dealt Confucianism a body blow. In the meantime, new cults strove to harmonize the ancient religious heritage of the people with the cultural elements that were newly acquired from the countries of the East and the West.

II. THE NEW CHINA

The quest for a harmony in the intellectual realm between Confucian philosophy and Western objectivism was matched in the political realm by the efforts made at the turn of the century under leaders such as General Chang Tso-lin (1873–1928), who worked toward greater homogeneity of organization.

Having thus received its first spark, modern nationalism was developed by Chiang Kai-shek and under the Communists became a united and aggressive movement.

Professor Fuang Yu-lan [22] underscored the forces inherent in modern Chinese self-analysis. In the very titles of his books, namely *New Rationalism, New Inquiry on Man,* and *New Investigation into the Way,* there is a hint of the modern rationalist trends. The meaning of Chinese culture and the essence of Confucianism, in all their strength and weakness, were thus brought to light.

These and similar writings seemed to concede that in the category of demonstration and interpretation, Chinese philosophy was outstripped by the Hindu and the Western. Its central theme was not what man possesses but rather what he is. It attached little or no importance to epistemology and was hardly concerned at all with the pursuit of knowledge for its own sake.

Nor did Chinese philosophy contrast man with the universe or

[22] *History of Chinese Philosophy,* 2 vols., 1930–1933; vol. I, tr. Derk Bodde and Henri Vetch, Peiping, 1937.

seek to develop a logic of its own. It subordinated metaphysics to human affairs, limiting its scope to what was considered the major problem of thought, namely how men can live together. But whereas Chinese philosophy was not systematic in form it was, nevertheless, systematic in content; and although traditional in form it was progressive in essence.[23]

The intellectual agony of New China in the philosophical domain had its counterpart in the military, political, social, and religious aspects of existence.

Awakened from the slow rhythm of her past by the new stimuli compelling revolutionary change, China proceeded along the course of reinterpretation and reëmbodiment whereby the old religion and culture began to assume more vital forms. Such was the humanistic China, resurrected by the touch of Western science and aroused by the democracy of the modern world. Although not a Confucianist himself, Sun Yat-sen (1866–1925), leader of the Chinese Revolution and founder of the Republic, made an attempt in his writings to show with well-ordered arguments that it is much easier to do than to know.[24]

New China is best understood, therefore, as an Oriental society whose underlying philosophy is Confucianism. The institutions, customs, ideals, religion, and current history of the Chinese presuppose the existence of basic Confucianist concepts as a method for social control. No one can understand Chiang Kai-shek, or Mao Tse-tung for that matter, without understanding Confucius. Confucianism began as a means of bringing social order out of the chaos of warring states. Unifiers of China are, therefore, irresistibly attracted to Confucianism as a frame of reference.[25]

That China turned to Russia instead of to Western democracy does not necessarily mean that she thereby made a choice of an ideological character. It does mean, however, that those swayed by their Communist leaders believe that their freedom from foreign intervention is better served if they look toward the Kremlin. To work for the freedom and independence of China is, therefore, a

[23] Chan Wing-tsit, *Philosophy—East and West*, pp. 24–25, 144–145.
[24] Shao Chang Lee, *Encyclopedia of Literature*, Shipley, ed., vol. II, p. 1171.
[25] Cf. John King Fairbank, *op. cit.*, p. 59.

duty to be discharged resolutely and prayerfully by all who long for the peace of the world.

It is quite unlikely that Communism will succeed in the extermination of Old China. Remaining still as a reminder of the archaic tradition is a linguistic system, the repository of Confucian authoritarianism. Three basic factors are detectable beneath the crust of Communism: (1) A peasant rebellion against status and privilege; (2) A Marxist dialectic which drew its vitality from the tragedy of the masses and in Confucianist humanism discovered forceful, albeit doubtful, support for its materialist pronouncements; (3) The upsurge of a genuine nationalism in China incensed by the intervention of foreign powers and the lack of temerity on the part of the country's rulers.

III. THE RELIGIOUS CONTENT OF CONFUCIANISM

The religious content of this system may be ascertained through inquiry into its conceptions of God, man, and immortality as well as its notions on creation, evil, and ethics.

1. *The Conception of God.* The original religion of the Chinese consisted in the worship of a number of inferior deities subordinated to the Supreme Being. The Divine Magnet has everywhere drawn the human spirit out of the dross of materialism and toward the eternal God.

The conception of God, upheld by the early Chinese, was a peculiar theism of their own. It acknowledged a Supreme Being conceived impersonally as Tien (Heaven) and personally as Shangti (Ruler Above). In the mysterious world of the unseen, Shangti was supported by a caste of spirits and deities; in the visible world, he was served by the sages generally and by the Emperor as his chief vicegerent. Only the Emperor of China had the right to officiate at the sacrifices offered to Shangti. The Supreme Being was accessible to all men, however, in the form of the impersonal Tien.[26]

At the dawn of her history, therefore, China was a nation whose rulers maintained a variety of monotheism, marred by an animistic worship of hills and rivers and by a polytheism evidenced in the adoration of many deities. The classics leave little doubt, however,

---

[26] W. E. Soothill, *The Three Religions of China,* London, 1913, pp. 126–130.

that a personal god, supreme over all, was also revered. The more frequent occurrence of Tien's name, as compared with that of Shangti, seems to suggest that although the two were essentially one, the tears and supplications of the common folk, barred from the latter, could only be addressed to the former.

Having no spiritual intercourse with the Supreme Being, the common man's conception of God came to be confined to the impersonal Heaven. An increasingly large number of objects, feared and worshiped, began to occupy the center of the religious stage as polytheism and animism acquired menacing proportions. Then Confucius arose, and like Socrates found the company of many gods and spirits loathesome. His soul longed for the moral God who alone satisfies the religious thirst of men.

Confucius failed in the purely religious domain because he lacked the vision to bring his disciples into living communion with the Eternal. Hence, the tide of ancestor-worship, deepened by the advent of Buddhism, grew into an overpowering swell.

2. *Man.* Confucianism exhibits a keen interest in man, his nature, and destiny.[27] In line with other Oriental systems of thought, it taught that man's nature was originally good, its degeneracy being the outcome of ignorance and a beclouded mind.

A confirmed humanist, Confucius explained evil as human selfishness, delusion, and incapability. When a pupil asked him about death and service of the spirits, he replied, "Till you have learnt to serve men, how can you serve the ghosts? . . . Till you know about the living, how are you to know about the dead?" [28]

According to him, the comprehensive program of humanism was true manhood; and that was the central idea of Confucianism. True manhood was mastery over self and the endeavor to restore the moral order. "The true man," in his judgment, "wishing to establish his own character, also seeks to establish the character of others." [29]

Being true to oneself and reciprocity were the logical foundation of this unmistakable humanism. Hence, the indubitable conclusion

[27] Andrew Chih-yi Chang, *Hsüntzu's Theory of Human Nature and Its Influence on Chinese Thought,* Peiping, 1928.

[28] *The Analects,* tr. Waley, 11:11.

[29] Chan Wing-tsit, *op. cit.,* p. 27.

that the basis of the Confucianist system lay in the moral realm, that is, in human experience itself.

3. *Immortality.* Knowing nothing like the Christian doctrine of immortality, Confucianism affirmed, nonetheless, that upon death the soul returned to the heavenly, active principle by which it was formed. Primarily concerned with man's earthly career, Confucius refused to answer questions about the hereafter, and talk about the spirits often annoyed him.

Yet the Chinese masses held to their worship of the spirits, abetted by the concession which the Master himself made to the ancestors. From this the concept was revitalized that the dead continue to take interest in the affairs of the living.

Consequently, the cult of ancestors became the folk religion of China and, as such, received the constant support of traditional Confucianism. In keeping with the admonition of Confucius, sacrifices to ancestors were considered an expression of reverence, loyalty, and tenderness.

It would appear, therefore, that whereas Confucianism was reticent on the subject of personal immortality, it encouraged devotion to the dead. This devotion was crystallized in concrete form around the family tablet and the adoration of Confucius.

While not officially declared to be divine, Confucius was revered in a manner often approximating worship. Built around his name was a cult which lasted from 195 B.C., when the founder of the Han Dynasty, Kao-tsu, personally offered sacrifice to the Sage, down to the abolition of the rite in 1905.

4. *Creation.* The concepts of man and immortality were read in the light of certain cosmological affirmations. As communicated by Confucius the picture of life, its origin and meaning, left a number of gaps which his successors undertook to bridge. Among the gaps which he had left open was the one pertaining to creation. In the latter part of the fourth century B.C., the yin-yang theory was developed in order to meet this lack. But the maturing of a cosmology, complete with literary support and philosophical argument, had to wait till the twelfth Christian century.

During that century, Chu Hsi, the Thomas Aquinas of Confucianism, advanced the view that the universe and its every part were composed of the two principles *Li* and *Chi*. Coeternal, infinite, distinct, and inseparable, these two principles formed the ground-work of creation. Conceived as the psychic principle, *Li* was an *élan vital* of dynamic energy. *Chi* was represented as the material form and substance of all things.

Operating in unison, these two principles were purportedly manifest in two modes, the yin and yang. Yin was negative, dark, cold, passive, and female; yang was positive, light, active, and male. Evident in the five agents—water, fire, wood, metal, and soil—the two modes were believed to exist behind the multiplicity of beings and objects.

The first pair of each specie were thus the products of spontaneous generation, and from them came all others by a process of transformation. Prior to the original pair, the yin and yang were in a state of perpetual motion, now separating and now coming together in order to give rise to the five agents which are at the basis of all things. Throughout this process, all beings, including inanimate things, are held together by the psychic principle *Li*.

Men are created equal since they share the same psychic principle. In its philosophical interpretations, this theory gave rise to three schools differing insofar as their emphases fell upon mind, reason, or empiricism.

Bearing the impress of Mencius (371–286 B.C.), this cosmology had already been sensitive to Buddhist teaching when Chu Hsi gave it permanent form. Despite the inequalities of Chinese society, he insisted that men are equal, their differences arising from the intrusion of the material principle, *Chi*. Sincerity was, therefore, the highest virtue because it made possible the eradication of the physical obstruction represented by *Chi*.

5. *Evil*. It is clear, then, why Confucianism explained evil as selfishness, delusion, and incapability. In the neo-Confucianism of Chu Hsi and Wang Yang-ming (1473–1529) the distinction between good and evil was made foreign to ultimate reality, and sin was apprehended as an incidental defect. Since man produces evil, it was argued that he can stamp it out. Like most other Oriental religions, Confucianism knew nothing of original sin, redemption.

forgiveness, sanctification, and the atonement. Man causes his own downfall and can work out his own salvation.

The three terms used to denote evil in Chinese—*tsui, O,* and *kuo*—mean respectively sin, evil, and transgression. Not one of these words nor any combination of them carries anything like the connotation of the word sin in Christianity.[30] Actually, Confucius and his immediate disciples occupied themselves with the inculcation of virtue rather than with discussions of the nature and consequences of sin.

He pointed out, however, that sin against Heaven leaves man in a state of utter hopelessness. To this, Mencius added a clarification: "Even though a man be evil (O), if he fast and wash he too may serve God (Shangti)." [31] But the Master had already defined transgression as error of judgment when he said, "To err and yet not to reform, this may indeed be called error." [32]

In short, neither the pre-Confucian nor the Confucian classics specify the predicament of the sinner, evil-doer, or unrepentant transgressor. Implied throughout is the notion that such a man will find himself in a tragic state and that he must extricate himself by returning to the harmony of nature.

6. *Ethics.* The ethical code of Confucius is practical, not heroic; prosaic, not poetic; commanding respect, but not admiration. In its religious and moral essence, it resembles the wintry silver of the moon rather than the glow of the sun, golden and warm. It leaves little to the imagination.

His five cardinal virtues are kindness, rectitude, decorum, wisdom, and sincerity; the prince was regarded as the chief exemplar of these virtues. Since Confucius had been a courtier, it is easy to understand why he conceived of virtue as streaming from the lofty height of the court down to the level of the people. Yet neither pleasure, honors, nor wealth represent the highest good, but virtue, the foundation of true happiness attainable through the earnestness of the individual will.

In keeping with other Oriental systems, Confucianism conceived

[30] Soothill, *The Three Religions of China,* pp. 248, 256–267.
[31] *Book of Mencius,* IV, 2:25.
[32] *Analects,* 25:29.

of ethics against the background of philosophy rather than revealed truth. Humanism, common sense, practical living, a rather constant emphasis on morality and character as the supreme good, moderation in nearly all things, these are the accents that mark the utterances of Mencius and the neo-Confucianists, if not Confucius himself. Through it all runs an all-pervading and natural love of life.[33]

Morality was ingeniously set in historical and cultural perspective by means of the five personal relationships: subject-ruler, father-son, husband-wife, elder-younger brother, and friend-friend. Within the framework of these relationships, the cultivation of virtue and perfect humanity meant that man's family was regulated, the state well-governed, and the whole nation made happy and stable. Righteousness was thereby conceived as virtue in operation. Reënforcing and supplementing each other these two ethical concepts, virtue and righteousness, were taken together, the first relating to the character of man, the second to his attitude in a given situation.

Man's proper attitude to others was crystallized in the concept of reciprocity which Confucius enunciated in these words, "Do not to others what you do not want done to yourself." [34] The positive aspect was brought out in the Golden Mean which was also ascribed to the Master: "To set the example in behaving to a friend, as I would require him to behave to me." [35] It is to be noted, furthermore, that righteousness was understood as becoming effective through propriety, that is, through doing everything profitable to the community and wholesome to the individual.[36]

In general, human relations under a given set of circumstances were to be governed by duty—that is, the demand of man's own nature in response to the challenge of the situation. Yet the prevailing sentiment seemed to be that only as man appropriated for himself the cosmic virtue of harmony did he discover his duty and learn how to exercise it. Such was the inward mood of Confucianist ethics, the contours of whose utopia, envisioned in the *Canon of*

[33] Charles A. Moore, *Philosophy—East and West,* p. 252.

[34] *Analects,* 15:23.

[35] *Doctrine of the Mean,* 13:14.

[36] Francis C. M. Wei, *The Spirit of Chinese Culture,* New York, 1947, pp. 78–93.

Rites, directed attention to a society wherein people governed themselves and the ruler only served as a titular head.

IV. A CRITICAL EVALUATION OF CONFUCIANISM

A life and an art, Confucianism, with its beliefs and institutions, constitutes a certain ritual rhythm comprising the restraints and metaphysical doctrines commonly identified with Chinese society and automatically accepted by the people. Into this rhythm, the Chinese were born and within its orbit found an art of living, wisdom, and security. No ignorant outsider may challenge the rhythm of Confucianism without at least taking pains to examine its worthwhile character and originality.

Like ancient Greece, China produced a massive civilization. The wise and truly great philosophers of the two countries believed that the whole fabric of life, including government, was an art epitomized in such arts as music and the dance. The Emperor himself was regarded as the apex of an entrancing system of music and ritual. The harmony and equilibrium which Confucius desperately sought to inculcate are so inextricably related to the selfsame poetry and music against which he was prone to rebel, that the aesthetic character of Confucianism needs no proof.[37]

In their practice of ethics and politics the Chinese are noteworthy among the nations. Whereas India, lacking a continuous political unity, gave herself to explorations in the realm of spiritual dynamics and the meaning of existence, China was content to focus attention on the main problem of the individual and the community.

Under the aegis of a tradition that lasted longer than any political organization known to India, China welded her people together in an unrivaled historic unity. And since we must ascribe Christianity —the soul of Western culture—to a divine origin, we must inevitably credit the Chinese for their matchless achievements. In the field of human relations as well as in their political maturity and the radiance that permeates their social ethics, their heritage stands alone.

In their long succession, the Confucianist scholars sanctioned

[37] Reginald F. Johnston, *Confucianism and Modern China,* London, 1934, pp. 100–110.

the worship of Heaven, and the adoration of ancestors as well as of Confucius. Yet despite the lofty conceptions of the Master, the religion which bore his name, insofar as it was a religion at all, was a composite wherein the anthro-cultural presuppositions of China were mediated. The findings of China's galaxy of thinkers coalesced with the magic, superstition, nature-worship, and idolatry of a primitive society. The golden rule and sincerity of Confucianism, its reciprocity, righteousness, and consciousness of duty are noble traits which drew their power, however, from man's confidence and self-assurance instead of from his humility before the Eternal and obedient faith in God's perfect gifts of grace.

If further support of this evaluation of Confucianism were necessary, the writings of Chinese and Western scholars would offer positive substantiation. Hu Shih [38] (1891–   ), one of China's creative thinkers, specified that the Chinese word for religion (*chiao*) conveys the idea of teaching or a system of teaching. He declared that the Chinese draw no distinction between the theistic religions and the purely moral teachings of the sages. Indeed, the word *chiao* was freely applied to Buddhism, Taoism, Islam, and Christianity as well as to Confucianism. They are all recognized as systems of moral teaching.

Religious essence, centering in morality and "the way of the gods," was, therefore, conceived merely as a sanction to ethics. Thus, the first and foremost philosopher of China, Confucius, was the founder of naturalism, and the second, Laotzu (whom critics date in the third rather than the sixth century B.C. of the traditionalists), was an agnostic. Motzu (*ca.* 479–381 B.C.), on the other hand, dissatisfied with the rational, natural, and agnostic trends in Chinese religion, established the system of philosophic and spiritual values known as Mohism; he revived the ancient religion of Shangti and, purifying the cult, he imparted to it a more personal albeit pragmatic character.

This, together with the intrusion of Buddhism, failed to alter the essentially humanistic genius of Confucianism. Filial piety, the core of Chinese devotion, did not go beyond the view that the human body—the concrete inheritance bequeathed by parents—was sacred.

[38] *The Chinese Renaissance,* Chicago, 1934, pp. 78–93.

Reverence of ancestors, the glorification of parents, and loyalty to superiors seemed to stem from the central theme of filial piety. As a well-defined religion, this was deemed adequate without much further recourse to the gods or any other form of supernaturalism.

The German philosopher and mathematician, Gottfried Wilhelm von Leibnitz (1646–1716), willingly conceded, nevertheless, the basic vitality of Confucianism. In a collection of data about China, *Novissima Sinica,* issued by the Jesuits in 1697, Leibnitz made a classical citation of Confucianism. It said in effect that although the West surpassed China in mathematics, astronomy, logic, and metaphysics, the Chinese surpassed the West in the ordering of life and in state morals.[39] Yet as enlightened and passionate a defender of China as Madame Chiang Kai-shek [40] described the seven deadly sins of her people as self-seeking, "face," cliquism, defeatism, inaccuracy, lack of discipline, and evasion of responsibility.

From the establishment of the Republic in 1912 to the rise of Communism, the impact of the West upon China has been the greatest single factor determining her political organization. Where the Western impact was not channeled through the educational, cultural, and spiritual agencies of Christianity, the outcome has generally been violent and disruptive.

The introduction during the past century of Western technology and thought owed a heavy debt to the efforts of Christian missionaries. The growth of a periodical religious press, to cite a single example, sponsored by Protestants and Roman Catholics, evoked in many indigenous circles a continuing response which bore telling results in the modern literature of the country.[41]

The basic lesson of the recent past is that the healing of China is primarily the healing of a soul whose sickness is reflected in the eclipse of the three major religions of the land. Confucianism, the erstwhile coördinator of religion, culture, and learning, is in a state of lethargy and flux; Taoism, once the source of mystical insights and inspiration, is today callous to its own morbidity; and Buddhism, which in the past promised to bring the Chinese enlight-

[39] Lewis Hodous, *op. cit.,* pp. 18–19.
[40] May-ling Soong Chiang, *China Shall Rise Again?* New York, 1941, p. 38.
[41] Rudolph Lowenthal, *The Religious Periodical Press in China,* Peiping, 1940.

enment on the deep mysteries of life, death, and eternity, is on the decline.

Offshoots and foster children have struggled to supplant the old faiths. Among them are nationalism and paganism, animism and revolution. If it be true that to labor for the political independence and integrity of China is to serve the cause of international peace and security, it is equally true that to strengthen the Christian forces within her borders is to bring a breath of fresh air to China and Asia and to contribute to the furtherance of religion, freedom, and the truth in the Far East and the whole world.

CHAPTER IX

MYSTICISM AND EFFORTLESS
SPONTANEITY: TAOISM

Early Taoism was closer to Confucianism than is usually supposed, since the concern of both was with life. Yet whereas Taoism taught that the preservation of life came from following nature, Confucianism discovered the fulfillment of life in the development of man.[1] Confucianism was a determinism in the sense that it viewed Heaven as the basic principle which gave direction to human life; Taoism maintained that the Tao—the vivifying principle—was the source of the universe.

As a philosophy, Taoism today is in a state of utter disruption, with long life and the vision of the Tao as its last remaining assets. Much like Confucianism, it conceived that a thing was produced by the Great Ultimate (Tao) through the interaction of the universal principles of activity and passivity; meantime, true reality passed on "like a galloping horse."

As a religion, Taoism is something else. It is alchemy, nature-worship, charms, mystical breathing, and the promise of longevity. In imitating Buddhism, it developed into a primitive cult with polytheism, meditation, monasticism, and transmigration of souls among its salient features.

The fatalism, pessimism, and transitoriness of life which Buddhism seemed to sow wherever it went, evoked a marked change in the Taoist outlook. Under the leadership of Chuang Tzu (*ca.* 369–295 B.C.) and his successors, the Taoists countered the Buddhist conception of the momentariness of existence with a conception of their own. Theirs was essentially a theory of spontaneous living, its chief aim being to let life take its course. Riches and glory, life and death, must not be allowed to confuse the basic issue of

[1] Chan Wing-tsit, *Philosophy—East and West*, pp. 24–25, 88, 144–160.

existence. Since nature had a program of its own, man can best arrive at blessedness through effortless conformity with the Way (Tao).

Tradition traced the origin of Taoist doctrine to the same Chou epoch which had produced Confucius. That Laotzu (lit., old master) flourished in the sixth century B.C., that he was an older contemporary of Confucius, that he was keeper of the archives at the Chou court, and that he was founder of Taoism, are affirmations which need to be taken with scholarly reserve. Recent criticism has established, on purely historical grounds, the likelihood that Laotzu lived about 300 B.C.[2]

The earliest known biography of Laotzu was composed almost five centuries after his death. There is a distinct possibility that the outline of his personal circumstances and the biographical data surrounding his name owed something to those imaginative Taoists who regarded him as their chief authority.[3]

In the upshot, the philosophical affirmations of Taoism proved less enduring than the religious. Its power rested increasingly on the assurance it held out on the subject of personal immortality and the control of hostile spirits. Thus Confucianism and Taoism—although at times irreconcilable—existed side by side with little or hardly any friction, the first a social philosophy and the second a mystical interpretation of life. Tempted to set up their own sect, the Taoists established, during the closing epoch of the Later Han, a state in the territory which at present forms the provinces of Shensi and Szechwan in Central China.

In a deeper sense, however, Taoism constituted a revolt against the ritualism and detailed regimen of the classics. It was as such an escape from traditionalism and the dead hand of the past. For a while, it drew its support from the popular demand for a more substantial religion than Confucianism provided. In its quietism and distrust of aggression, it expressed the wishes of the humble folk and emerged as an embodiment of revulsion against autocracy in China and Confucianist bureaucracy.

[2] Homer H. Dubs, "The Date and Circumstances of the Philosopher Lao-dz," *JAOS,* vol. 61, no. 4, December, 1941, pp. 215–221.
[3] Latourette, *A Short History of the Far East,* pp. 90–91, 107, 166.

Partly under the impact of Buddhism, the Taoists erected temples, developed a pantheon, recruited a priestly class distinguishable by its garb, and upheld belief in heavens and hells. Claiming descent from a Taoist sage of the Han Dynasty, the so-called Taoist pope exercised jurisdiction over a loosely knit national congregation.

Although it had some influence on the magic and religious thought of Japan, Taoism did not rise there as an independent sect. Even in China, its cradle, the effective dynamism of the Taoists has long exhausted itself and if it figures at all in the national spiritual economy, it is only in a degraded and much reduced form allied to primitive religious institutions.

I. The Literary Deposit

The present Taoist canon,[4] consisting of 5,845 rolls in 1,120 Chinese bound volumes,[5] is equal to the Buddhist sacred texts in size but less admirable in content. Rooted in Chinese antiquity, it has had a long history, having already been codified under the Han. In A.D. 1281 Kublai Khan of the Mongol Dynasty—patron of Buddhism at the expense of Taoism—ordered the Taoist texts burned along with the wooden blocks from which they were printed. The effectiveness with which the order was executed is not, however, known.

Kublai Khan's decree made an exception of the *Tao Te Ching,*[6] the primary text of Taoism. Ascribed to Laotzu, it consists of sayings derived from various sources and embedded in older material. Dealing with the Tao, ethics, and government, it embodies mystic poetry and epigrams of a high order and was probably first compiled in the latter part of the fourth century B.C.

Chuang Tzu,[7] one of the most brilliant Taoist intellects, occupies a high place among the ancient philosophers of mankind. The work ascribed to him, the *Chuang Tzu Book,*[8] consists of thirty-three

[4] Published in Shanghai, 1925.

[5] Tr. James Legge, the leading Taoist texts including *The Tao Te Ching* and *Chuang Tzu's Book* are available in *SBE,* vols. 39 and 40, New York, 1927.

[6] Arthur Waley, *The Way and Its Power: A Study of the Tao Te Ching,* London, 1934; Lionel Giles, *The Sayings of Lao Tzu,* London, 1926.

[7] H. A. Giles, *Chuang Tzu: Mystic, Moralist, and Social Reformer,* Shanghai, 1926.

[8] Lionel Giles, *Musings of a Chinese Mystic,* London, 1911.

chapters and may be divided into three parts: an inner core from
the pen of Chuang Tzu himself, an external part composed by the
philosopher's pupils, and a miscellany of chapters from a later date.
A spurious work of the third Christian century, the *Lieh Tzu* [9]
carries the concept of the Tao to the point of fantastic mecha-
nism.

The *Tao Tsang,* fundamental for the study of Taoism, remains
relatively unknown in the West. A large collection which has passed
through many editions, it was published twice during the Ming
period (A.D. 1368–1644). A new collection of Taoist texts was in
progress in 1937 when China sustained the first onslaught of
Japanese arms.

Although these books bore no signature and were held by some
to have come down from Heaven, they had for one of their authors
the celebrated Ko Hung (*ca.* A.D. 270–350), who was largely responsible for making Taoist philosophy a vehicle for alchemy and
the quest for longevity.[10]

II. China's Mystics

Mysticism, with its pantheistic emphasis, has not been generally
at home in the West. Western mystics seemed generally to reëcho
their Eastern rivals, particularly in their witness to the essence of
the one reality in all and through all. In his doctrine that all things
emanate from the ineffable First Being, Plotinus betrayed reliance
on Indian ideas. The light of theism shone too brightly in the West
for a philosopher, even if he were of the stature of Spinoza, to
give pantheism wide currency.[11]

The standard mysticism of the East—Hinduism, Buddhism, and
Taoism—did not inculcate communion between the individual,
immortal soul and the living God. They taught instead some form
of identity between self and Ultimate Reality, by means of mystical
procedures initiated by men.

Thus in Hinduism, the mystical goal consisted in complete identity with Brahman. In Buddhism we note a mysticism of becoming,
whereby the path leads to nirvana, the seeker becoming Buddha,

[9] *Taoist Teachings from the Book of Lieh Zu,* tr. Lionel Giles, London,
1947.
[10] Chan Wing-tsit, *op. cit.,* p. 51.
[11] George P. Conger, *Philosophy—East and West.* p. 241.

that is, not the Buddha nor any one of the many Buddhas, since mathematical distinctions will have ceased to exist.

Taoist mysticism occupied a position midway between the Hindu conception of identity with the World Soul and the Buddhist plan of becoming. The chief representatives of mysticism in the history of Chinese religion, the Taoist mystics aimed at unity with the Tao, and that was the main characteristic of Taoism setting it apart from its sister Chinese religion.

The Taoist mystics abandoned observation and dialectic in favor of the trance as the chief source of knowledge. They evolved a philosophy of passivity, expressed in the concept of *wu-wei* (action by inaction), an effortless, do-nothing, and non-interference program.

Chuang Tzu emphasized that it is heavenly to rule an empire without straining any effort. According to him, to teach an empire without exerting effort was synonymous with virtue. The *Tao Te Ching* referred to the superlative excellence of Heaven and Earth, and observed that neither speaks. Spontaneity became the badge of mysticism and of holiness. To busy oneself with no business was the hallmark of the mystic and saint.

The withdrawal of the Taoists from the arena of action and public affairs gave the Confucianists full rein and, engrossed in their effortlessness and spontaneity, the mystics of China receded into the background having wilfully chosen to bow off the social stage.

III. The Political and Popular Expression of Taoism

It must be pointed out, however, that the Taoist mystics repudiated the moral and legal restraints implicit in the Confucianist system. They developed the theory of a small state with a minimum of political activity. Mention has already been made of Emperor Shih Huang, China's first unifier, who favored Taoism owing to its emphasis on the principle of spontaneity and non-interference. The first Han emperor also favored Taoism, which throughout the period of this dynasty was the only religion that really stood up against the Confucianists.

Early in the third Christian century, a dynasty of Taoist popes arose in the family of Chang, lasting until its dispossession by the Communists in 1927. Officially recognized in A.D. 748, these popes had established their headquarters at Lung Hu Shan in the southeastern province of Kiangsi, whence they exercised jurisdiction over the believers living in families as well as geomancers, fortunetellers, and quack doctors.

Popular Taoism assimilated to itself the cult of the Immortals, which had sprung up on the shores of Shantung. Allegedly inhabiting the mountains of Central Asia and the Isles of the Eastern Sea, these Immortals were believed to have access to a garden where the peach tree of life throve; they also had knowledge of the elixir of life. Hermits who experimented in the field of longevity incidentally made a contribution to dietetics and pharmacopoeia.

The functions of folk Taoism's local gods and spirits—which peopled the countryside and performed the role of intermediaries between men and the Ruler Above—included the power to shorten or lengthen life.

IV. PRESENT-DAY STATUS

According to a Chinese proverb, "He who wishes to know the future must first make himself familiar with the past." In seeking to understand the present-day status of Taoism, it may be useful to weigh its role under the Manchus who, until the twentieth century, were the last great foreign rulers of China.

Kang Hsi, the second Manchu emperor, who ruled A.D. 1662–1722, had received the emissaries of the French Louis XIV and the Russian Peter the Great; Jesuits as well as Chinese scholars assembled at his court. In his famous Sacred Edict,[12] Kang Hsi defined Taoist teaching as pernicious and consigned it to a contemptible position among false doctrines. Of the Taoist secret orders, he wrote:

"Lascivious and villainous persons creep in secretly among them; form brotherhoods; bind themselves by oaths; meet at night and disperse at the dawn; violate the laws, corrupt the age, and impose on the people." [13]

[12] K'ang Hsi, *The Sacred Edict,* London, 1819.
[13] Eloise Talcott Hibbert, *Jesuit Adventure in China during the Reign of K'ang Hsi,* New York, 1941, p. 238.

Taoist secret societies had a long record. The White Lotus Society (Pai Lien Chiao) goes back to the Mongol (Yuan) Dynasty (1279–1368). During the last century and a half, the Society of Heaven, Earth, Man (San Ho-hui) had eight rebellions to its credit. In time of turmoil and social unrest, the secret orders provided the subversive pattern for China's current events. With their emphasis on meditation and their peculiar ethical tone, the societies were the nurseries of sedition and anarchy.

From the days of Chang Tao-ling (fl. in the first and second centuries A.D.)—reckoned as the real founder of Taoism and a descendant of Chang Liang who had played a major role in the establishment of the Han Dynasty—Taoism had incorporated all manner of popular beliefs and institutions as well as many skills and arts.

In its modern form, it found expression in two schools, the Southern with its so-called papacy which lasted until 1927, and the Northern dating from the fifth Christian century. Chang Tao-ling, patron saint of the Southern Taoists, does not enjoy great honor among the members of the Northern branch which seems to be primarily concerned with the practice of meditation, metaphysical speculation, and mystical breathing.

Taoism in its more elevated aspect offers a laissez-faire gospel, a line of least resistance that Toynbee [14] describes as a worship of Chance which, however, "differs from ours in deriving from a less sordid origin."

But even if the Tao were "the way the universe works," and ultimately something very like the Eternal in the abstract and philosophical sense, it is, nonetheless, impersonal and aimless. For the "Great Tao is like a boat that drifts; it can go this way; it can go that." [15] The road to a harmony with the Tao is a philosophy often wedded to magical rites and the control of malevolent demons and forces. The inborn faith of the believer in a true and gracious Creator was therefore squandered.

Taoism is demonstrably doomed in China, but that is not the same as saying that it is already a vanished religion.

[14] *A Study of History,* Abridgement, p. 445.
[15] Arthur Waley, *The Way and Its Power,* pp. 30, 34.

CHAPTER X

PSYCHOLOGICAL ETHICS AND PROTEAN UNIVERSALITY: BUDDHISM

A PROTEST against and an offshoot from Hinduism, the family of religions collectively known as Buddhism attained its universality in the Far East largely through its inherent tendency to make easy compromises. Practically extinct in India, its cradle, Buddhism retains wide influence in China, Tibet, Korea, Japan, Burma, Ceylon, and other neighboring countries.

The overwhelming majority of Buddhists belong to the group of sects designated as the Mahayana branch. Although in its early history Buddhism reportedly sent missionaries to the Near East and North Africa, the great theistic faiths—Zoroastrianism, Judaism, Christianity, and Islam—proved more insurmountable than the mountain barriers, and no lasting result was achieved.

Today there are no recognizable communities of Aryans and Semites professing Buddhism. Even in the lands of East Asia, where this religion made her astonishing conquests, Buddhism, despite occasional revivals, is generally quiescent. In 1935 an estimate of the Buddhists in the world was placed around 214 million. Numerically Buddhism thus holds fifth place among the great religions of the modern world,[1] with an approximate twenty per cent of Asia's population.

There is not a single unchangeable doctrine in Buddhism. Favoring rapid expansion was its remarkable facility for adaptation, evolution, and transformation. Without pretending to impose a clearly defined artistic expression of its essence, it molded the native mentalities to its peculiar theme. Amidst the variety of

[1] D'Espières, *Les religions dans les différents pays du monde*, Brussels, 1935; cf. Joseph Etienne Champagne, *Manual of Missionary Action*, tr. Roy L. Laberge, Ottawa, 1948, pp. 114–115.

cults and doctrines, this theme may be discovered in the physiognomy of the Buddha whose repose, appeasing mild gesture, and ecstatic mood arise wherever Buddhism takes firm root.

I. The Origin of Buddhism

India of the sixth century B.C., as in the twenty-six subsequent centuries, was dominated by the caste system. At the top of the social ladder stood the Brahmans, custodians of the Hindu religion with its multiplicity of beliefs, practices, and ceremonials. The once potent gods and goddesses were reduced to a position secondary to that of the Brahman priesthood. Members of the other castes found themselves at the mercy of the Brahmans in all matters pertaining to faith and worship.

The defects of the Hindu religious structure did not elude the Brahmans themselves, who were quite conscious of the fact that their own power and prestige had left the gods in a state of eclipse which reduced their usefulness to the common man. Consequently, the Brahmans sought a Supreme Being who would be worthy of contemplation and adoration.

The former eschatology had envisioned a heaven for the devout and a hell for the reprobate. Now an all-encompassing doctrine of transmigration engendered an appalling air of pessimism and raised serious doubts whether, after all, life was really worth the living. To the enervating Indian climate were added the melancholy strains of an endless round of existence, an everlasting cycle of birth and rebirth.

In the view of many thoughtful people, salvation came to signify release from the dreadful necessity of returning to this seemingly purposeless and futile tragedy of existence crystallized in karma (law of the deed), an eternal chain of cause and effect. The deeds of countless previous incarnations were conceived as the determining factor shaping each new birth.

The philosophically inclined Brahmans, who numbered within their ranks thinkers of great ingenuity, turned to a philosophy of monism purporting to offer a sane solution to the baffling problem of transmigration and the endless round of existences.

At its core, Brahmanical monism was committed to the view that ultimate reality was one, unchanging, indivisible, impersonal, and without parts or qualities. This reality was Brahman, sometimes referred to as Atman (self) and as Brahman-Atman, that is, Universal Soul. "That, O soul, art thou"—was the great affirmation of Hindu philosophy.

Release from karma was less the product of study and more the reward of a beatific vision, a mystical experience of discernment whereby the individual soul, whatever it might be, was absorbed in an oceanic depth of eternal being. Then, and only then, did man receive the assurance that rebirth and returning to tragedy were halted, that existence was an illusion, and that the vision of ultimacy was meaningful.

There were Hindu thinkers who rejected this monistic interpretation of religion. But the exponents of monism found boundless joy in the mystical path and ascetic experience. In the meantime, the vast majority of India's population continued to live by a religion that consisted in sacrifices, idolatry, and magical rites.

1. *The Buddha (563–483* B.C.*).* Such was the spiritual atmosphere into which the man was born who was later recognized as the Buddha (the Enlightened One). He was also known as Sakyamuni, that is, Sage of the Sakyas, a noble clan of Northeast India constituting a small aristocratic republic south of the present-day Nepal border. The son of a prince, his real name was Siddhartha Gautama and he belonged to the Kshatriya (ruling) caste.

At the age of twenty-five, Siddhartha determined to exchange his wealth and privilege for a homeless and ascetic existence. His first act of self-humiliation was renunciation of family ties and worldly possessions. He left wife and child and became a wanderer. In his quest after deliverance from the shackles of reincarnation, he came to the conclusion that birth could only lead to misery. Since the succession of births was an endless story, he undertook to find release in a new domain of religious experience.

For seven years he wandered about, engaged in fasting and mortification of the flesh. At last he gave up that technique as utterly futile.

One day, as he sat under a pipal tree near the village of Uruvela, the present-day Bodhgaya south of Patna, he experienced an absorption wherein the redeeming knowledge of deliverance from rebirth unfolded to him.[2]

Whether or not to communicate to the world the great themes about human destiny which had arisen within him was the subject of protracted inner debate. Having finally set his mind upon preaching his doctrine, he went to Benares where he delivered his great sermon. There, too, he won his first converts and met the five disciples who formed the inner circle of monks around whom many lay adherents banded themselves.

The earliest source on the Buddha and his message is the Tripitaka (Three Baskets) consisting in the Vinayapitaka (rules of the order), Suttapitaka (discourses of the Buddha), and Abhidhammapitaka (treatises on the doctrine). Written in Pali, which bore to Sanskrit a relation like that of Italian to Latin, this text is in the dialect of northeast India, the ecclesiastical language of Buddhism. But it was not until 247 B.C., that is, 236 years after the founder's death, that the first evidence for the existence of the Pali Canon came to light.[3]

2. *Fundamental Themes.* In his teaching the Buddha emerges as a compassionate rationalist. He was a reformer whom Albert Schweitzer recognized as the Martin Luther of Hinduism.

The Buddha's most revolutionary theme was the denial of the existence of both the universal and individual souls, thus signalizing his complete break with the Brahmanical doctrine of redemption. If Hinduism is best understood as a philosophy of "thatness," then original Buddhism most certainly was "thusness." [4] According to the Buddha, the spirit should only be concerned with what was of direct and practical significance, that is, only with results wrung directly from evidence. From this central theme, two corollaries were deduced.

First, that in terrestrial joy there is no real joy, for all life is suffering. Unlike Brahman philosophy, his did not explain deliverance from karma and reincarnation on the basis of liberating the

[2] Albert Schweitzer, *Indian Thought and Its Development,* London, 1936, p. 89.

[3] E. J. Thomas, *The Life of Buddha as Legend and History,* London, 1927, p. xix.

[4] Junjiro Takakasu, *Philosophy—East and West,* p. 69.

soul from the world of senses. Rather did he stress the need for the drastic suppression of desire on the basis of a curtailment of life through the disavowal of the will-to-live and all human longing.

Secondly, he breathed into Hinduism a new breath of life conveyed in his ethics. Though not limited to theory, this ethics was essentially psychological and therefore incomplete even if compassionate. He was probably the first to express the idea, a fundamental law in the history of religion, that the ethical spirit in itself implies energy, the release of which produces an incalculable impact upon mankind. Thus to endure enmity, and to forgive evil, not only leads to moral perfection but sets forth a new and lofty standard in the world.[5] But to the extent that the Buddha's ethics did not put love into operation, it failed to demand realistic and disinterested love and therefore differed widely from that of Jesus.

India and Hinduism took pause and for centuries waited uncertain as to the true meaning and intent of the Buddha. In the end India cast off his life-suppressing theme, retaining only the ethics.

II. DEVELOPMENT AND SCRIPTURES

1. *Divergence from Hinduism and Jainism.* When the beloved disciple of Buddhism, Ananda, expressed concern at the imminent death of his Master, strange words fell from the Buddha's lips:

> I am not the first Buddha who came upon earth, nor shall I be the last. I came to teach you the truth, and I have founded on earth the kingdom of truth. Gautama Siddhartha will die, but Buddha will live, for Buddha is the truth, and the truth cannot die. He who believes in the truth and lives it is my disciple and I shall teach him. The truth will be propagated and the kingdom of truth will increase for about five hundred years. . . . In due time another Buddha will arise, and he will reveal to you the self-same eternal truth which I have taught.

"How shall we know him?" asked Ananda. To this the Buddha replied, "The Buddha that will come after me will be known as Maitreya, which means 'He whose name is kindness.'" Thus did the Buddha point to One greater than himself whose manner is kindness and whose name is love.[6]

[5] Albert Schweitzer, *op. cit.*, pp. 106–120.
[6] Cf. E. H. Brewster, *The Life of Gotama the Buddha*, London, 1926, pp. 189–199; Paul Carus, *The Gospel of Buddha*, Chicago, 1896, pp. 217–218.

Like Mahavira, that other reformer of Hinduism and the founder of Jainism, the Buddha rejected the Vedic scriptures, the system of caste, the claims and pretensions of the Brahmanical priesthood, and the monistic interpretation of religion and human destiny which centered in the conception of Brahman-Atman. In common with the teaching of Mahavira, that of the Buddha had an atheistic import, and like it preserved the Hindu view of transmigration, karma, and pessimism. Unlike Mahavira and Jainism, however, the Buddha rejected the belief in the eternity of the soul. How he could deny the existence of the soul and at the same time maintain a valid belief in transmigration is the classic paradox of primitive Buddhism.

2. *The Four Noble Truths.* A woman whose son had died still hoped, as she sat mourning by his corpse, that he would live again. She went to see the Buddha and begged him to restore her boy to life. The Master told her to bring him a handful of mustard seed from a home where grief had not struck. In vain did the anguished mother go about from house to house only to be told that bereavement was common to all. At last one night, as she watched the city lights, she knew the simple truth that grief is universal to all families and persons, that it was selfish of her to mourn as though she was the only one who suffered. Therefore she had her child buried and sought refuge in the Buddha.[7]

Despite the apparent placidity of his countenance and agnosticism of his thought, the Buddha was gravely concerned with the problem of suffering. In his first sermon, delivered in the Deer Park outside Benares, he formulated the celebrated Four Noble Truths.

This, O monks, is the Noble Truth of Suffering: Birth is suffering; decay is suffering; illness is suffering; death is suffering. Presence of objects we hate, is suffering; separation from objects we love, is suffering; not to obtain what we desire is suffering. . . .

The Noble Truth of the cause of suffering: Thirst, that leads to rebirth, accompanied by pleasure and lust, finding its delight here and there . . . thirst for pleasure, thirst for existence, thirst for prosperity. . . .

The Noble Truth of the cessation of suffering: the complete cessation of thirst—a cessation which consists in the absence of every pas-

[7] See Millar Burrows, *Founders of Great Religions,* pp. 97–98.

sion—with the abandoning of this thirst, with the doing away with it, with the deliverance from it, with the destruction of desire. . . .

The Noble Truth of the Path which leads to the cessation of suffering.[8]

The Four Noble Truths occupy a place in the foreground of Buddhist teaching. But the excessive importance attached to them by Western research tended to crowd out certain other equally important elements in the Buddhist system of religious thought.[9]

3. *The Eightfold Path.* When the Buddha contemplated the world of change and transmigration—as Hinduism conceived it— he formulated the Four Noble Truths concerning suffering, its cause, extinction, and the path leading to freedom. The four truths, then, consisting of the way to salvation gave rise to eight stipulations which were to govern the conduct of the believer:

Right belief, right aspiration, right speech, right conduct, right means of livelihood, right endeavor, right memory, right meditation.

Comparable to the Beatitudes rather than the Decalogue, since they contain no prohibition, the foregoing injunctions breathed an air of noble freedom. Except for the teaching of Jesus, which stands alone and peerless, the words of the Buddha, as enunciated in utterances such as those cited here, lifted him above all contemporaries and successors in India and the Far East. He detached, however, the life of perfection from its source of divine power and made hardly any provision for the reality of God's grace.

4. *Nirvana.* Hindu philosophy had conceived nirvana as final emancipation, the extinction of the flame of life upon union with Brahman. Nirvana (Pali nibbana) indicated in primitive Buddhism, however, the dying out in the heart of the threefold fire of raga, dosa, and moha, that is, passion, hatred, and delusion. Involved in Buddhist nirvana, furthermore, was a beatific spiritual vision and liberation from the necessity of future transmigration.

Nirvana was, therefore, release from liability to suffering and from mortality, the highest this-worldly and other-worldly goal

[8] Cf. T. W. Rhys Davids and Hermann Oldenberg, *Vinaya Texts,* pt. I, *SBE,* vol. IV, New York, 1899, pp. 95–96.

[9] James Bissett Pratt, *The Pilgrimage of Buddhism,* New York, 1928, pp. 17 *sqq.*

attainable. Not only men, but gods also, where their existence was at all envisaged, were held to be in need of this process of salvation. Whether nirvana implied total extinction or merely annihilation of consciousness is a controversial issue, a moot case in view of the doctrine's ambiguity. At any rate, nirvana did imply escape from repeated existences.

A distinction may be drawn between nirvana and pari-nirvana, the first relating to this world and the second to the hereafter. If nirvana was release through emptiness and the voiding of self, it also was joy and peace of mind. It ought to be emphasized, furthermore, that teachings on the nature of self and nirvana were communicated to the laymen in readily grasped metaphors. The laity were admonished to show affection to the monks, and the monks were instructed to teach the layman the truth that he could comprehend, while both were to refrain from evil doing.

5. *The Buddhist Canon.* There is actually no authoritative canon of sacred literature acknowledged by all Buddhists. Varied and voluminous, the Pali Canon is the most famous, serving as the standard bible of Hinayana Buddhists in Ceylon, Burma, Siam, and Cambodia. Dating from about 20 B.C., its textus receptus embodies the doctrines of primitive Buddhism as they are contained in the Three Baskets.[10]

In Nepal, Tibet, China, Korea, and Japan, the Mahayana Buddhists have other canons based in the main on a Sanskrit original represented by the few extant books and fragments.[11] Also in use are a number of non-canonical writings partly accessible in English translation.[12]

III. EXPANSION IN EAST ASIA

1. *Monk and Congregation.* The response to the Buddha's teaching was heartening. Converts from his own Kshatriya caste rose to

[10] The short *Dhammapada* (way of virtue) was the first part of the *Tripitaka* to be translated into English, Max Müller, 1870; later, W. W. C. Wagiswara and K. J. Saunders, *The Buddha's Way of Virtue,* New York, 1912. Portions of the *Tripitaka* are in 2 vols. of *SBE,* where some non-canonical writings are also included, and in 5 vols. of the *Pali Text Society Translation Series.*

[11] See Edward J. Thomas, *The Life of Buddha,* New York, 1927, pp. 27 *sqq.*

[12] H. C. Warren, *Buddhism in Translation,* Cambridge, 1896.

sixty and quickly multiplied to include members of the lower castes as well as many Brahmans. The growth in membership called for the enactment of rules to govern behavior in the order (*sangha*). A concise summary of the Buddhist faith, the initiate's confession was "I take refuge in the Buddha, I take refuge in the truth (*dhamma*), I take refuge in the order."

The monk vowed obedience to the Ten Precepts,[13] a decalogue enjoining a middle course between asceticism and self-indulgence. The first five precepts proscribed murder, theft, immorality, falsehood, and intoxication. The others demanded moderation in eating (no meals after midday); forbade looking at dancers, singers, and actors; discouraged the donning of garlands, the use of perfume, and ornaments; warned against sleeping on high or broad beds; and prohibited the possession of gold or silver objects. Public confession before a fortnightly assembly was ordained in the case of anyone who violated a precept.

The laymen, from whom the fabulous wealth and earthly possessions of the Buddhist monasteries came, were required to observe only the first five precepts. Completely ignored at first and debarred from participation in religious life, women were reluctantly allowed to form nunneries.[14]

2. *The Lesser Vehicle: Hinayana.* The older form of Buddhism, reproachfully dubbed Hinayana (lesser vehicle) by the more powerful though later school styled Mahayana (greater vehicle), was nontheistic and avidly monastic. More nearly akin to the older tradition of the faith, however, it is justifiably named Early Buddhism; and since it chiefly survives in Ceylon, Burma, Siam, Cambodia, and the Malay Archipelago, it has been called Southern Buddhism. The historical significance of Hinayana is enhanced by its Pali Canon, the primary documentary source on original Buddhism.

Tradition preserves the record of several epochal Buddhist councils which were held in the period following the Buddha's death. One of these dealt with controversial matters of doctrine and was

[13] Edward J. Thomas, *Buddhist Scriptures,* London, 1913, p. 52.
[14] Charles Eliot, *Hinduism and Buddhism,* 2 vols., London, 1921, vol. I, p. 160.

convoked under the patronage of Emperor Asoka (*ca.* 272–232 B.C.), the ruler of Magadha who had subjected the whole of India to his authority. Grieved by the human misery which his incessant wars had caused, Asoka reportedly determined to embrace Buddhism. A permanent contribution which he made in the propagation of the faith resulted in the planting of Hinayana in Ceylon.

Along with its conservative teaching and rigid discipline, Hinayana developed a more flexible and popular religious outlook demonstrated in its heavy reliance upon the adoration of the Buddha, which had a strong appeal to the masses. The Master's high prestige with the people culminated in his enthronement as a divine, omniscient, and compassionate figure whose many incarnations and superb qualities caught the public fancy, fired his followers' zeal, and considerably enlarged the scope of Hinayana.

3. *The Greater Vehicle: Mahayana.* Far surpassing popular Hinayana in its departure from the original teaching of the Buddha was the course taken by that other branch of the faith described as Mahayana. Reared in Northwest India, the Mahayana doctrine was sharpened in those early disputes which focused on issues such as the nature of self, immortality, and the person of the Buddha. About the beginning of the Christian era, Mahayana acquired its distinctive character, emerged as a vibrant new expression of Buddhism, and vied with Hinayana in claiming for itself a more authentic version of the Master's teaching.

In its expansion across Central Asia, China, Tibet, Korea, and Japan, Mahayana Buddhism exhibited the marks of a protean religion, ever adapting itself to new circumstances and wantonly assimilating religious elements that were incompatible with its essense. This propensity for radical change may be closely examined under the five headings of scripture, vicarious suffering, theistic pretension, metaphysics, and agnosticism.[15]

With regard to scripture, Mahayana acknowledged, as has already been intimated, the co-existence of several canons derived from an almost extinct Sanskrit original.

The concept of vicarious suffering was developed into a theory of

[15] A. K. Reischauer, *Great Religions of the Modern World,* pp. 106–109.

salvation integral to the doctrine. This was envisaged in the peculiar phenomenon of Bodhisattvas, diligent and courageous beings, perfect and qualified to become Buddhas, who chose nevertheless to remain seekers after enlightenment in order to save others. Energetically and sacrificially pursuing the highest wisdom, the Bodhisattva type represented the aspiration after supreme knowledge whether among laity or monks. Compassion thus became the central human value of Mahayana Buddhism, articulated through the Bodhisattva, which turned the gaze of the devout from the past to the future, from Buddha Sakyamuni of history to a realistic experience of enlightenment and Buddhahood, and from the notion set forth in the Pali Canon that only a few may hope to attain enlightenment to the free promise of a terrestrial and celestial career of bliss open to all who follow in earnest confidence.[16]

The theistic pretension of Mahayana was detectable particularly in the doctrine of Amitabha, a Buddha of eternal life offering salvation, who in popular religion at least acquired the character of a theistic deity. This orientation was thwarted in the end by the emergence among the scholars of the view that the eternal Buddha, together with the ideas of paradise and immortality, was merely an accommodation to the limitations of the finite mind.

A highly speculative metaphysics characterized Mahayana. Knowledge, in short, was conceived in two categories, absolute and relative. Only relative knowledge was possible in the communication of religious truth to the people, the absolute being far beyond their grasp.

A pervasive agnosticism which pretended to tolerate contradictory notions, on the assumption that they were necessary expressions of man's total ignorance, was bound to confuse the vision of ultimate reality and gradually to lead toward the elimination of religious essence. Thus, a cynical skepticism, the outgrowth of Mahayana agnosticism, proved inimical to the cause of religion and retarded the progress of the believer in the realm of faith. The net result was the deadening of spiritual life and the displacement of the light by obscurity and of truth by disillusionment.

[16] Clarence H. Hamilton, "The Idea of Compassion in Mahayana Buddhism," *JAOS*, vol. 70, no. 3 (July-September, 1950), pp. 145–151.

IV. THE CONTEMPORARY BUDDHIST STRUCTURE

1. *A Religion in Dissolution.* Beginning as an Aryan faith, Buddhism in the course of a few centuries overran much of India. Partly due to corruption in morals but mainly through uncongeniality to the Hindu soul, it had practically disappeared by the twelfth Christian century from the land of its birth. About that time, Islam had established itself in Central Asia and India, where it proved a deadly foe to Buddhism.

Today, three religions, Islam, Buddhism, and Christianity, claim universality, respectively, in Western Asia and North Africa, the Far East, and the Western world. Whereas its influence remains widespread in East Asia, Buddhism as a religion is in a state of retrogression. Despite astonishing conquests in Africa, China, and Indonesia, Islam's primacy as a living faith is in grave doubt.

Even with all her sins and divisions, Christianity stands as the most vital custodian of religion in the modern world. With the assurance of faith and the perspective which history bestows, the followers of Jesus Christ believe that He holds the key to the future. They persevere in the confidence that since in Him the heart of the Eternal is opened to all men, the unity of men is possible when they open their hearts to Him and to each other in humble obedience and consecrated service.

Behind contemporary Buddhism stands an incontrovertible record. There was, first, the founder and his precepts, whence sprang, with varying degrees of fidelity to the original and shades of opinion and emphasis, the multiple structure of sects and schools.

In the age of Asoka (*ca.* 250 B.C.), a spectacular popularization of the Buddhist doctrine was achieved, and for the layman the note of an eternal world order was sounded. Later on, Mahayana gained by its less austere interpretation of the faith the goodwill and esteem of multitudes among the Northern peoples of the Far East; proclaiming itself the Great Way, it looked upon the Hinayana followers of the Narrow Way with unrepressed disparagement.

Among the Hinayanists, however, particularly the Theravada (School of Elders) in Ceylon, measurable vitality persists. Although their rivals have long accused them that they neither attained

Arhatship (sainthood) nor understood the true meaning of the Bodhisattva, these Elders have won the respect of Oriental and Western scholarship, their eminence resting upon the painstaking care whereby they cultivate the study of the Pali Canon and preserve its text.

Sharp distinctions occurred within the ranks of Mahayana, which in its classical expression had given rise to the Halfway type of sect (*ca.* 50 B.C.–A.D. 50), the Paradise devotees (*ca.* A.D. 100), and the Full Mahayana group (*ca.* A.D. 100–400). The last variation on the Buddhist theme involved primary concern with the nature of reality and centered in a monist interpretation of religion. In the sixth Christian century a pantheistic realism, championed in China by Chi-i and his followers, dominated the Mahayana scene. Since A.D. 700, these trends seemed to dissolve into a sensuous polytheism and magic cults, giving birth to Tantric and Shakti forms of worship.[17]

Although Chinese Buddhism could, in the twentieth century, boast that thousands of its monks and nuns were engaged in religious meditation and scholarly pursuits if not active service, the indisputable fact, supported by internal evidence, shows that for over a millennium—that is, since the Tang Dynasty—this religion has been in virtual decadence.[18]

2. *Centers of Contemporary Vitality.* (a) *Southeast Asia.* Dating from the beginning of the Christian era, if not earlier, the Hinduization of Southeast Asia—including Ceylon, Burma, Siam, the Indochinese Peninsula, Malaya, Indonesia, and the Philippines—meant the extension of Indian culture and institutions to these lands. Hindu and Buddhist cults were inevitably introduced. Powerful folkways and religious traditions, emanating from India, swallowed up the native cultures of this area much as the footprints of an elephant swallow up those of all other creatures.[19]

In Ceylon, the Senghalese, who are of Aryan-Dravidian descent and constitute the principal stock of the island, are mostly Hina-

[17] Kenneth J. Saunders, *Epochs in Buddhist History,* Chicago, 1924, pp. xiii, xiv.

[18] Latourette, *A Short History of the Far East,* p. 486.

[19] Kenneth Perry Landon, *Southeast Asia: Crossroad of Religions,* Chicago, 1947, pp. 3, 61.

yanists. Not only was the Pali Canon first reduced to writing here, but here, too, the Ceylonese Chronicles which transmitted much of early Buddhism's lore were composed. Here too, Buddhaghosa, the fourth-century scholar and author, wrote a famous exposition of the faith which became standard throughout the Hinayana world. Therefore, Ceylon deservedly ranks as a nerve center in the Hinayana domain of Southeast Asia, a region aptly described as the cultural Mediterranean of the Far East.

Beyond the crudities of folk-religion in Southwest Asia, Hinayana Buddhism created a religious structure whose value is still to be recognized in the twin features of sadness and quiet joy. "In joy we live, hating none; let us live in the midst of those who hate, unhating; in the midst of those who ail, let us live in perfect health; having nothing yet we possess great riches." [20] Indeed, the forcefulness of the early sangha (monastic) community is still cherished and retains a moderately compelling dynamic effect in all the area.[21]

(b) *Tibet.* Lamaism, with its Tantric infusion of sex symbolism, is the form which Buddhism assumes in Tibet and Mongolia. Originating in the tenets of Mahayana, it was introduced into Tibet during the seventh century by Padmasambhaira. Allied with Shivism and the native Shamanism of Central Asia, Lamaism developed into a peculiar religious type noted for its degradation.

Among the ritualistic peculiarities of Lamaism is the use of a prayer wheel, flags, rosaries, and bells, as well as the practice of a form of baptism and confirmation. A monstrous distortion of the original Mahayana, Lamaism provided the Buddhas, Bodhisattvas, and the Master himself with spouses.

Dominating the hierarchy is the Lama (one who is superior). The Grand Lama at Lhasa acquired in the sixteenth century the title Dalai (ocean, i.e., measureless, profound). He presides over the Yellow branch of Lamaism, to which is opposed the Red with its own titular head known as the Teshu Lama. Under these two dignitaries are several orders of monks and nuns.

The success of Lamaism in Tibet facilitated its spread in China, Russia, and along the borders of India. As a phenomenal example

[20] Cf. *The Dhammapada,* tr. Max Müller, ch. xv, pp. 197–200.
[21] K. J. Saunders, *Buddhism in the Modern World,* London, 1922, pp. 28–29.

of Mahayana's protean quality, Lamaism deserves notice if only because of its abominable and coarse character. From its Tibetan stronghold on "the roof of the world," it continues to propagate its demonolatry and stands as an anomaly among the religions of the modern world.

(c) *Japan.* Proceeding out of India, Buddhist speculation with its ramification in art, literature, and religion, reached Japan as early as A.D. 552 through China and via Korea. Its position as an established state religion was defined under the Tokugawa Shogunate by a decree issued in 1614.

Having undergone some change in their course which brought them to Japan, the Chinese varieties of Mahayana included the Pure Land sects with their chief interest in heaven, the Western Paradise of Amitabha; the intuitive sects, particularly the Chou school whose offshoot in Japan is known as Zen Buddhism, noted for its devotion to country and emperor as well as for its mystical elements; the rationalist sects which emerged in Japan as Tendai, a philosophical idealism devoted to the pursuit of the truth in utter disregard of what was viewed as an artificial discrepancy between Hinayana and Mahayana; and the True Word sects, with an emphasis on mystery which in Japan acquired the name Shingon, a powerful order finding a place in its constellation of divinities even for Shinto figures. Tendai and Shingon were largely responsible for the wedlock, enduring for a thousand years, consummated between Buddhism and Shinto.[22]

In its distinctly Japanese expression, Buddhism came to the forefront through the teachings of the thirteenth-century monk, Nichiren (1222–1282), a passionate patriot and visionary who set out to debunk both Tendai and Shingon as well as the Pure Land and Zen sects. He spoke with an authority based on the Lotus sutra (a sermon of the Buddha) and strove to express, within the Buddhist framework, the cultural and nationalist genius of his people; all of which accounts for modern Japan's revived interest in him.[23]

Zen Buddhism had also claimed to transmit the Buddhist essence

---

[22]Charles Eliot, *Japanese Buddhism,* London, 1935, pp. 321–431.
[23] Masaharu Anesaki, *Nichiren: The Buddhist Prophet,* Cambridge, 1916; *History of Japanese Religion,* London, 1930, pp. 378–379.

directly from the Master rather than from any document or rite. It defined religion as experience, claimed no belief in gods, and upheld the two pillars of Great Wisdom and Great Compassion, exalting the humility of begging and the importance of work. By constantly negating the logical system upon which the modern mind has been nourished, contemporary Zen seeks to attain a higher affirmation of the truth as it sees it, namely that of intuitiveness as opposed to intellectual understanding. It holds forth a practical, disciplined truth which in the view of its modern expounder, Daisetz T. Suzuki,[24] is like a gong that is struck and whose vibrations instantly follow; if men are not alert, they fail to catch them.

In its broad outline, Japanese Buddhism revolves about three main principles. First, that man is in error and ignorance and must seek to reform himself by opening his understanding to the truth; knowledge of the truth comes by enlightenment, the key word in all Buddhist piety. Secondly, to turn from error and to aspire toward enlightenment means to escape from suffering and achieve bliss. Thirdly, with the attainment of bliss, the seeker shall cease from evil and apply himself to good accomplishments.

It is obvious that these principles, as they were implemented in Japanese Buddhism, were far from identical with Christian teachings.[25] That in essence they prescribe a view of divinity which is at variance with that of revelation and the Christian interpretation of religion is self-explanatory.

3. *Mahayana's Perennial Gift: Accommodation.* Scholars are not agreed on the exact date when Buddhism entered China. The middle of the first Christian century has been proposed as a time fitting the circumstances which attended the event.[26] At any rate, the impact of Buddhism upon the culture of China has generally been circumscribed and did not penetrate the depth of social and political consciousness. It was an impact limited to the spheres of

---

[24] *The Essence of Buddhism,* London, 1946; see also his *An Introduction to Zen Buddhism,* Kyoto, 1934; *The Training of the Zen Buddhist Monk,* Kyoto, 1934; *Manual of Zen Buddhism,* Kyoto, 1935.

[25] A. K. Reischauer, *Studies in Japanese Buddhism,* New York, 1917, pp. 183–184.

[26] Francis C. M. Wei, *The Spirit of Chinese Culture,* pp. 100–110, 118.

art, literature, and speculative philosophy, and involved perennial accommodation.

Even within the speculative and philosophical field, the contrast between India and China was remarkable. There was India's other-worldliness and the all but purely this-worldly concern of China. The disparity came to the surface particularly in Buddhism's denial of life and Confucianism's affirmation of its importance. The Buddhists held out the monk's ideal, whereas the Confucianists placed emphasis upon the family. When Mahayana Buddhism had finally lodged itself in their midst, the Chinese somewhat belatedly realized that it was a threat to their social structure.

It ought to be remembered, furthermore, that Buddhism only acquired prestige in China during the third Christian century under the barbarian invaders who succeeded the collapse of the Later Han. When the Tang Dynasty restored native ascendancy, the fortunes of Buddhism began to show progressive decline.

Although its contributions to China outweigh those of Taoism, Mahayana Buddhism is confronted today with the obstacles of skepticism, secularism, and a mundane approach to existence. Through its monks and nuns, monasteries and temples, revivals, and sporadic resurgence of the gift for accommodation, Buddhism barely manages to keep alive. The most notable of its Chinese creations is a female Bodhisattva, the goddess of mercy Kuan-yin who, as an abstraction of the principle of kindness, endears the faith to the common people.[27]

It has already been observed that the average Chinese recognizes the existence of three religious forms in his country: Yu Chiao, the religion of the scholar based on the teachings of Confucius; Shi Chiao, the religion of Buddhism; and Tao Chiao, religion of the Way based on the teachings of Laotzu. There are besides 30 million Moslems in China and over a million Christians.[28]

Not only is Buddhism thus recognized by the common man, it has also had an altogether distinguished though limited role. Whereas it served no holy end in lifting the spiritual consciousness of the people, it tended, nevertheless, to promote a love of morality.

[27] John King Fairbank, *op. cit.,* p. 114.
[28] Cheng Tien-Hsi, *China Moulded by Confucius,* London, 1947, pp. 47–48.

In the aesthetic realm, it directed the mind to the love of beauty in nature and contributed to the advancement of art and literature.[29]

The Buddhist monks hastened the development of block-printing in China and made possible the issuance, on May 11, 868 of the world's first printed book, *The Diamond Sutra,* by Wang Chieh.[30] In their peculiar relationship to Chinese culture, the several Buddhist sects may yet serve Christianity in its approach to the country's spiritual problems. Cleansed from their impurities and corruption, these sects may some day become an artery through which the truth of the Gospel will flow into the blood stream of China's corporate life.

4. *Buddhism in the Modern World*. Historical parallels between Buddhism and Christianity are not lacking. The Hindus rejected Buddhism as the Jews rejected Christianity. Jesus attacked the established priestly order of His country; the Buddha rebelled against the sacerdotalism of the Brahmans and the monist philosophy of the Upanishads.

The anthropocentric barrier to religious growth was manifest in both Palestine and India. In Palestine, a religious and ethical institution, steeped in the Jewish racial consciousness, barred the fulfillment of divine illumination represented by Christianity; in India, the old and deep-rooted pattern of Hindu life militated against the permanent establishment of a new religion. In both instances the impact of the universal upon the particular, the ideal against the temporal, and the spiritual against the natural was repudiated.

Nor does it come as a shock to the Christian student of religious history that it was the Buddha as saviour of the world who ultimately triumphed in the Far East. In his qualities of gentleness and compassion, in his message of virtue and deliverance from sorrow, the suffering masses of Asia believed they had discovered the light they hoped for. Edwin Arnold's *Light of Asia* is a poetical exposition of Buddhism which interpreted the life of the Buddha as saviour. But the failure of Buddhism in this respect is due to the fact that it only offered a substitute where the Eternal had provided a reality.

[29] A. Beal, *Buddhism in China,* London, 1884, p. 259.
[30] Shao Chang Lee, *Popular Buddhism in.China,* Honolulu, 1939, p. 9.

In the lands of the Far East, such as Japan, China, and Tibet, Buddhism failed to satisfy man's religious hunger because it held out merely a partial expression of saving power. It tended, moreover, to emphasize the worthlessness of existence, presenting a negative evaluation of destiny. To be sure, it faced squarely the problem of suffering, afforded a measure of escape from sorrow, made a claim to enlightenment, placed an emphasis on ethical living, and supported an ethical code. Although the Buddha pretended to know nothing of prayer, the system which he established made room in its later stages and metamorphosis for this essential aspect of all religion.[31]

In Japan, more than elsewhere in our time, the source materials for the study of Buddhist thought have been preserved. Junjiro Takakasu [32] (d. 1945), a leading authority in the field, gave an analysis of Buddhist philosophy under the four categories of realism, nihilism, idealism, and negativism—that is, being, non-being, both being and non-being, and neither being nor non-being. He admitted that Buddhism makes no room for the Eternal and denied that the Buddha was really deified.

Yet the concept of God was not actually abandoned; what Buddhism has to say about ultimate reality and the principle of true reality is strikingly close to what a Western philosopher might say about God as the Absolute. Indeed, the concept of the Buddha, once he has entered nirvana, comes near to belief in him as a supreme personal being.

Mahayana Buddhism upholds Amitabha, for the worship of millions in Japan, as an Eternal Supreme Being. In short, Buddhist ideas on the nature of the human self and on self-creativity—that is, saving oneself through one's own efforts—leave little doubt that the purpose of this religion, its emphasis on impermanence and non-ego, notwithstanding, is to perfect man's character through perfect wisdom and cultivation of the highest personality.

That is not to say, however, that the disparity between Christianity and Buddhism can be easily bridged. While it is conceivable

---

[31] K. J. Saunders, *Buddhism in the Modern World,* London, 1922, pp. 29, 42.
[32] *The Essentials of Buddhist Philosophy,* W. T. Chan and C. C. Moore, eds., Honolulu, 1947.

that both Jesus and the Buddha might have conceded some of the ontological arguments for the existence of God current in their day and based on the necessity of perfect being in nature, their teaching was anything but identical. The intention of the Buddha, the nature of his person, and the essence of his message do not imply or suggest a definitive encounter with the Eternal whose revealed truth in Christ means a reconciliation between God and man. Whereas a realistic confrontation between man and nature is to the everlasting credit of Buddhism, its silence on the essential relation between the Creator and the creature deepens the sense of religious emptiness.

CHAPTER XI

VISION OF THE SELF-REVEALING
GOD: JUDAISM

W<small>HEN</small> Theodor Herzl, prophet of modern Zionism, aroused leading Europeans in favor of a Jewish national home in Palestine, he
discovered in the person of William H. Hechler, Chaplain of the
British Embassy in Vienna, a tower of strength. Hechler had been
a tutor at the court of the Grand Duke of Baden and knew the
German Kaiser personally.

In 1898 when Herzl, leading a Jewish delegation, waited in
Jerusalem to see Wilhelm II then on a state visit to the Holy Land,
Hechler stood beside the great Jew. With tears in his eyes, he
blessed the Jewish delegation in the name of the God of Abraham,
Isaac, and Jacob.[1] The fact that the precursors and successors of
Hechler are legion perhaps warrants the opinion that Zionism dur-
ing the nineteenth and twentieth centuries received strong Chris-
tian support.

Although opinion in Christendom was not unanimous on this
controversial issue, the impact of those who favored the Jewish
nationalist movement was considerable and decisive. More than a
symbol of the world's secular tragedy, Palestine provided an index
of the spiritual dynamic, or lack of it, that stirred Christianity in its
dealings with two great religions of the modern world, Judaism
and Islam.

The need for better understanding of modern Judaism is press-
ing. Both as a non-Christian religion which falls under natural
theology and as a Scriptural faith which shares with Christianity
the special revelation of God, Judaism occupies a strategic position in the history of religion. The elements of a fresh reappraisal

[1] Joseph Patai, *Star Over Judaism: The Life of Theodor Herzl,* tr. Francis
Magyar, New York, 1946, pp. 212–213.

must include its Biblical fountainhead, historical development, and distinctive character, and touch upon its difference from Christianity.

I. THE BIBLICAL FOUNTAINHEAD

Originally designating any member of the tribe or kingdom of Judah, the name Jew, particularly after 538 B.C. and the return from the Babylonian Captivity, indicated membership in the new Hebrew commonwealth. Judaism as a religion, consisting in all that was set forth in the Law and the Prophets, expounded in the Talmud, and interpreted by the rabbis, held the Jewish community together and offered the Jews the basis of unity when their national existence was disrupted and the Temple destroyed in A.D. 70.

Almost two thousand years of dispersion did not shake the Jew in his allegiance to the God of his forebears. Intermarriage with other peoples might change the racial affinities of the Jews, but common belief in the one God of Israel gave them unity and persistence. Revealed in the Torah, demonstrated in Hebrew annals, and wrought out by the faithful through centuries of misery, this belief inspired the Jew. Wherever he went, he carried his concept of the fatherhood of God and exalted among the nations the principles of peace, justice, and law.

1. *Abraham's Repudiation of Idolatry.* Rooted in the Old Testament, this vision of God is traceable to the experience of Abraham with the Eternal who gave him the promise of a great destiny, repeated later to Isaac and Jacob. The God of Israel, is, therefore, the initiator of Hebrew religion and history as a blessing to all mankind.

Abraham's response to the call of the Eternal, and his obedient departure from the Mesopotamian land of his birth, are recognized in the Bible as a supreme example of true faith.[2] Having accepted the challenge of the truth, he was granted a habitation in Palestine where his offspring became a nation great for its disavowal of idolatry and deep longing for the city of God.[3]

Setting their religious standards in the light of the truth given

[2] Gen. 12:1–8.
[3] Heb. 11:8–10.

them, the seed of Abraham exerted a powerful influence as they communicated the Biblical knowledge of God to the nations. Born a Jew, Jesus Christ arose as Saviour of mankind, and His church took its first visible form within the Jewish community of Palestine.

The mass of the Hebrew people frequently proved vulnerable to paganism. Yet from the time of the Judges onwards, a remnant had kept the faith and, fearing the Lord, thought upon His name. Of these, Malachi[4] spoke exultantly:

And they shall be mine, saith the Lord of Hosts, even mine own possession, in the day that I make; and I will spare them, as a man spareth his own son that serveth him.

2. *Backsliding Israel.* Israel's proneness to evil mirrored the helplessness of every mortal as he stands before the holiness of God. A golden calf of some kind was sure to make the people sin.[5] In Canaan, the temptation to confuse the true religion with the worship of the native gods, and in folk religion a confrontation between Baal and Jehovah, were inevitable.[6]

As the cruder types of idolatry withered away, more refined forms lifted their heads. It was against the infiltration of ungodliness in the guise of hypocrisy and spiritual atrophy that the Prophets fulminated.[7] Acting both as the conscience of Israel and the indomitable champions of the true religion, the Prophets were God's watchmen and warners of the people.[8]

False diplomacy and political ineptitude culminated in national ruin, yet the Priests seemed unperturbed. Although the Prophets had warned that God refused to be bribed with innumerable sacrifices and rivers of oil, yet empty ceremonials, lacking in penitence and a radical change of heart, gained centrality at the Temple and in the worship services.[9] Jeremiah [10] cautioned against the notion that all would be well so long as the Temple stood.

Six centuries later and under altogether different circumstances,

[4] 3:17.
[5] Ex. 32:1–6.
[6] 1 Kings 18:21.
[7] Jer. 2:13; Is. 5:13–14.
[8] Jer. 6:16–18; Ezek. 3:17–19.
[9] Is. 1:11–17; Jer. 7:21–26; Hos. 6:6; Mic. 6:6–8.
[10] 7:3–7.

the struggle between the Prophets and the Priests was resumed. Rome now ruled Palestine as part of the Province of Syria, albeit through petty vassals such as Herod the Great (37–4 B.C.). The conflict which in this era raged between the champions of the true faith and the clerical parties, focused in the opposition which Jesus met at the hands of the Priests and Pharisees.

3. *The Rise of Judaism.* Encircled by a rich though pagan culture, the Jews had sought refuge during the Babylonian Captivity in their peculiar heritage calculated to set them apart from the majority of the population. This centripetal drive was manifest in heavy accent upon the observance of the Sabbath, ceremonial worship in the synagogues, and punctilious fulfillment of the Law.

Subsequent to their return to Palestine and the restoration of their national life, the Jews persisted in the effort to preserve their religious and cultural institutions intact. To that end, the hallowed and bitter memories of their past were woven into the Temple ceremonies and festivals.

Formalism and conservatism loomed as primary motifs in the growing self-consciousness of Jewry. In keeping with this spirit, its religious tradition began to reflect that legalistic and exclusive character by which it has been generally known.

If there was a single mundane principle regulating Judaism, it must have stemmed from the need which the Jew felt to defend himself against foreign contamination. It was in response to that need that the major parties and orders of early Judaism appeared. Precisely that role of national and religious self-preservation was performed, with different approaches and unequal success, by both the Sadducees and Pharisees.

4. *The Sadducees and Pharisees.* The sect of the Sadducees, owing its origin to the fourth century B.C. and its name to Zadok, high priest of Solomon,[11] constituted a priestly aristocracy which during the lifetime of Jesus exercised political control sustained through collaboration with the Romans.

Doctrinally conservative, they rejected the traditions of the Elders and regarded the validity only of the written Law of Moses.

[11] Louis Finkelstein, *The Pharisees: The Sociological Background of Their Faith,* Philadelphia, 1938, vol. II, p. 663. Ez. 40:46.

Although their power collapsed with the destruction of the Temple, their spirit and mentality lived on.

Sadducean theology denied the resurrection of the dead, personal immortality, and retribution in the hereafter. Stung by Jesus' claim to authority over the Temple, they tried to snare Him into the admission that the resurrection which he taught led to absurd results.[12] Their old feud with the Pharisees enabled Paul to split the Sanhedrin (supreme court) by wringing from their foes partial support for his preaching.[13]

The Pharisees had separated themselves, as their name implies,[14] avoiding association with impure things, ideas, and persons. Christ condemned their religious exhibitionism, hair-splitting legalism, and hypocrisy but nowhere implied that every Pharisee was thereby automatically indicted.[15] As a matter of fact, the subsequent history of Judaism is a monument to Pharisaic achievements. We have it on rabbinical authority, however, that many Pharisees were a disgrace to the order.

Josephus[16] credited the Pharisees with penetrating insight and minute interpretation of the Law; their formulations, in contrast to those of their Sadducean opponents, bore the stamp of greater exactitude in the exposition of the Law. The impact of Pharisaism upon Palestinian Jewry during the two centuries preceding Christianity may be seen from its influence in Galilee which, in a hundred years, was changed from a district where relatively few Jews lived into a land as Jewish as Judaea.

Jesus sparked the relationship between Christianity and Judaism in his decisive encounters with the Pharisees, foremost exponents of Judaism in his day.

Think not that I came to destroy the law, or the prophets: I am not come to destroy, but to fulfill. For verily I say unto you, Till heaven and earth pass, one jot or one tittle shall in no wise pass from the law till all be fulfilled. Whosoever therefore shall break one of these least commandments, and shall teach men so, he shall be called the least in

---

[12] Mark 12:18–27.   [13] Acts 23:8.

[14] George Foot Moore, *Judaism,* vol. I, Cambridge (Mass.), 1932, pp. 60–62, 193–194.

[15] Mark 23:1–28.

[16] *Jewish War,* I. 5. 2, 110; II. 8. 14, 162; *Antiquities,* XVII, 2. 4, 41.

the kingdom of heaven: but whosoever shall do and teach them, the same shall be called great in the kingdom of heaven. For I say unto you, That except your righteousness shall exceed the righteousness of the scribes and Pharisees, ye shall in no case enter into the kingdom of heaven.[17]

In interpreting the Gospel in terms of the prevailing theology of his time, Jesus placed the Pharisees in the foreground of the historical setting of His message.[18] Sympathy to the Pharisaic system at its best will therefore reveal much of the true meaning of Christianity.[19]

Following His death and resurrection, Pharisees such as Nicodemus and Joseph of Arimathaea became devout believers. Even Gamaliel, the most eminent Pharisee in the Sanhedrin and a contemporary of Jesus, showed Peter and John consideration when in peril. In a memorable episode Jesus had drawn the line, however, between the congeniality of Pharisaic doctrine to his message and its disparity with it:

And when he was demanded of the Pharisees, when the kingdom of God should come, he answered them and said, The kingdom of God cometh not with observation: Neither shall they say, Lo here! or, lo there! for, behold, the kingdom of God is within you.[20]

Unlike Jesus who belonged to the "poor of Israel" whose piety was nourished by the Psalms, Prophets, and Apocalyptic literature, Paul was "a Pharisee, the son of a Pharisee." [21] Although Paul fought for the right of Gentile Christians to freedom from the Law, he himself submitted to its requirements and did not question the obligation of converts from Judaism to be circumcised. Yet on the road to Damascus, the light that shone upon him made him a new man who owed allegiance to Jesus Christ rather than to the observance of the Law; and that was the center of his faith.

In sum, though he did not acknowledge Christ, the genuine Pharisee loved God with heart, soul, strength, and mind, and his neighbor as himself.[22] That is the reason why Paul, even after his

[17] Matt. 5:17-20.
[18] Lev Gillet, *Communion in the Messiah,* London, 1942, pp. 4-6.
[19] R. Travers Herford, *Pharisaism,* London, 1912, pp. 3, 33.
[20] Luke 17:20-21.   [21] Acts 23:6.
[22] J. Jocz, *The Jew in the Bible,* London, 1947, pp. 20, 54.

conversion, remained a Jew.[23] In his encounter with the Samaritan woman, Jesus Himself conceded that "salvation is from the Jews," yet affirmed that "neither in this mountain nor yet at Jerusalem," shall men worship the Father, but "in spirit and truth." [24]

5. *The Messiah*. The heart of the Christian interpretation of Judaism centers in the Messiah and draws upon this religious Biblical fountainhead. Paul and the Gospels affirm that Jesus is the Messiah, the Christ of God, preacher of the kingdom of heaven, and the Incarnate Son of God who gave Christianity its essence.

In its original Hebrew and Aramaic connotation which applied to any person anointed to rule as king,[25] the word Messiah had no special significance until it came into vogue as title of that scion of David's house and lineage who should rule in the future kingdom of perfection. The Old Testament did not at first use the word in this special sense, for it was only after the exile that the Jews developed the concept of the Messiah as the one anointed and empowered to establish God's kingdom at the end of time.[26]

Envisaged in two phases, this Messianic kingdom was to bring high spirituality to a universal level under the leadership of Judaism; it was also to be a glorious national restoration of Israel. The fusion of these two phases constituted the basic contention of Jewish Messianic thought.[27]

Arising in the Greek period and deriving its strength from Jewish and non-Jewish sources, this Messianic belief foreshadowed, despite its dubious character, some of the truths of Christianity.[28] Early in His earthly ministry, Jesus stood, one Sabbath, in the synagogue at Nazareth and identified Himself as the Messiah.[29]

As the New Testament knew Him, Jesus was more than the announcer of a renewal in Israel, an expansion of the inner dispositions of the Pharisaic soul. The kingdom He brought was not

---

[23] A. Deissmann, *St. Paul*, tr. L. Strachan, London, 1912, p. 98.

[24] John 4:21, 23.

[25] 2 Sam. 1:14, 16; 7:13.

[26] Cf. Dan. 9:25.

[27] Meyer Waxman, *A Handbook of Judaism: As Professed and Practiced Through the Ages*, New York, 1947, p. 17.

[28] W. O. E. Oesterley, *The Jews and Judaism During the Greek Period*, London, 1941, p. 160.

[29] Luke 4:18–21; Is. 61:1–2.

primarily an answer to the deep longings of the Jewish community, nor indeed was it to be a supernatural development at the end of time. Both the eternity and eschatology of the Bible, on the one hand, and a faith unfolding in the days of his flesh, on the other, were joined together and formed into an expression of God's will and truth for man.

Precisely this unique Messiahship of Jesus, the Jewish portraits of the Messiah had failed to grasp.[30] Jewish Messianism inspired no one to say with Paul, "Do nothing through faction or through vainglory, but in lowliness of mind each counting other better than himself; not looking each of you to his own things, but each of you also to the things of others. Have this mind in you, which was also in Christ Jesus: who existing in the form of God, counted not the being on an equality with God a thing to be grasped, but emptied himself, taking the form of a servant being made in the likeness of men; and being found in fashion as a man, he humbled himself, becoming obedient unto death, yea, the death of the cross." [31]

For this kind of Messiah one looks in vain through the writings of the rabbis and the Jewish religious tradition.

II. The Historical Development

Inextricably linked to a land and people,[32] Judaism is a religion historically represented by a variety of beliefs and institutions interpreted on the authority of sacred literature and reflecting contact with alien cultures. Regarded with the highest admiration, its interpreters, who flourished about the dawn of Christianity, were in a position to survey the epic of their ancient race and to set its pace for many centuries to come.

Indeed, Judaism is as much the product of the interpreting fathers Hillel, Shammai, and Akiba, as it is the descendant of the Old Testament sages and prophets. Thoroughly human and vocationally alive, these early Fathers kept close to the social life of their people and, in keeping with a practice common among the doctors of Jewish religion, gave a third of their day to such manual labor

[30] Harry Emerson Fosdick, *The Man from Nazareth*, New York, 1949, pp. 28–29.

[31] Phil. 2:3–8.

[32] 2 Macc. 2:21; 8:1; 14:38; Gal. 1:13, Esth. 2:5; 8:17.

as shoemaking, wood-cutting, or masonry, devoting the rest of it to more strictly spiritual pursuits.[33]

1. *Hillel, Shammai, Akiba.* During the reign of the first King Herod, the foremost authority among the Jews was Hillel (*ca.* 60 B.C.–A.D. 10) whose grandson, Gamaliel, teacher of Paul and head of the Sanhedrin, once interceded in behalf of the disciples of Jesus when they were in danger. [34]

An immigrant from Mesopotamia, Hillel began life in Jerusalem as a laborer. A maxim in the Talmud said that a Jew "should always be as meek as Hillel and not as quick-tempered as Shammai." His was evidently the manner of the polished Pharisee who represented the dominant element of the order. His career (30 B.C.–A.D. 10) [35] led to the presidency of the Sanhedrin, and tradition recognized him as *nasi* (prince) although his one verifiable title is *ha-zakan* (elder). In contrast to his colleague, Shammai, he advocated a milder interpretation of the Halakah (oral law). Hillel contributed traditions which enriched the Babylonian Talmud, fortified the intellectual structure of Judaism, and restored the Jewish system of Scripture exegesis which became the embodiment of rabbinical religious and moral thought.

Shammai's title to fame rested upon his controversies with Hillel, punctilious concern for the Sabbath, profound learning, and the founding of a rigorist school Beth, (house of) Shammai. Born in Palestine he participated in his country's political and religious drama. An incident gives point to his peppery character: A heathen who sought admission to Judaism was thrown out by Shammai who considered the applicant's conditions outrageous; but when the man applied to Hillel, the latter by sweet reasonableness made a convert of him. In keeping with the stern and uncompromising standards of their master, the Shammaites strove, despite their gluttonous enjoyment of the Sabbath on every weekday, to maintain a stringent code of procedure, and in their intense patriotism forbade collaboration with Rome or anyone who condoned her cause.

Akiba ben Joseph (*ca.* A.D. 50–132), the Palestinian *tanna*

---

[33] Kaufmann Kohler, *The Jewish Encyclopedia,* vol. III, p. 359.
[34] Acts 5:34 *sqq.*
[35] W. Bacher, *The Jewish Encyclopedia,* vol. VI, pp. 397–400.

(teacher) and father of rabbinical Judaism, definitively established the Old Testament canon. Of comparatively humble parentage, he married the daughter of a wealthy Jerusalemite whom he had allegedly served as a shepherd. Having transgressed Hadrian's edict against the practice and preaching of the Jewish religion, he was executed and became a celebrated martyr.

Although Akiba had acknowledged as the Messiah Bar Kokba (son of the star) who had risen against the forces of Hadrian,[36] his consuming pursuits were primarily academic. Largely through his counsel and direction, Aquila (fl. *ca.* A.D. 117–138) provided the Greek-speaking Jews with a rabbinical Bible, and the Targum was revised.

Convinced that the Old Testament, regarded by the Christians as integral to Scripture, no longer could serve as the only intellectual and confessional bond of Jewry, he undertook to produce a new bond on the basis of the Halakah, emblem of Judaism's capacity for change and secular orientation. Whereas the former Halakah had grown out of the internal struggle between Pharisee and Sadducee, that of Akiba reflected the contest between Judaism and its external rivals, Hellenism and Christianity.

2. *Talmudic Judaism.* Subsequent to the fall of Jerusalem in A.D. 70, the history of rabbinism unfolds in three distinct periods, Talmudic, Gaonic, and medieval.

Properly speaking, the Talmudic period was the time when the several parts of the Talmud were put together. Its beginnings were marked by the age of the Tannaim (pl. of *tanna,* teacher) and their fellow Pharisees, authorized by Titus to organize a Sanhedrin at Jabneh (Jamnia) in the vicinity of Jaffa, where the Palestinian Talmud was in due course evolved.

In the meantime, the Jewish center of gravity had shifted to Mesopotamia where the Resh Galutha (Exilarch), head of the Eastern Jews, resided, and the Babylonian Talmud, excelling its Palestinian rival in wealth of material, subtlety, and popularity, was developed.[37] Here a distinct contribution was made by the

---

[36] Louis Ginzberg, *The Jewish Encyclopedia,* vol. I, p. 305.
[37] G. F. Moore, *Judaism in the First Centuries of the Christian Era: The Age of Tannaism,* 2 vols., London, 1927.

Amoraim (pl. of *amor,* speaker, A.D. 200–500) whose interpretations of Talmudic writings made for greater clarity. With the formulations of the Saboraim (the Reflective Ones) in the half century A.D. 500–550, the Babylonian Talmud was brought to completion.

The Gaonim (pl. of Gaon, excellency, title reserved for the president of a Jewish academy) attained their prime during the sixth to the eleventh centuries. Assuming the onerous defense of Judaism in the early Islamic period, the Gaons also figured in the internal controversies of Judaism, particularly those provoked by the Karaites.

In opposition to the Rabbinists and Talmudists, the Karaites adopted the watchword, "Back from Tradition to Scripture." [38] Partly in revolt against the rabbis and possibly under the influence of Islamic theology, their chief spokesman, Anan ben David, had advocated about A.D. 765, adherence to the Written Word. Avoiding an absolute break with tradition, Karaism was nevertheless a throwback to Sadduceeism and throve on the rejection of oral tradition. In modern times, considerable Karaite colonies flourished in Damascus and Cairo; and Imperial Russia at times played off Karaite against Rabbinist. [39]

The most distinguished Jew of his time, Saadia ben Joseph (A.D. 882–942), became Saadia Gaon who added a new dimension to Jewish history. [40] Born in Egypt, he had studied in Palestine, Syria, and Iraq, and finally rose to the presidency of Sura, one of the two great academies of Iraqi Judaism. His *Book of Beliefs and Opinions* [41] was an attempt to interpret Judaism as a rational body of beliefs. The greatest Talmudist of his age, he reconciled Arab culture with Judaism, relied upon the findings of the rationalist Mutazilites, and checked the disruptive influence of the Karaites within catholic Israel. His was, therefore, a role comparable to that of Philo who had reconciled Hellenism with Judaism.

3. *Medieval Effervescence.* Beginning in the rabbinical response to Karaism and Islam, medieval Jewish rationalism culminated in

[38] J. Furst, *Geschichte des Karaerthums,* 3 vols., Lepizig, 1862–1869.

[39] Lev Gillet, *Communion in the Messiah,* pp. 220–221.

[40] Judah Goldin, *The Jews: Their History, Culture and Religion,* Louis Finkelstein, ed., vol. I, New York, 1949, pp. 194–200.

[41] Tr. Samuel Rosenblatt, New Haven, 1948, p. xxvi.

Maimonides, then gradually receded as theology and mysticism supplanted philosophy in the attempt to reclaim the Jewish tradition for new generations.

Judaism was quickened in the Western world by the Arab conquest of Spain where Solomon ben Gabirol (*ca.* 1021–*ca.* 1070) composed his unforgettable sacred lyrics, and Bahya ben Pakuda (d. *ca.* 1140), leaning on al-Ghazzali (d. 1111), produced *Duties of the Heart,* an ethical treatise of profound insight. Joseph Halevi, who was born in Toledo and died in Palestine after 1140, was a poet and rationalist, relentless in his rebuke of those philosophers who veered Judaism away from its religious anchorage.

Moses Maimonides (1135–1204) emerged as the great medieval philosopher and codifier of Hebrew law. Setting aside traditional rabbinism, he endeavored to spiritualize Judaism.[42] His *Guide to the Perplexed* offered confused minds an interpretation which, in its allegorical details, was as old as Philo. An unconscious intermediary between Arab Aristotelianism and Christian Western theology, he drew from his knowledge of philosophy a rational interpretation of Scripture. Yet Judaism owed him its only widely accepted creed, formulated in thirteen articles in an appendix to his commentary on the Mishna of Sanhedrin.

It may not be without significance, however, that the last voices of Spanish Judaism included Hasdai ben Abraham Crescas (1340–1410) and Joseph Albo (1380–1444) both of whom sought to rescue the faith from the throes of philosophy through their appeal to revealed religion.

4. *The Scriptural, Talmudic, and Mystical Components.* In its historical development, the Jewish religion may be understood in the lights of its Scriptural, Talmudic, and Mystical monuments.

(a) Scrupulously preserved by the rabbis, the Old Testament became the heritage of Christianity and mankind.[43] From pre-Maccabean times down to the Middle Ages, Jewish scholars devoted

---

[42] Isaac Husik, *A History of Medieval Jewish Philosophy,* Philadelphia, 1941, pp. 236–311.

[43] E. Levine, *The Parting of the Road,* F. J. Foakes Jackson, ed., London, 1912, p. 310.

themselves to the Masorah,[44] the determination of the Biblical text, with critical notes and diacritical reading.

Two tendencies governed the development of the canon, the one critical, reducing the number of sacred books, the other conservative, calculated to retain the precious monuments of the faith. Rooted in the exegesis initiated by Hillel and culminating in the work of Akiba at Jamnia, the textus receptus of the Hebrew Bible, provided with Masoretic apparatus, was completed between the fifth and eighth centuries.[45]

Fixed by 200 B.C. but not completed till the early second century of our era, the Hebrew canon comprised the books of the Old Testament and eliminated certain writings such as the Apocrypha, even those which had been included in the Alexandrian Greek canon of the Septuagint.

Along with the text went its interpretation, commonly allegorical as the works of Philo and Maimonides prove, or mystical as in the case of Spinoza. Standing within this tradition, Moses Mendelssohn in 1773 published a German translation of the Pentateuch aiming to restore to it the natural and historic meaning of the Old Testament. That modern Judaism longs for God as He speaks in the Bible was evidenced in Moses Montefiore's English translation, *The Bible for Home Reading,* and in a similar translation of the Hebrew Bible for Austria and Germany made in 1925 by Martin Buber and Franz Rosenzweig.

(b) Centered in the Talmud [46] was the body of Jewish canonical and civil law which, though not found in the Old Testament, was nevertheless ascribed to Moses, the Elders, and Scribes. Also incorporated were the decrees of the Sanhedrin, the courts of law, and such alien legislation as had become regulative for Jewry.

The Talmud consists of the Mishnah (text) and the Gemara (commentary). Reproducing the same text, the two Talmuds (Babylonian and Palestinian) differ in the commentary. Having

[44] C. Ginsburg, *The Messorah,* London, 1880–1885.

[45] Critical Masoretic text, *Biblia Hebraica,* ed., R. Kittel *et al.,* Stuttgart, 1937.

[46] Abridged Eng. tr. of Babylonian Talmud, M. Rodkinson, 16 vols., New York, 1896–1903. See A. Lukyn Williams, *Talmudic Judaism and Christianity,* London, 1933, pp. 32–34.

practically superseded its rival, the Babylonian Talmud is noted for the high authority of its Gemara. The chief supplement to the Talmud is the Midrash (exegesis) which includes the Halakah (oral law) and the Haggadah (homiletical and anecdotic), a non-literal exposition of Scripture.

Offsetting the formalism, casuistry, and mystical trends that had set in, the Talmud expressed the desire of the believer for the experience of God in daily life and promoted the rationalist character of Judaism.

(c) Jewish mysticism had an early expression in the lore concerning Ezekiel's [47] heavenly throne-chariot (Merkaba). Its pattern of Hasidism (saintliness) ultimately merged in the Cabbala (mystical tradition). The eighteenth-century Hasidic revival might have been a reaction against rabbinic legalism, but it drew its vitality from the remote Jewish past. Philo spoke, in *De Vita Contemplativa,* of pre-Maccabean Hasidim (mystics) who did not sacrifice like priests but kept themselves in a priestly state of holiness.

The Biblical concept of Shekinah (divine indwelling) lent itself to speculative interpretation as a path to God, and Hellenistic influence inspired, for instance, the concept of angels as the words of God and the mystical doctrine of wisdom. Cabbala became an esoteric system, known only to the elect, who deemed their special knowledge revelation grounded in and illuminating the Torah.[48]

Although the first mystical treatise, the *Yetsirah* (Creation),[49] dated from the sixth Christian century, Judaism's major source on mysticism, the *Zohar* (Brilliance),[50] a commentary on the Pentateuch, has been ascribed to the Spanish Moses de Leon (1250–1305).[51] Rich in metaphor and undoubtedly reflecting centuries of mystical brooding, the Zohar projected the idea of a sphere, a whole realm of divinity underlying the phenomena of sense perception.

[47] Ez. 1 and 2.

[48] A. E. Waite, *The Secret Doctrine in Israel,* London, 1913; *The Holy Kabbalah,* London, 1930.

[49] Tr. W. W. Westcott, *Sepher Yezirah,* London, 1893.

[50] Tr. H. Sperling, M. Simon, and P. Levertoff, with Introduction by J. Abelson, 5 vols., London, 1931–1934.

[51] Gershom G. Scholem, *Major Trends in Jewish Mysticism,* New York, 1946, pp. 186–204.

III.   THE DISTINCTIVE CHARACTER OF JUDAISM

The vision of God, His nature, unity, and self-revelation to the sages, prophets, and fathers, is the central affirmation around which the distinctive attributes of Judaism arise.[52]

1. *The Torah*. Philo (*ca.* 20 B.C.–A.D. 54), the Hellenistic Jewish philosopher, pointed out that mankind, from East to West, showed aversion to foreign institutions; yet, centered in the Torah, the Jewish institutions attracted Barbarians and Greeks, dwellers on the mainlands and islands of Europe, Asia, and the whole inhabited world.[53]

Whereas conservative Judaism today is concerned with Israel, and Reform sets its gaze upon the vision of God, the Orthodox Jews are primarily devoted to the Torah,[54] finding in it their articles of faith, confession, and creed. To the Orthodox Jew, the whole Torah is Sinaitic in inspiration and authority. To toil in the Torah, which may denote the Law or all the Hebrew Bible, is to devote oneself to the study and interpretation of the Holy Book and thereby to earn reward in this world and the next.

But the Torah does not stand alone as the supreme authority of the faith. An equilibrium was struck between the canonical character of the Torah and the decisive authority of the Talmud, constituting a distinctive aspect of Judaism.[55]

2. *People and Land*. The Jewish Polish scholar, Nachman Krochmal (1785–1840), originated, largely under Hegel's influence, the idea of Jewry's mission in the modern world. Influenced also by the Italian philosopher of history, Vico (1668–1744), Krochmal conceived of the two branches of history as that of the nations and that of Israel. Essentially a secular thinker, his system of thought reduced Judaism to the level of the nations which elevate their anthropocentric assets and make themselves an object of wor-

[52] A. Lukyn Williams, *The Doctrines of Judaism Considered*, London, 1939, pp. 13 *sqq.*

[53] Cf. Harry Austryn Wolfson, *Philo,* vol. II, Cambridge, Mass., 1947, pp. 187–195.

[54] Bernard Harrison, *Annals of the American Academy of Political and Social Science,* March, 1948, p. 32.

[55] Leo Baeck, *The Essence of Judaism,* New York, 1948, pp. 22–23.

ship. Martin Buber [56] has shown this to be the dilemma of contemporary Judaism.

There was hardly an epoch in Jewish history when Judaism represented a racial homogeneity.[57] The disparity between the Sephardic Jew and the Ashkenazi in medieval and modern times had its counterpart in the difference between Palestinian, Babylonian, and Alexandrian Jews in antiquity. Yet from its earliest inception, Judaism considered the link between its people and land vital to the preservation of religious stamina.

This dual allegiance to land and people explains the career of Theodor Herzl and Chaim Weizmann, leading architects of the State of Israel which came into being on May 15, 1948. Restraining the thoughtful, however, is the conviction that Israel is not a nation like the other nations. It is to ascend from the biological law of power, glorified in national existence, to the dimension of truth and righteousness, that the Chosen People were called. Israel was chosen to be a true people and that means God's people.

3. *Messiah and Eschatology.* The erstwhile fundamental doctrine of the Messiah has lost ground in modern Judaism. Reform and even Conservative Jews have renounced the concept of a personal Messiah with its eschatological verbiage and centered their attention on a Messianic era when the kingdom of peace and progress shall become a historic reality.[58]

In his twelfth creedal article, however, Maimonides asserted the belief in the coming of the Messiah. Whereas supernatural qualities were not as a rule ascribed to him, the Messiah was to rely on the will of God and excel in human perfection.[59] To be expected as a descendant of the House of David, he will die leaving a son and heir; and surpassing all rulers in the exercise of justice and wisdom, he will usher in the political independence of the Jewish nation which in turn will introduce universal peace.

The crux of the matter is that Jewish Messianism is at variance with Christianity both in tense and consequence.[60] Born out of

[56] *Israel and the World,* New York, 1948, pp. 197, *sqq.*
[57] Leo Baeck, *op. cit.,* p. 72.
[58] I. Epstein, *Judaism,* London, 1939, p. 7.
[59] M. Friedlander, *The Jewish Religion,* London, 1937, p. 160.
[60] Abraham A. Newman, *Great Religions of the Modern World,* pp. 241–245.

varied experiences and mystical moods, it directed Jewish aspirations toward the end of days, yet, avoiding the supernatural, redemptive, and truly eschatological emphasis, it was restricted to the phenomenal and epochal features of history. In the loss of even this insubstantial messianism, one discovers the seeds of religious deterioration in a modern Judaism whose urge to have done with the expectation of a personal Messiah makes belief in immortality and personal resurrection increasingly difficult for the non-Orthodox Jew.[61]

4. *Sin and Human Perfectibility.* Confronted with perfection, man discovers the sordid quality of his nature, and his encounter with the Redeemer removes him from the depth of tragedy to fellowship with God. Actually, therefore, the conviction that man has set himself irreparably in opposition to his divine origin and to his Lord cannot be fully disclosed save to one who believes in God through Jesus Christ.[62]

Although the Hebrews had a deep consciousness of personal and communal depravity, Judaism did not take so grave a view of human nature. Repudiating the reality of original sin, it failed to grasp the true significance of the Cross and Resurrection.[63] Having conceived of sin as the fate prepared by the individual when he disavowed his essence and made himself a mere object, Judaism pointed to original sin as that myth long shattered by the Prophets.[64]

Thus making light of the Biblical story of the Fall, Judaism upholds a meliorism, a doctrine of human perfectibility which sounds strange on the lips of a people who know at firsthand the progress of cruelty and reaction in the world. Determined to avert the paralysis of original sin, Jewish thought denies the possibility that any such obstacle could cast its shadow upon history or impinge upon the intention of modern Judaism to lead the human procession toward freedom, justice, and brotherhood.[65]

[61] Philip S. Bernstein, *What the Jews Believe,* New York, 1950, p. 15.
[62] Emil Brunner, *Man in Revolt,* tr. Olive Wyon, New York, 1939, p. 114.
[63] A. Roy Eckardt, *Christianity and the Children of Israel,* New York, 1948, p. 48.
[64] Leo Baeck, *op. cit.,* pp. 161–162.
[65] Abraham A. Newman, *op. cit.,* pp. 246–250.

5. *The Sabbath and Festivals.* The importance of the Sabbath, festivals, and holy days as a distinctive expression of Judaism moved Samson Raphael Hirsch, the nineteenth-century German rabbi, to declare that "the catechism of the Jew is his calendar." [66]

Instituted in the Decalogue [67] as a day of rest lasting from Friday evening to the next sundown, the Sabbath extended to the common man the privilege of leisure and lofty living and raised Hebrew standards to a level elsewhere unknown. The six services which signalize the day's sanctity are climaxed in the Kiddush, a benediction uttered by the head of the family over the bread and wine, preceding the Sabbath meal. [68]

Similar to the Sabbath are Passover, Pentecost, and Tabernacles, which were originally pilgrim festivals requiring the celebrants to go up to Jerusalem on foot. Beginning with the New Year, a ten-day penitence ends with the Day of Atonement (Yom Kippur). Following a lunar calendar, the cycle includes, other than special days marking the beginning of the month, fasts and mourning, Hannukkah and Purim, the first commemorating the victory over the Greco-Syrians in 165 B.C. and the second the deliverance of the Persian Jews from destruction in the days of Queen Esther.

Whereas Jesus and His disciples observed these days, He made the Sabbath subordinate to human welfare. [69] Paul emphasized that to return to the formalism of the festivals was to fall back to a sub-Christian level. [70] Therefore the Christians adopted as their Sabbath the first day of the week, the day on which Christ rose from the dead. [71]

6. *The Synagogue: Center of Worship, Study, and Assembly.* Whether the synagogue arose during the Babylonian exile or the subsequent Persian period, it owed its origin to the prayer meetings which the prophets organized in the days of the first Temple for the purpose of devotion and exhortation. [72] Not only the later

[66] Philip S. Bernstein, *op. cit.,* p. 17.

[67] Ex. 20:11.

[68] W. O. E. Oesterley and G. H. Box, *A Short History of Rabbinical and Medieval Judaism,* London, 1920, pp. 187–196.

[69] Mark 1:21–25; 2:23–28; 3:1–6.

[70] Gal. 4:9–11.   [71] Acts 2:1; 20:7.

[72] Louis Finkelstein, *The Jews: Their History, Culture, and Religion,* vol. II, p. 1354.

synagogue but the church and mosque, as well, trace back to those early Hebrew assemblies. With the Dispersion, the synagogue rose to prominence as center of worship, learning, and assembly.

The emancipation of the Jew, in the wake of the American and French revolutions, gave birth to congregational synagogues, free from political pressure and reorganized by laymen instead of rabbis. But a strong social consciousness did not arise in modern Judaism until the upsurge of Zionism and the revival of Jewish education.[73] Thus, despite the curb which secularism laid upon the synagogue, it retained its ascendancy in Jewish ethical and religious life.[74]

Liturgically and otherwise, the debt of the Church to the synagogue is unquestioned. The phrase "Our Father who art in heaven" with which Jesus prefaced the Lord's Prayer, is Jewish.[75] Indeed, the Christian recognizes some of his own litanies in the Shema, "Hear O Israel, the Lord our God, the Lord is One," Judaism's central prayer; and in the Kaddish, "Exalted and hallowed be the name of God throughout the world . . . May his kingdom come, his will be done," the prayer by which Judaism honors the dead.

This common ancestry does not, however, spell the identity of church and synagogue. Whereas the synagogue is committed to the study of the Torah and derives its strength from the vision of God and fidelity to the welfare of Jewry, the church is the body of Christ and, in common allegiance to Him, its members find their fellowship and their concern for others. The Conservative Jew has, therefore, tended to equate learning and nationalism with worship and the purely religious function of the synagogue;[76] and describing themselves as Sadducean, Reform rabbis, while regarding Jesus as a "great teacher of morality and an artist in parable," believed that any religion which led men to the good life was true.[77]

---

[73] Ismar Elbogen, *A Century of Jewish Life,* tr. Moses Hadas, Philadelphia, 1945, pp. 92–96.

[74] Abraham A. Newman, *op. cit.,* p. 257.

[75] Morton Scott Enslin, *Christian Beginnings,* New York, 1938, p. 102.

[76] Simon Greenberg, *Religion in the Twentieth Century,* Vergilius Ferm, ed., New York, 1948, p. 327.

[77] Louis I. Newman, *ibid.,* pp. 320–322.

IV. CHRISTIANITY AND JUDAISM

The Christian religion is absolute truth because it inculcates faith in Jesus Christ, the perfect revelation of God, in whom both the absolute meaning of life and the expression of divine activity appeared in the flesh and remained as after his death and resurrection he ruled as supreme Lord of life.[78] Did this Christianity stem from the first-century Judaism which prevailed among the Jews of Palestine and Egypt? Judaism repudiated the Incarnate Lord, made a break with the new religion, and set itself apart from Christianity.

From the beginning of his ministry, Jesus bore the reproach of the Pharisees because he challenged their conception, or conceptions, of religion. Although the first Christians shared the Hebrew religious heritage, their religion was not the daughter of Palestinian Judaism. Nor was it the daughter of Egyptian Judaism whose foremost representative Philo had, of course, taught the existence of a being intermediary between God and man; but that intermediary, the Divine Word, was not God and, according to Philo, remained a stranger to the flesh.[79]

Inherent in the redemptive work of God made known in Jesus Christ, the New Testament is not only free from traceable Gentile religious influence [80] but also independent from the Jewish tradition, though fulfilling the promises to Israel.[81] Ignoring hostility, Christians have therefore longed for the salvation of a people whom the Eternal had chosen and honored.

The Old Testament was made the storm center of Jewish-Christian controversy largely because Christianity interpreted the ancient revelation in a manner which was at variance with the exegesis of the Scribes and Pharisees and essentially defferent from the teachings of Philo and his Alexandrian colleagues who had per-

[78] John A. Mackay, "Christianity and Other Religions," *Protestant Thought in the Twentieth Century*, Arnold S. Nash, ed., New York, 1951, p. 284.

[79] M. J. Lagrange, *Le Judaisme Avant Jésus-Christ*, Paris, 1931, pp. 587-591.

[80] H. J. Cadbury, "The Present State of New Testament Studies," *The Haverford Symposium on Archaeology and the Bible*, Elihu Grant, ed., New Haven, 1938, p. 19.

[81] On the essential unity of the New Testament message, see Floyd J. Filson, *One Lord, One Faith*, Philadelphia, 1943.

fected their knowledge in the light of Hellenistic thought and philosophy.

A man of towering intellectual genius and formidable erudition, it may be assumed, had intervened and enabled the Christians to defeat the rabbis and subtle Alexandrian Jews at their own arguments. Who might this man of genius be? He could hardly have been the man Jesus who though he quoted Scripture yet left no written record or scholarly work, and though his fame as a preacher and miracle maker had won him the title of rabbi yet really claimed no philosophical training or versatility as a worldly thinker.

Was this genius Paul whose arguments, now cast in rabbinical vesture, now taking a more incisive and personal form, actually introduced novel explanations and strange new insights? But the Jews themselves denied Paul recognition as an interpreter and dismissed his theology as an intrusion of Greek mysticism. Careful examination of the Greek religions and of Paul's Christianity proves that his theology was the outcome of faithfulness to the New Testament,[82] and that Jesus Christ was his clue to the understanding of the Old Testament.

That Jesus Christ is the clue to the Old Testament means as little from a Pharisaic Jewish and purely rational viewpoint as it does from the viewpoint of his assumed philosophical genius. Neither the Jew nor the rationalist can on the basis of isolated Prophetic texts learn what the Incarnation means. Christianity cannot be deduced from the Old Testament revelation through a rational interpretation.

So long as Paul understood the Scripture according to his own mind and in the light of Pharisaic erudition, he remained a Pharisee. In order to grasp the full meaning of the Hebrew scriptures, he needed a new revelation, Jesus Christ. That the Incarnate Lord is the fulfillment of the Old Testament revelation means infinitely more than its natural and historic culmination in Him since He filled the ancient texts with a new content hitherto unknown to man and beyond the capacity of mortal creativity. More than the logical conclusion of the Covenant, He was its completion and perfection. In short, transcending the rabbinical schools and wisdom of

[82] J. Gresham Machen, *The Origin of Paul's Religion,* New York, 1921.

the age, He established contact with the Old Testament from above and beyond the religious structure of Judaism.

Jews there have always been who, recognizing that the Old Testament bids them look for a Prophet who will come as the Messiah, received Christ as Lord and adored Him in penitence and faith as personal Saviour and friend. But they could scarcely discover Him unless they had trusted in the faithfulness of God to show them the way, unless they had seen the breach that separated mundane Judaism from the Old Testament revelation, and, above all, unless they had known that the ancient light, like the daybreak, offered little if it did not bring in the splendor of the morning.

CHAPTER XII

THE SOVEREIGNTY OF ALLAH, HIS BOOK,
PROPHET, AND PEOPLE: ISLAM

ISLAM is the religion, ideology, and folkway of some 300 million
inhabitants of important regions in Asia, Africa, Europe, and the
islands of the seas. Since they do not formally worship Mohammed,
their prophet, but acknowledge him only as God's emissary, it is
obvious why Mohammedans prefer to be known as Moslems, that
is, believers in Islam which means surrender and submission to the
sovereignty of God.

The global community of modern Islam spreads out in a ring
of many lands encircling the planet along its warm belt. Among
the predominantly Moslem nations of the Middle East are Egypt,
Saudi Arabia, Syria, Jordan, Iraq, Yemen, Turkey, and Iran, as
well as Afghanistan and Pakistan. In the West Pacific, the United
States of Indonesia (which in 1950 became a member of the United
Nations) is overwhelmingly Moslem. There are besides considerable Moslem communities in Lebanon, Albania, Yugoslavia, the
U. S. S. R., China, India, the Balkans, Africa, and elsewhere.

At the end of World War I, the collapse of the Ottoman Empire,
leading Islamic power since the fifteenth century, dealt the traditional orthodoxy of Islam a mortal blow. The declarations of the
congresses held at Cairo and Mecca to determine the future of
the Caliphate which had been cancelled by the Kemalist Turks on
March 3, 1924, constitute the swan song of Islamic theocracy. The
Islamic peoples began thereafter to move steadily toward secularism, sectionalism, and Westernization. A set of nationalisms, such
as the Turkish, Arab and Pakistani types, replaced the old theocracy.

In the meantime, the Russian Revolution of 1917 had spelled
chaos in the Moslem soul. The 40 million Moslems of Russia

received cultural autonomy. Two Moslem republics, Daghestan and Azerbaijan, emerged in the Caucasus, and five in Central Asia— Uzbek, Kazakh, Turkmen, Tadzhik, and Kirkhis. Other Moslem communities, scattered in the Caucasus and Siberia, received similar status under Communist control. Subject to Soviet secularism and materialism, the development of these states, much as in Turkey, proceeded from anything but the common Islamic tradition.

Greater changes still were the outcome of World War II. Thirty million Moslems in China were caught in the web of the Civil War. By virtue of their autonomy, they were free to establish closer ties with their brethren in the Near East. Actually, a few students came to complete their studies at Cairo's famed Azhar, the world's foremost Islamic seminary. But the general position of China's Moslems was far from satisfactory, especially after 1949 when the high tension involved in dual allegiance to Islam and Communism began to mount. In the Near East the several Arab states won independence and joined the United Nations. But perhaps the greatest single development which highlights contemporary Islamic history took place in 1947 when Pakistan, a nation of 70 million Moslems, emerged as a vigorous new state and became a full partner in the British Commonwealth of Nations.

Noteworthy present-day movements in the political arena are the Arab League and the Moslem League, the former founded in 1945 and the latter dating back to 1906. Still in its infancy, the Arab League nevertheless weathered dissension among the leaders and remained intact against the terrific odds of débâcle in Palestine. Thanks to the outstanding contribution of Mohammed Ali Jinnah (1876–1948), the Moslem League became a force effective in ordering the lives of Moslems who inhabit the Indian subcontinent.

This awakening of Moslem nations, their gradual emancipation from the yoke of illiteracy and isolation and their liberation from imperialism, is one of the major signs of our time. The two sources of weakness which continue to foil the powers of growth are, on the one hand, secularism and socialism and, on the other, the stubborn resistance of the traditionalists in almost every walk of life. Dynastic and petty national strife have frustrated the desire for coöperation and service of a common cause. All but dead is that pan-Islamic spirit which marked the turn of the century.

If they are to resist Communist infiltration and meet the challenge of the world crisis, the Islamic peoples will need to muster all the stamina at their command. The crisis presents Islam and the Moslems with a golden opportunity to make good on all they cherish. If Islam today, as many of its enlightened spokesmen profess, is animated with a real desire to work for the goals of freedom, equality, and peace, it can carve for itself a place of honor among the nations by putting its own house in order and by courageously opening its doors to reforms insuring religious liberty and freedom of conscience, free enterprise and the betterment of the poor man's lot.

An intelligent understanding of the problem facing Islam requires an analysis of its religious content, historical dynamic, and twentieth-century structure.

I. THE RELIGIOUS CONTENT

1. *The Transmutation of Diverse Religious Traditions.* The basic picture of early Islam projected a religion which bore striking resemblance to Judaeo-Christianity, and a culture more intimately related to the Hellenistic and Aramaic traditions than to the ancient Orient separated from it by a thousand years.[1] The Koran and Tradition betray oral knowledge of a Hebrew religion which was taken to include the New Testament.[2] Any religious or intellectual elements, deriving from Biblical antiquity or the Iranian and Indian heritage, were surpassed in importance by those drawn from Syrian and Greek sources. The triumph of Islam in the seventh century has not been injudiciously regarded as the judgment of God upon a degenerate Near Eastern Christianity.[3] Whether in the Koran or subsequent biographies of the prophets, Islam knew the Bible mainly through the Apocrypha and Haggadah.[4] Thus,

---

[1] W. F. Albright, *JAOS,* vol. 60, no. 3, September, 1940, pp. 300–301.

[2] C. C. Torrey, *The Jewish Foundation of Islam,* New York, 1933, pp. 1, 8.

[3] Richard Bell, *The Origin of Islam in Its Christian Environment,* London, 1926, pp. 1, 212.

[4] D. Sidersky, *Les Origines des Légendes Mussulmanes dans le Coran et dans les Vies des Prophètes,* Paris, 1933.

while it represented a reversion to primitive Arabian monotheism and preserved pre-Islamic rites such as circumcision and the procession around the Kaaba, Islam was essentially a composite faith, its overtones constituting only a repercussion from Biblical religion.

(a) *Mohammed (ca.* A.D. *571–632).* Having started life as an orphan in Mecca and learned hardship at first hand, the Arabian Prophet became a man of leisure at twenty-five through his marriage with Khadijah, a rich and noble widow of matronly virtues. At forty, his meditations matured into a vast conception of God and His role in history. Mortified by the idolatry of the Quraysh, his own tribe, and its aristocracy, sponsors of the center of fetishism and pilgrimage at the Kaaba, he roundly denounced the ancient paganism and all it meant.

That their trusted kinsman and one-time fellow-businessman, Mohammed, should preach a message disruptive of their commercial interests and oblivious to their social status was more than his tribe could countenance. Undaunted by their ridicule and fury, he intensified his efforts and organized a compact body of supporters. The decisive event in Mohammed's life and in the new religion took place in September, 622, when, unwilling to yield to his people's intimidation and open persecution, he fled to Medina, city of his maternal uncles, and thereby initiated the Moslem era. Received with honor, he eventually occupied in Medina the seat of a ruler before whose tribunal disputes between Moslems, Jews, and pagans were arbitrated. Prophetic though his claims continued to be, he had come to wield increasingly the sword of a theocratic statesman intent upon the regulation of state affairs and upon defeating his foes. When he died on June 8, 632, Mohammed bequeathed to his followers a legacy of Arab unity which, despite his religious acumen and political sagacity, was shackled by the wedlock of religion and government and burdened by the ambiguity of his instructions regarding a successor.

Dissatisfied with the medieval portrayal of Mohammed as an impostor, Western scholarship furthered, from the middle of the nineteenth century, a more trustworthy and objective evaluation of his life and faith. Carlyle reversed the conventional European approach when he introduced the founder of Islam as a prophet-hero.

Objective criticism, however, has revealed Mohammed, in the opening stages of his apostleship, as a warner and reviler of the people, a preacher of an eschatology, bearing the accent of eternity, who called men to worship God, basing his arguments on the reality of heaven and hell, the last day of judgment and retribution.[5] In Medina the prince dwarfed the preacher, and the worldly, materialist aspect of Islam drew permanent form from the personal life of the founder. Islamic theology knows nothing of that cult of the Prophet which folk Islam wove around the person of Mohammed, lifting him far beyond his claims. The orthodox Moslem view is that an unlettered (*ummi*) though brilliant and faithful man, Mohammed became the instrument of revelation through the express purpose of Allah.

(b) *The Koran.* Constituting the message of Mohammed and the chief source on his life, the Koran (from Arabic *al-quran,* reading, recital) in its 114 suras (chapters) is regarded as uncreated, the replica of an eternal, celestial original. While not sharing this view of mechanical revelation which divests Mohammed of responsibility for the creation of the Book, critical research is clear that the Koran is the product of a sincere and brilliant mind. Into its making Mohammed put the commitment and exalted vision of a passionate seeker after the truth.

The first Koranic utterances were memorized or written perhaps on palm leaves and tablets of stone. The emergence of rival collections moved the third Caliph (successor of Mohammed), Uthman (644–656), to canonize the Codex of Medina. Early in the tenth century, an authorized version was established in Baghdad.[6] Throughout the sacred text, Moslems recognize the speaker as Allah who in choosing Arabic as a medium ennobled this language and made it something more than the Latin, Greek, or Hebrew of Islam.

These are the signs of the perspicuous Book. Verily, we have revealed it, an Arabic Koran; haply ye may understand. We tell thee

[5] Tor Andrae, *Mohammed: The Man and His Faith,* tr. Theophil Menzel, London, 1936, pp. 71 *sqq.*
[6] Arthur Jeffery, *Materials for the History of the Text of the Koran,* Leyden, 1937, pp. 1–10.

the best of stories, in inspiring thee with this Koran, though thou wert before it among the heedless.[7]

Regarded as the standard miracle of the faith, the Koran sets forth the precepts and legislation of Islam. It was largely due to its influence that the various dialects of the Arabic-speaking peoples have not fallen apart into distinct languages as did Latin in producing the Romance languages.

No one, save by the authority of the Koran, may speak about the spiritual realm. Basically, the Moslems are Koranists. Islam thus came into being, a religion without an ecclesia, without clergy, and without a central see. Yet largely through the ironclad dogmatics of Koranic theology, this religion has been able to tighten the legalistic scriptural belt around its body.

2. *Principal Affirmations.* Characteristic of Islam are a number of clear-cut affirmations which, particularly insofar as the being of God is concerned, set it apart from the religions of India and the Far East. Where Judaism projects the vision of God, the Lord and Father, as one, and where Christianity teaches that God is love revealed in the Person of the Redeemer, Islam affirms that God is great—*akbar*—which literally means greater, that is, than anything and anyone conceivable.

> Say, "He is God alone!
> God the Eternal!
> He begets not and is not begotten!
> Nor is there like unto Him any one!"[8]

In its protest against polytheism, the Koran singled out the Trinity, the divinity of Christ and His Sonship, for attack as aspects of tritheism.[9] Echoes of the Arian, docetic, and Nestorian heresies are the probable background of the Koran's assertion that Jesus[10] was only a man, that He was the Messiah but not the Crucified and Risen Lord, and that He will return but not as Lord of life and immortality.

---

[7] Koran 12:1-3. Koranic references are to the translation of E. H. Palmer, Oxford, 1900. Other noteworthy translations were made by Rodwell (1861) and Richard Bell (1937-1939).

[8] Koran, 112.   [9] *Ibid.,* 5:16; 19:36.

[10] D. B. Macdonald, *The Encyclopedia of Islam,* M. Th. Houtsma *et al.,* ed., 4 vols. and supplement, Leyden, 1913-1938, vol. II, p. 524.

Islam's doctrine of God knows nothing of a Mediator, and Koranic Christology, though paying reverence to Jesus as man and messenger of God and as the Word and Spirit of Allah, forswears nevertheless the Incarnation and hence renders void the redemptive purpose of God. Indeed, this is the parting of the road between Islam and Christianity. Christians base their faith on the belief that the essence of religion is made absolute in the divine means of grace, apart from which the idea of God and revelation is left in jeopardy within the mechanical and rational dimensions.

The hereafter, and the resurrection of the body, are the subjects of another affirmation. Throughout its history, Islam has been a religion of reward and punishment, boldly maintaining that the final day of reckoning will be a terrible convocation.[11] However, since the meaning of life and the divine initiative of the Eternal are not seen in the light of God's mercy, grace, and love, disclosed in Christ, the fire reserved for the damned is not balanced by the vision of holy joy and blessed fellowship with the Father reserved for the redeemed who rest in the assurance of God's peace.

To be sure, Islamic eschatology, with its florid description of paradise, shows dependence on the Syriac Christian idiom. Its absolution (*kaffara*) and oblation (*qurban*), however, seem to be more indicative of an approximation between the speech of Christians and that of Jews than of a real grasp of the deep significance of the Christian doctrine of the atonement.[12]

A third affirmation relates to Mohammed as the last (seal) of the prophets. An unlettered man, he was the choice of God and conveyor of revelation to mankind. Unlike the poets, soothsayers, and magicians of pagan Arabia, he was hailed as a child of destiny, the Prophet of Allah.

"We have not taught him poetry, nor was it proper for him." [13]

That he was foretold in the Biblical accounts, which Jews and Christians have meantime perverted, is an Islamic view that is fully unsubstantiated.

[11] Koran, 81:1-15.
[12] J. Windrow Sweetman, *Islam and Christian Theology*, pt. I, vol. I, London, 1945, p. 35.
[13] Koran, 36:69.

A fourth affirmation concerns the Koran as the clear, decisive, and absolute truth. That Moslem scholars today may through scientific criticism study the Koran objectively only at the risk of personal peril, leaves little doubt that the Book continues to retain its sacrosanct ascendancy through intellectual coercion and imposed authority rather than through freedom of conscience and reasoned faith.

Finally, there is the affirmation concerning the community of believers including all who believe in Allah, His Prophet, Book, and the Day of Judgment. This is the justly celebrated brotherhood of Islam wherein all barriers of race, color, tongue, and status are tossed aside. Yet Islamic brotherhood is not a peculiarly spiritual fellowship of the forgiven and redeemed; much less is it the beloved community of those bought with a price and whose inner peace and forgiveness are translated into love of friend and foe and concern for the welfare of others.

From Cairo to Karachi and from Casablanca to the Sulu Sea, these principal affirmations are written into the ritual performances of the faithful, the so-called five pillars of Islam: profession of faith, worship, alms-giving, fasting, and the pilgrimage. And wherever the muezzin calls the believers five times daily to worship Allah, these affirmations provide the motivation behind Scripture, worship, theology, and ethics, in a world rocked by secularism and robbed of its idealism and faith by the penetration of materialist dogma.

3. *Dogmatics.* The simplest formulation of dogmatics in a given religion is normally contained in its creed. Though intended for the devotees themselves, a creed often springs from a combative desire to silence the dissident in the light of orthodox doctrine.

In the case of Islam, the earliest creed, crystallized in sentence and formula, was embedded in the Tradition (*Hadith*), that is, the so-called *Logia Muhammadis.*[14] A body of oral and written literature, Tradition represented the practice of the Prophet and his companions; and although padded with unreliable, if not actually falsified, entries, served as a mirror of Islamic religious history in

[14] A. J. Wensinck, *The Muslim Creed,* Cambridge, 1932.

the seventh century.[15] Various other works of unequal merit began to appear when in the form of homily, biography, history, commentary, or creed, the articles of faith were expounded.

The Confession, together with the four other Pillars, provided the groundwork for a dogmatic creedal exposition of the Islamic religion. Thus, (1) the Confession, namely, there is no God but Allah and Mohammed is His Apostle, remains the primary article of faith. (2) Performance of ritual prayer and (3) payment of alms are also articles which determine effective witness. (4) Prescribed at an early date of the Prophet's regime in Medina, was the Fast of Ramadan which, together with (5) the Pilgrimage, constituted acts of piety involving creedal significance.

The dogmatic crisis of the eighth and ninth centuries revolved about the controversy over predestination and free will and led to protracted discussion of the justice, attributes, and essence of God. It was an epoch of reaction against the rigid transcendentalism of the Koran. The contagion of post-Augustinian theology and the catalysis of Greek ideas, introduced by Christian and Jewish converts, proved irresistible and produced a rationalist trend within Islamic thought.

Added to these factors were others such as increasing intercourse with paganism and the rich heritage of India and Central Asia, the rise of sects and the stormy annals of a militant theocracy, which accelerated the demand for a more adequate theology. A distinction was eventually drawn between formal observance of Islam and inner religious experience. Convincing answers were sought with a sense of utmost urgency to the questions who is a Moslem, what constitutes polytheism, and what is the greatest sin?

The quest for the marks of Islamic catholicity and orthodoxy ended in a consensus that the heinous and mortal sins which the Prophet condemned included polytheism, magic, unlawful manslaughter, spending the inheritance of orphans, usury, desertion from battle, and the slandering of chaste women.[16] Even if it did not succeed in breaking through the battlements of the Islamic religious structure as it later did in medieval Christendom, Arab

---

[15] Alfred Guillaume, *The Traditions of Islam,* Oxford, 1924, p. 10.
[16] Wensinck, *op. cit.,* p. 39.

philosophy was nevertheless a goad urging the Moslem theologians to restless endeavor and more consistent thought.

4. *Folk Religion.* A critique of Islam will not only intimate its disparity with Christianity but take seriously its failure to transform the mentality of the millions who constitute the bulk of believers. Folk Islam registers the resurgence of paganism alongside a superficial affiliation with the exalted articles of faith.

In its agricultural, pastoral, and nomadic expression, folk Islam does not represent a uniform religious pattern. Yet the Islamic masses of the Middle East, Pakistan, Africa, and Indonesia, share in part the marks of that primitivism dealt with earlier in this work.[17] Little susceptible to the influence of new ideas and the necessity for change, they have discovered in the absolutes and authoritarianism of the Koran a safeguard against stimulation from the outside world.[18]

Sharply in contrast with the monotheistic emphasis of Mohammed is the overlay of superstition, sanctioned magic, veneration of saints, and shrine worship which marks popular Islam.[19]

The persistence of the tribal spirit with its institution of blood revenge, surpassing the vendetta of Corsica and the Kentucky mountaineers in ferocity yet quite negligible in comparison with the destructive international feuds of the West, seems to be rooted in a pagan individualism which Islam could not tame. In the Fast of Ramadan, the Shiite Passion Play, and the Friday Assembly, Islam offers the teeming masses a rallying point and an exit for long-repressed emotions.

A new vision, coupled with drastic measures, is needed if the tragedy of the Moslem masses is to be relieved. Education cannot perform the operation needed, apart from a self-critical reformation of Islam. The leaders insist on the preservation of a status quo in religion, the masses are apparently impervious to idealism, and the Westernized classes who have drunk deep at the founts of secularism and materialism are skeptical about spiritual forces.

Speaking realistically, and from a purely human viewpoint,

[17] See above, pp. 22–23, 40–48.

[18] J. S. Trimingham, *The Triumph of God,* Max Warren, ed., London, 1948, pp. 256–261.

[19] Samuel M. Zwemer, *Studies in Popular Islam,* London, 1939, pp. vii-viii.

Islam's best hope for the immediate future seems to lie in a friendly orientation toward Christianity.

II. The Historic Dynamic

When Abraham Kuyper (1837–1920), the Dutch theologian and statesman, returned from a visit to the eastern shores of the Mediterranean, he began to compose his three-volume *Pro Rege,* an interpretation of Christ's kingship in every domain of existence. In the Moslem world, Kuyper had discovered that the name of Mohammed usurped the place of Allah in the affections of the masses. The faithful Moslem paid homage to Mohammed about four to five times during each of the 1800 to 2500 prayers which he annually offered. Built around this unmitigated reverence for the Arabian Prophet was a historical dynamic discernible in Islam's political organization and sects, as well as in its philosophical and cultural expression.

1. *Political Organization: The Caliphate.* An extreme and skillful structural simplicity marked the political organization of Islam [20] which centered in the Caliphate,[21] a system of government peculiar to this culture, making the Caliph (successor of the Prophet) the chief administrator of the realm.

The Caliphates of Medina (A.D. 632–661), Damascus (661–750), Baghdad (762–1258), Cordova (756–1031), and that of the Ottoman Turks which came to an end on March 3, 1924, were all Sunnite (orthodox) and maintained that the Caliph succeeded only to Mohammed's secular role. The schismatic Shiites, of whom the Moslems of Iran form a solid block, conceived of the Caliphate as an Imamate, that is, an expression of legitimacy and divine investiture, the Fatimid state of Cairo (*ca.* 909–1171) having been their only major Caliphate.

Although the Caliphate is now defunct as are the blood-stained annals of an institution long haunted by dynastic troubles, the basic issue of separation between religion and politics still hangs like a ghastly specter over Islam. Enlightened Moslems have discrimi-

[20] A. L. Kroeber, *Configurations of Culture Growth,* pp. 695–696.
[21] On the history of medieval Islamic empires, see P. K. Hitti, *History of the Arabs,* London, 1949.

nately wondered whether Allah really willed that the religious welfare of His people should ever be placed at the mercy of any Caliph, state, or government.

Grounded in the Koran and Tradition, political theory in Islam also drew, in its later stages, upon the concepts of government set forth by Plato and Aristotle.[22] The Moslem philosopher, al-Farabi [23] (d. 950), who witnessed the decline of the Abbasid Caliphate of Baghdad, propounded a theory of the ideal state. Influenced by Platonic doctrine, he envisioned his ideal state as a hierarchy, under God, ruled by a virtuous Caliph, counseled by a corps of philosophers who were steeped in the metaphysical knowledge of the First Principle. Salvador De Madariaga, in a brilliant volume entitled *Spain,* wrote that the mighty and refined Caliph of Cordova must have looked down on the petty, warring kingdoms of Northern Spain much as the President of the French Republic looks down upon the Moroccan tribesmen.

2. *Sects: Sunnites and Shiites.* Constituting the majority of Moslems, the Sunnites were the main actors in the long drama of Islam. Indicating orthodoxy, the form, Sunnite, derives from *sunna,* that is, the custom, tradition, and usage of the Prophet and his companions. With the rise of the Ottoman Turks who captured Constantinople in 1453 and overran Egypt in 1517, Sunnites continued for another half-millennium as the stalwart champions of Islam. Since the two World Wars, even without Caliphal authority, they have asserted themselves in national and international affairs, particularly in Pakistan and the Arab countries.

Armed with their orthodoxy, the Sunnites formed four canonical schools of legal interpretation which fought off medieval heresy and stood like a brass wall against rationalism. Since the Renaissance, however, the old light began to burn low, self-righteousness, mediocrity, and contempt for others proving no match against the adversary in an age of free inquiry and experimental science. Fanaticism supplanted conviction, jealousy and hatred replaced good will, and superstition dethroned religion.

[22] Thomas W. Arnold, *The Caliphate,* Oxford, 1924, pp. 121–128.
[23] Friedrich Dieterici, *Alfarabis Abhandlung über den Musterstaat,* Leiden, 1895, p. 122.

The great divide between Sunnite and Shiite Islam is the personality of Ali, Mohammed's cousin and son-in-law.[24] Those who supported Ali's claim to the Caliphate came to be known as his Shiites (partisans). Invoking Mohammed's will and testament in favor of Ali, the Shiites contended that the election of abu-Bakr, Omar, and Uthman, who had preceded him in office, had happened in default. To this day, Shiism has its own leading shrines at Najaf, Kerbela, and Kazimain, in Iraq, and at Mashhad and Qum in Iran.

Shiite theology proceeded from the assumption of Ali's divine appointment and argued to the conclusion that the Imamate (pontificate) of Islam, which could not be ascribed to the Sunnite Caliphs, was the birthright of some seven or twelve Imams (pontiffs) including Ali, his two sons, Hasan and Husain, and certain other descendants. Around the memory of Ali and his allegedly legitimate heirs, all of whom suffered violent death, Shiism recovered several concepts lost to Sunnite Islam, such as that of a mediator between the believer and God, vicarious suffering, and the dogma of a now-concealed, later to return, Imam.

The articulate center of non-Arab malcontents, especially of Iranians conscious of their cultural superiority, Shiite Islam became a thorn in the Sunnite side. Among its offshoots are the Druzes of Syria and Lebanon, the Assassins of medieval notoriety, the Ismailis whose name has been popularized by their titular head, the fabulously rich Agha Khan, and his son, and the Bahais whose religious propaganda has reached our American shores.

3. *Philosophical and Mystical Leaven.* The attempt to crack the shell of orthodoxy was not monopolized by Shiism, for philosophy and mysticism had their own parts to perform. That despite their relatively peripheral character, the philosophers and mystics were able to set a process of leavening in motion meant that though Islam was an Arab religion in the non-Arab world [25] it was no less a hybrid in religious essence than in cultural content.

Arab philosophy is traceable to the studies of Jewish and Syrian Christian scholars. Having acquired classical philosophy and sci-

---

[24] Consult Dwight M. Donaldson, *The Shiite Religion,* London, 1933.
[25] W. Wilson Cash, *The Expansion of Islam: An Arab Religion in the Non-Arab World,* London, 1928.

ence mainly through Syriac intermediaries, the Moslem thinkers fashioned these into a new synthesis observing the demands of their own era and religious outlook. It was an era when Asia Minor was a Christian country with Constantinople as capital and when the Iberian Peninsula, together with Sicily was the home of Islamic cultural effervescence. It would hardly have been accurate at that time to speak of the Moslem East and the Christian West.[26]

An international body, the Arab philosophers recognized as their ranking representatives the Arab, al-Kindi (d. 850), the Turk, al-Farabi (d. 950), and the Persian, Avicenna (980–1037). The achievements of these luminaries, who lived in the Near East, were climaxed in the contributions of Averroës (1126–1198), a Hispano-Arab, and Maimonides (1135–1204), a Jew. The same Greek impact which had agitated the theologians concerned with the problem of free will and predestination, and produced the rational school of Mutazilites, now led the major philosophers to intriguing subjects such as being, creation, knowledge of God, and the reality of the First Intelligence. Repudiated by the religious scholars of Islam, Arab Aristotelianism fared better in Europe, where it fitted into the scholasticism and humanism of Thomas Aquinas.[27]

More effective were the Sufis (mystics) who in the twelfth century created the beginnings of a vast reorganization in Islamic life corresponding to the monastic orders of medieval Christendom. Influenced by the philosophers in his early career, al-Ghazzali (1058–1111), Islam's greatest theologian, turned in his maturity to Sufi mysticism and, in his *Revival of Religious Sciences,* enunciated the fundamental affirmation that religious knowledge must inevitably depend upon revelation.[28]

Truly universal in outreach and implication, Sufism opened the Moslem heart to the love of God and, in its gnosticism, incarnationism (*hulul*), and renunciation, established a record of faith in divine immanence and pantheism. But this theosophy, with its Greek, Christian, Buddhist, and monastic ingredients, was a dan-

[26] Christopher Dawson, *The Making of Europe,* New York, 1945, p. 168.

[27] Etienne Gilson, *The Spirit of Medieval Philosophy,* tr. A. H. C. Downes, New York, 1940, pp. 178–188.

[28] Louis Gardet and M. M. Anawati, *Introduction à la Théologie Mussulmane,* Paris, 1948, pp. 67–72.

gerous game to play in Islam which looked upon the notion of union with Allah as a rank heresy.[29]

Contemporary Islam knows many a mystic, but the old Sufi whose wisdom, learning, and cultural eminence reflected honor upon the orders and all who tread the path, has long since vanished from the scene. Instead of the stately mystic poets of Persia and the brilliant Arab Sufis, one encounters at present a class of imitators who have lost the fire of the masters, and a variety of mendicants, dervishes, magicians, and selfish practitioners.

4. *Classical Culture and Expansion.* Arnold J. Toynbee [30] draws an illuminating comparison between the Christian and the Islamic civilizations. Going back to Hellenic civilization, modern Christendom in its Western and Eastern branches arose after the intermediary appearance of the Roman Empire, the Christian Church, and the wandering peoples. In like manner, Islamdom is an heir to an antique parent, the Syriac civilization which became resplendent in the time of King Solomon and Hiram of Tyre; it also branched out into the affiliated Arabic and Persic divisions; and between the current Islamic civilization and the ancient Syriac appeared the intermediaries of the Baghdad-centered Abbasid Empire, the Islamic "Church," and the wandering peoples.

In the chrysalis of Arabic and Persic Islam, comparable to Eastern and Western Christendom, one sees the Sunnite-Shiite groupings and the Islamic duality represented by Arab and non-Arab societies. Saudi Arabia, Egypt, Iraq, Syria, Palestine, North Africa, the Sudan, and Yemen fall into the Arab society; Turkey, Iran, Afghanistan, Turkestan, Pakistan, Malaya, and Indonesia constitute the non-Arab society. An outer ring, made up of Islamic Negro Africa, Moslem Russia and China, as well as other isolated communities in Europe, the Philippines, Japan, and the Americas, envelops the Crescent of Islam.

Representing the last great florescence of Near Eastern culture, Islamic civilization developed from the seventh to the thirteenth century, its creativity having terminated by A.D. 1050 as the suc-

[29] A. J. Arberry, *Sufism: An Account of the Mystics of Islam,* New York, 1950, p. 93.

[30] *A Study of History,* Abridgement by D. C. Somervell, pp. 15–16.

cess of the First Crusade, a half-century later, seems to indicate.[31] It issued forth in a new religious enthusiasm, centered in the Koran and Tradition and supplemented by the pre-Islamic heritage of lyrical poetry.

Although as a religion Islam contained little novelty, its distinctive character was inherent in the personality of the founder, the glorification of the Arabic tongue, and a striking cultic simplicity. Arab in speech, though frequently not in blood, the key figures of Islamic culture contributed along verbalizing rather than experimental lines. The lack of visible aesthetic art, ordinarily construed as the result of theological proscription, was probably due to more complex and less obvious causes. Except when produced in an anti-clerical mood and setting, sculpture, painting, and drama were conspicuously absent.

In its higher aspects, this eclectic and verbalizing civilization made signal contributions in theology, literature, philology, philosophy, science, and architecture.[32] Simplicity of organization, variation on a central organizational motif, followed the principle of repetitiveness rather than complexity. And since the Middle Ages there have been few re-creations of Islamic culture, the Iranian and Turkish movements having relied heavily on ethnic revival and formed conscious secessions from the more genuinely Arabic-Islamic tradition.

III. TWENTIETH-CENTURY ISLAM

Having survived the Mongol invasion of Baghdad (1258), this Islamic system, whose militant defenders till the close of World War I were the Ottoman Turks, stood in sharp contrast with Christianity. As already noted, the Redeemer was ignored, largely because Islam knew nothing of original sin and its founders and interpreters were oblivious to the problem of evil and sidestepped the need of the soul for forgiveness, a personal Saviour, and prayer as an eventful intercourse with the Eternal.

The aesthetic, human, and spiritual aspects of Moslem life, like

---

[31] A. L. Kroeber, *op. cit.*, pp. 695–697.

[32] See George Sarton, *Introduction to the History of Science,* 3 vols. in 5, Washington, 1927–1928.

the theological, were made more deserving of Christian compassion by the grave stagnation which overtook Islam during the period of Western upheaval. If al-Ghazzali, Avicenna, and Averroës had excelled their peers of the Latin West and rendered decisive contributions to the Christian philosophy of the age, leading to the enrichment of scholasticism and the incorporation of Aristotelianism in the thought pattern of Thomas Aquinas, the picture was now radically altered. Sixteenth-century Islam saw no rehabilitation of theology, experienced no religious revival, knew no Reformation or Renaissance, and produced hardly anyone equal to Martin Luther, Erasmus, or John Calvin.

The impact of Western civilization, political, technological, economic, intellectual, and religious, together with the resurgence within Islam itself of movements such as Wahhabism, Pan-Islam, and political agitation, often disruptive and divisive, produced twentieth-century Islam.[33] But the development of contemporary Islam has scarcely gone beyond the recovery of its religio-political heritage, manifest in the recrudescence of medieval encomiums of Mohammed and the formal observance of the cult,[34] supplemented occasionally by secular passion and nationalist fervor.

1. *Arab Theism.* The followers of Mohammed, ibn-Abd-al-Wahhab (1691–1787), constitute the Wahhabi sect of Islam which inveighs against innovations and advocates return to the pristine faith enshrined in the Koran and exemplified in the career of the Prophet. Ruled by the wily and realistic King ibn-Saud, the Wahhabis have carved for themselves in Peninsular Arabia a highly strategic though primitive state, embracing on the west the cities of Mecca and Medina which are sacred to Moslems everywhere, and on the east the internationally important oil deposits of the province of Hasa.[35]

The Wahhabis of the eighteenth and nineteenth centuries were

[33] H. A. R. Gibb and Harold Bowen, *Islamic Society and the West,* vol. I, pt. 1, London, 1950, p. 11. Maurice Gaudefroy-Demombynes, *Muslim Institutions,* tr. John P. MacGregor, London, 1950, pp. 208–216.

[34] See G. H. Bousquet, *Les Grandes Pratiques Rituelles de L'Islam,* Paris, 1949.

[35] H. St. John Philby, *Arabia and the Wahhabis,* London, 1928; *Arabia,* London, 1930.

firebrands who rose against a corrupt and decadent Islam, preaching the right of the believers to close their ranks and resist alien infiltration. Puritanical in its Islamic emphasis, Wahhabism elicited a reactionary response throughout the Moslem world. But worldly-wise King ibn-Saud channeled the religious enthusiasm of the Wahhabi brotherhood to more profitable secular ends.[36]

2. *Egyptian Rehabilitation of Theology.* The reformation of Islamic theology was left to Egypt and produced the nineteenth-century, pan-Islamist al-Afghani (1839–1897) and his disciple, Mohammed Abdu (1849–1905), who achieved recognition as the chief theologian of modern Islam.[37] Although these pioneers inspired interest in Koranic studies and religious renewal, neither critical Koranic scholarship nor profound spiritual awakening have yet been achieved.

As a matter of fact, today the more liberal wing of the reformers are secularists inclined to emulate the example set by Turkey but giving rise to popular fronts such as the Moslem Brotherhood, with a discreditable record of political and social arson.[38] Whereas the sober intellectual finds in the legislative sanctions and generally reactionary Islamic temperament a deterrent to the development of an Islamic theology based on private judgment, the more youthful spirits seem satisfied with a negative interpretation of their faith along anti-Western lines.

3. *Turkey Reborn.* Turkey's reforms, to which successive generations of literati had contributed, finally released under Kemal Ataturk (d. 1938) the forces which established a state. Thus within the historic confines of Asia Minor new Turkey comprised the irreducible minimum of land which every Turk recognized as his homeland.[39]

The literary seeds of Turkey's modern nationalism were sown by Zia Gokalp (1876–1924), the intellectual father of *devrim,* the stream of rejuvenation including both revolt and reform. As the Prussians of his day regarded themselves as the élite of Germany,

[36] K. S. Twitchell, *Saudi Arabia,* Princeton, 1947, pp. 88–109.

[37] Charles C. Adams, *Islam and Modernism in Egypt,* London, 1933.

[38] H. A. R. Gibb, *Mohammedanism: A Historical Survey,* Oxford, 1949, pp. 176–180.

[39] Donald Everet Webster, *The Turkey of Ataturk,* Philadelphia, 1939.

so Gokalp believed that the Turks were the leaders of Islamic peoples. The official translation of the Koran into Turkish was, according to Halide Edib, distinguished authoress and feminist leader of modern Turkey, in keeping with Gokalp's conviction that the progress, freedom, and democracy of the Western world were products of the Protestant Reformation. Neither Turkey nor any other Islamic country, he maintained, therefore, could travel the road of progress and obtain international stature without the advantage of a deep religious reformation.

Other views and insights competed with those of Gokalp. Faced with the choice between Islamic leadership and its implied conformity with the teachings of Mohammed, on the one hand, and the pursuit of the revolution along the lines of her national and military genius, on the other, Turkey chose the latter, and the story of her rebirth was not, therefore, that of Islamic revival.

4. *Iran Makes a Fresh Start.* When Reza Shah Pehlevi was summoned by the National Assembly of Iran to take the oath which enabled him in April, 1926, to ascend the Peacock Throne, a new constitutional state with an ancient and glorious heritage made a fresh start. If the Arabs are rightly reckoned as the creators of Islam as a religion, and the Turks as its militarists and lawgivers, then the Iranians are truly its artists and men of letters.

The literary soul of Iran in its ancient and medieval manifestations may be studied in two foremost creations, the *Avesta* and the *Shahuama,* the first as the bible of Zoroastrianism, the second a medieval historical epic of the nation's past. A host of other expressions of the Iranian spirit favored the schismatic character of Shiite Islam.[40]

The turmoil of the two World Wars notwithstanding, the aspirations of Iran for international recognition became evident in the dispute with Great Britain over the nationalization of the oil industry (1951). Religious fervor became an adjunct to nationalism. The earlier trend, taking a leaf from Turkey's revolution, had circumscribed Islam and struck for the purification of Persian from foreign, particularly Arabic, loan words. But intense patriotism and ultra-national hysteria drew upon the emotionalism of mullahs

[40] Donald N. Wilber, *Iran: Past and Present,* Princeton, 1948, pp. 208–211.

and Moslem fanatics. In that kind of atmosphere, the growth of a Shiite piety, balanced by sound learning, proved unfeasible.

5. *Pakistan: Nationalism and Rationalism.* Apart from the purely political and nationalist activity which preceded Pakistan's birth as a sovereign state in the summer of 1947, a considerable degree of religious leavening had taken place, sharpening the differences between the Moslem and Hindu.

Whereas the Hindu religion stemmed from the Sanskrit classics and Vedic wisdom, Indian Islam was mediated through Persian and Arabic, the language of the Koran and Islamic culture. India's Moslems, therefore, became increasingly aware that, whereas the speech of their Hindu neighbors was Hindi, their own vernacular, Urdu, though a variant of Hindustani, was actually written through the characters of the Arabic alphabet with certain modifications. In contrast to the metaphysical, other-worldly, and pessimistic overtones of Hindu society, was the pragmatic, this-worldly, articulate, and theistic faith of the Islamic community.[41]

The rationalism of Indian Islam and its religious regeneration date from the era of the Indian Mutiny of 1857. The Aligarh movement led by Sir Ahmad Khan (d. 1898), which brought forth a university and a potent cultural system, combined religious education with modern scientific knowledge. Sir Mohammed Iqbal (d. 1938), the most distinguished figure of modern Indian Islam, attained international fame and was recognized as a thinker, Sufi, poet, and writer. His *Reconstruction of Religious Thought in Islam* (1934), first published in Urdu, gave that language a new importance.

Of the three sectarian developments in modern Islam, Wahhabism, Bahaism, and Ahmadiya, the last emerged within the confines of Indian Islam. Its founder, Mirza Ghulam Ahmad, starting in the Punjabi village of Qadian in 1879, pressed his personal claims as Mahdi, Messiah, and avatar of Krishna, thus uniting in himself what Islamic theology had ever put asunder. In line with his self-proclamation as the likeness of Jesus, Mirza Ghulam proceeded to expound the doctrine of *jihad,* not as a holy war against non-Moslems but as a striving after righteousness. Taken together, the

[41] Percival Spear, *India, Pakistan, and the West,* Oxford, 1949, pp. 76–91.

two branches of Ahmadiya, one at Qadian, the other at Lahore, are regarded as the most aggressive and missionary-minded sect of contemporary Islam. Extending their activities into Africa, Europe, and the Americas, the controversialists of Ahmadiya preach an Islamic apologetic of revival and seek to impress their message upon the cultured classes, hoping to counteract thereby the application of rationalist and agnostic theories to Islamic doctrines.

Islamic liberalism in Pakistan has made possible, however, the continuance of Western influences. A measure of religious liberty has been guaranteed under the constitution. Progressive interpretation of the *Sharia* (Islamic law), forming the basis of political and juridical theory, has not been unfavorable to the growth of Christianity which claims more adherents in Pakistan than in any other Islamic country.

6. *Islam in the Far East: China and Indonesia.* The doors of constructive citizenship in China, opened to all races and creeds under Sun Yat-sen, and later under Chiang Kai-shek, led to the improved status of Moslems. But already shaken by the ideas of two revolutions, the far-away Turkish and, nearer home, the Chinese, the Moslems of China were soon startled to their wits' end by the tide of Russian Communism which desecrated their mosques and questioned their religious standards. Hence, their opposition to Moscow, concealed though it may have been at times, was no less vehement than was their resistance to the Japanese occupation of Chinese soil.

Thirty million strong, they inhabit Chinese Turkestan and, scattered through China proper,[42] form large constituencies in the interior provinces of the far west, Kansu and Sinkiang being their two leading strongholds.[43] Generally conforming to the country's way of life, they nevertheless stand apart as an alien minority pursuing its peculiar cultural heritage.

Chinese Moslems maintain contact with their co-religionists in the Middle East and, in their aversion toward Confucianist ethics and Buddhist worship, regard the mosque as the center of their religious community, their spiritual leaders being rated on the

[42] H. A. R. Gibb, *Mohammedanism*, p. 22.
[43] K. S. Latourette, *A Short History of the Far East*, pp. 122–123, 487.

basis of training in Arabic and Islamic studies.[44] Although Islam's first appearance in China dates back to the Tang Dynasty (A.D. 618–907), the origins of the contemporary Moslem community in the land are more recent.

Having made its way into Southeast Asia through easy compromise with local spiritism, Islam now lays claim to some 65 million adherents in the southern provinces of Siam, as well as in the Malay Peninsula and Indonesia. Moslem traders and Sufi teachers, who hailed from points such as Gujarat and Malabar in Southern India, attracted many followers to their faith by lowering the terms of admission.[45] Long subject to Hindu and Buddhist influence, this area, therefore, became in more recent epochs the scene of open competition between Christianity and Islam, each making some headway but neither winning from the other.

Indonesian Islam, which already existed when Marco Polo landed at the eastern coast of Sumatra in 1292, betrays a high degree of magic and pantheism, partly derived from the local environment and partly acquired in the course of its passage through India. Contact in more recent decades with the Sunnite orthodox theology of Mecca and Cairo has tended to mitigate these pagan proclivities. Yet loyalty to both India and Arabia aggravates the religious problem of Indonesia, where the resurgence of political nationalism and the revival of the heathen heritage of the islands have all but reduced Islam to a veneer. The eclectic character of their version of Islam notwithstanding, the Indonesian Moslems regard themselves as orthodox Sunnites and vigorously resist conversion to any other faith.[46]

IV. CHRISTIANITY AND MODERN ISLAM

The defeat of Ottoman Turkey in World War I shattered all hope for a pan-Islamic solidarity. Out of the débris of the colossus, however, a new *modus vivendi* was achieved under which the Arab, Turk, Persian, Pakistani, and others, learned to fend each

---

[44] Isaac Mason, *A Primer on Islam,* Hankow, 1928.

[45] Kenneth Perry Landon, *Southeast Asia: Crossroad of Religions,* Chicago, 1947, pp. 134–164.

[46] Hendrik Kraemer, *The Christian Message in a Non-Christian World,* New York, 1947, pp. 200, 269.

for himself. Increasingly, the strategy of relations with the outside world seemed to consist in resort to defense in depth and to the tactics of dispersal.

Christianity continued through the twentieth century to exert an impact upon Islam and the Moslem peoples. Totally apart from the Western political impact and that of Christian culture, as such, Christianity—that is, the religion of the followers of Jesus Christ —enjoyed a historic antecedence and continuity in the Middle East, the cradle of the two faiths. Indeed, Christianity stood alone as a religion whose roots were deeper than those of Islam, nationalism, and Communism, and which was of an earlier vintage than those types of Zionism, imperialism, and democracy which were invoked in the Moslem world.[47]

Perhaps the nature of the Christian impact upon Islam can best be examined in the Middle East, a region which to Christianity means infinitely more than the scene of its historic conflict with Islam. No greater responsibility devolved upon twentieth-century Christianity than that of the revival, reformation, and propagation of the faith in and about the land where the Good Shepherd walked and ministered. The exaltation of His name in the Middle East was a theme worthy of piety and commitment, even as it was fit for Christian scholarship and heroic endeavor.

That the influence of Christianity in this region was formidable meant that its historic relation with Western Asia was maintained and vindicated. It was a relation that went back to the era preceding the birth of Mohammed; and it was an influence woven into the inner texture of the Koran. Through the living testimony of Christian men and institutions, Christianity had contributed to the golden prime of the Caliphate. Research has abundantly shown that Christianity constituted, as it does today, a vital force creative in the lives of countless Moslem generations and in the total effort of Islamic peoples.

Religious impact may be defined as that impulse imparted, by one who enjoys a living knowledge of God's truth, to others whose spirituality is either dormant or morbid. Modern Islamic theology

[47] See George Sarton, *The Incubation of Western Culture in the Middle East,* Washington, D. C., 1951, pp. 17–18.

left little doubt that it was impotent, by the sheer force of its own resources, to stem the tide of decadence in the Moslem world. On the pietistic level, there was an ostensible surrender to the will of Allah, without much concern, however, for the cathartic purposes of the Creator. There was no real commitment to His love, no unselfish regard for the welfare of non-Moslems. Providence had been reduced to Fate and the fear of Fate which, in the language of Kierkegaard, is the fear of nothing, tended to vitiate the norms of ethics and public morality.

Christianity's first modern impact on Islam emanated from the strongholds of Eastern Orthodoxy, Roman Catholicism, and Protestantism—that is, from Czarist Russia, Europe, and America. At present, American Protestantism, acting through the Ecumenical Movement and the World Council of Churches, exercises a conspicuous leadership and responsibility in the Moslem world. Classical American culture bore the imprint of this Protestant dynamism which about 1820 was ready to leap into the Middle East.

Writing in 1900, Henry H. Jessup of the Syria Mission recalled the words of the 1849 report of the standing committee on the translation of the Bible into Arabic. A prophetic passage in that report had said:

The Arab translator is interpreting the living oracles for the forty millions of an undying race whose successive and ever augmenting generations shall fail only with the final termination of all earthly things. Can we exaggerate on such a theme? Is it easy to overestimate the importance of that mighty power that shall send the healing leaves of salvation down the Tigris, the Euphrates, the Nile and Niger; that shall open the living fountains in the plains of Syria, the deserts of Arabia and the sands of Africa; that shall gild with the light of life the craggy summits of goodly Lebanon and sacred Sinai and giant Atlas?

Fifty years since Jessup embodied those words in the documentary history of the Arabic translation of the Scriptures, the outcome of Christian missions in the Islamic Middle East may be discovered along six levels: (1) the level of Arab nationalism where the idea of autonomy was fostered; and (2) that of Islamic rehabilitation where Moslem thinkers were sufficiently fascinated by Christian thought to know what Islam must do in order to survive. (3) The level of the revival of Christianity through the resuscitation of indigenous communions, the Eastern Churches, and the replacement of their air of frustration and withdrawal with an awakened concern for the uplift of Islamic society. (4) The level of integrating the several competing impacts—British, French, Muscovite, Roman Catholic, and others—in an abiding unity of thought and purpose. (5) The integration of the cultural, religious, economic, and political phases of existence in a harmony calculated to halt the further deterioration of the Islamic heritage and social structure. (6) The establishment of a national evangelical Church, keystone of the Christian arch, which emerged as the principal missionary spearhead and exercised a priestly function in the consecration of the whole community.

When Christians speak of their strategy in the Moslem world, they inevitably mean that, confronted with hatred, bitterness, and rejection, they will pray for forgiveness and the power to forgive others, seeking always to use every open avenue to the Moslem heart in order to make Christ known in humble service, living witness, and self-sacrifice.[48] Remembering at all times that if we speak with the tongues of men and of angels about the Word that became flesh and dwelt among us; and that even if we behold His glory, glory as of the only begotten of the Father, full of grace and truth, but in the meantime we have not love, we shall surely reap nothing but failure, and our noble efforts in the end will become as a sounding brass or a clanging cymbal.

Only when the relation of Christianity to Islam is fashioned after the pattern of Christ's relation to us will the approach of the Christian to the Moslem be right.

[48] See James Thayer Addison, *The Christian Approach to the Moslem,* New York, 1942.

CHAPTER XIII

THE MAKING AND DYNAMISM
OF CHRISTIANITY

I. THE EFFULGENCE OF CHRISTIANITY

1. *The Advent and Message of Christ.* The Christian religion took visible form with the advent of Jesus Christ (*ca.* 5 B.C.–A.D. 30). In the small circle of humble folk, fishermen and other Palestinian Jews, the movement began as a revival within Israel. It assumed larger scope as it became the nucleus of a spiritual revolt against the vested interests of the priests and the several orders of rabbinical interpreters. The Gospels reverberate with the echoes of rebuke pronounced by Jesus against the Scribes and Pharisees.

The new religion broke into the open as a spiritual transformation, calling the convert to "walk in the newness of life."[1] It achieved initial success engendered by an absolute obedience of faith and confirmed in the exultation of kindred hearts. In the course of time, the converts were able to proclaim the message of their Lord for the healing of the nations. Christianity thus took its place as a determining factor in the advance of man toward freedom and truth. To both history and culture it imparted the dynamic of a new age and the impulse of a new creation in Christ.

Although riveted upon mystery and the Eternal, the message was easy to understand. It was the fulfillment of that call of the Eternal disclosed in nature, made known in the scriptures of the Old Testament, and now substantiated in the person and work of Jesus. "Today hath this scripture been fulfilled in your ears."[2] Although no mortal has yet complied with every Christian precept or attained perfection in the graces of faith, yet even a child can grasp the true spirit of Christianity.

[1] Rom. 6:4; 12:2; Eph. 14:21–24; Col. 3:9–10.
[2] Luke 4:21.

Enshrined in profound meaning and anchored in ineffable revelation, the message was nonetheless concrete and bore the marks of transparency. It combined the depth of eternal truth with the clarity of the temporal. For its ultimate source it relied completely upon God "who like as a father pitieth his children"; [3] and the Son who said, "Greater love hath no man than this, that a man lay down his life for his friends"; [4] and the Holy Spirit who enkindles a flame of sacred good will in the cold hearts of men that they may walk as children of light "in all goodness and righteousness and truth." [5]

The faithful disciples and early saints derived their vision of God from a living Person. The vision became more vivid with the passing years, for the Lord had promised to remain with them "always, even unto the end of the world." [6]

Along with the vision, came vitality discerned in the extraordinary events accompanying the birth of Jesus, His ministry, agony and passion, and resurrection, as well as in the compelling authority with which He spoke. As Saviour of mankind, Shepherd of lost souls, and friend of the bruised and sinful, Jesus bestowed the consciousness of life and the hope of immortality upon all who approached Him in faith and contrition. Beyond peace of mind He gave his followers the power to resist evil; and more than security, He offered those who in penitence confessed Him as Lord, the forgiveness of sins and the radiance of adventurous freedom from bitterness, despair, and the haunting fear of death.

These singular gifts of grace in a remarkable manner reflect the distinctive character of Christianity. Inherent in the hallowed episodes which constitute the Redeemer's earthly life, they take form from that transport of spiritual assurance centered in the Crucified, whose Cross is the emblem of suffering and whose Resurrection is the divine parable of victory over the world and its destitution.

2. *The Cross and Resurrection.* The Cross is the focus of holy

[3] Ps. 103:13.
[4] John 15:13.
[5] Eph. 5:9.
[6] Matt. 28:20. On early Christianity consult Adolf Harnack, *The Expansion of Christianity in the First Three Centuries,* tr. J. Moffatt, 2 vols., New York, 1904–1905.

and secular history, inscribed at the heart of Christianity, and sets forth against the background of salvation the abject nature of man's infidelity. It is the unforgettable reminder that Christian power was not ever to be wedded to pleasure, arrogance, wisdom, or ceremony. Outwardly, the Cross was defeat, inwardly it is always victory. In showing love to His torturers, Christ died with the words of perfect faith upon His lips.

But the Cross is invariably rejected by those who have no questions to which the Crucified is the answer. It is a scandal in the eyes of those who have neither the hope nor the expectation for which the Cross is the fulfillment.[7] A disclosure of the meaning of life and history, the Cross joins the Hebraic and Hellenic interpretations of life, the former with its insight that life was fulfilled in history and the latter which viewed life as transcending history.[8]

The earthly career of Jesus attains its zenith in the Resurrection, token of the eternity of life, the survival of personality, and the inexorable triumph of right over wrong.[9] The history of religion shows no parallel to this august and devastating event, august by virtue of its divine presupposition and objective, devastating in its influence on the religious structure of the race. Every other standard is shattered, and life takes on new meaning because Jesus Christ rose from the dead. Nothing in the spiritual saga of mankind ever took so firm a hold over so many minds for so long.

There is no other religion which can match the insights thus given the Christian on the subject of reward and punishment both here and hereafter; and a religion which lacks a heightened interest in the life beyond scarcely meets the inner thirst of man.[10]

The thought of Plato on immortality, the beliefs and institutions of the Egyptians and Persians, as well as the ideas of later Jewish Messianism, have all been largely superseded. Yet with all the revelations of modern science and against the subtle objections of natural philosophy, belief in the indestructibility of the soul per-

[7] William Temple, *Basic Convictions,* New York, 1936, p. 45.

[8] Reinhold Niebuhr, *The Nature and Destiny of Man,* vol. II, New York, 1943, pp. 6, 37.

[9] Adolf Harnack, *What Is Christianity?* tr. T. B. Saunders, London, 1901, p. 162.

[10] G. Lowes Dickinson, *The Greek View of Life,* London, 1909, p. 32.

sists. Freedom from the bondage of superstition and release from pessimism regarding the shape of things to come are the portion of all who believe that Jesus passed through the valley of death, and "that flesh and blood cannot inherit the kingdom of God; neither doth corruption inherit incorruption." [11]

3. *Christianity: The Redemptive Purpose of God.* Two concepts, that of the universality of the faith and that of the contemporaneity of Jesus Christ, fortified the Christians in their proclamation of the Gospel and transcended the centuries and the divisions which afflicted the Church. On the one hand, Christianity proclaimed itself the final and universal revelation of God, embracing within its preaching all and more than all that other religions offered; on the other, was its affirmation that men everywhere had immediate access to God through the Redeemer who, though He died centuries ago, still lives as the risen and exalted Lord who loves all men.[12]

Robed with these spiritual assets, the Christian wielded immense power.[13] His faith did not end in the domain of the intellect, the aesthetic, or the esoteric, but was calculated to be effective and creative. Thus during medieval times, Christianity forestalled the collapse of civilization and held high the torch of learning.

Christianity laid the foundations of greater progress when it explained the concept of a rational God who moves in an orderly universe. It was out of these humble beginnings, reaching their maturity in the dazzling feats of science, that nature's secrets were gradually unlocked and the enigma of human personality was partly unmasked.

Since the Renaissance, and despite her schisms, Christianity has stood as the chief custodian of freedom and democracy, our civil liberties being but deductions from the Christian doctrine of man. That Christians of every class and kindred today lead the human procession toward peace and the enforcement of human rights, is traceable to the redemptive purpose of God crystallized in the Covenant, the Church, and the thrust of Christian missions.

[11] 1 Cor. 15:50.
[12] A. Victor Murray, *Personal Experience and the Christian Faith,* London, 1939, p. 22.
[13] Georgia Harkness, *The Resources of Religion,* New York, 1936, pp. 76–80.

4. *Covenant, Church, Missions.* Deep were the roots of this redemptive message which dated back to the Covenant whereby the Eternal promised man favor and life subject to the fulfillment of well-defined conditions.[14] The Covenant assured man, on condition of obedience, that he should be saved from destruction.[15] To Abraham and his seed the Covenant granted national protection.[16] Consecrated on Mt. Horeb during the time of Moses, the promise was contingent upon keeping the Ten Commandments.[17]

The Covenant finds its proper setting and implementation in the strange and eventful world of the Old Testament. About fifteen centuries of religious development are later brought to fulfillment in Jesus; the ancient religious stream overflowed the limits of Israel and, forming Christianity, issued forth as the river of life, a New Covenant for all the nations.[18] From the beginning, the relation of Jesus to the Prophets was the chief reason why the Christians accepted the Hebrew scriptures as their own.[19]

The New Testament or the New Covenant, then, was the Gospel with happy portents for the cause of religion and the story of man. Reaching its summit in Jesus, the Prophetic line which led to Him made men feel about Him as they had felt about Moses and the Prophets, with this difference, however, that He was the Incarnate Lord in whom shone the face of the Most High, "portrait of the invisible God." [20] Such was the peerless and incomparable Christ, clue to the hidden treasures of religion.[21] At last men knew what God was like.

Vitally dependent upon the missionary incentive for its growth, the Church was basically conceived as a righteous remnant, a holy community of saints, the people of God who, because of their commitment to Jesus Christ, were set apart and altogether distinguished from the followers of other religions.

[14] Gen. 2:16, 17; 9:12, 15, 16.
[15] Gen. 6.
[16] Gen. 13:17; 15:18 and elsewhere.
[17] Deut. 5:2.
[18] Heb. 8:8–13; Gal. 4:21–31; John 7:39; 2 Cor. 3:6–9.
[19] Leroy Waterman, *Religion Faces the World Crisis,* Ann Arbor, 1943, p. 158.
[20] Col. 1:15.
[21] John Baillie, *The Interpretation of Religion,* New York, 1928, p. 466.

Enmeshed in the Jewish community, the early Church of Palestine regarded itself as the true Judaism, its members constituting the Israel of God. The admission of Gentiles touched off a storm of protest among the Jews, but Paul made it clear that salvation was primarily an individual experience. His characteristic conception of the Church as the Body of Christ had the strong implication of unity in diversity.[22]

From its very inception, Christianity faced the opposition of those who questioned the presuppositions of the Church. In the eighteenth century an open assault in the guise of historical criticism was made against the unique character of Christianity. Particularly under attack was the nature of the connection between the Church as the chief representative of religion, and history. Gotthold Ephraim Lessing (1729–1781), the German critic and dramatist, gave this assault its classical expression when he contended that no creed can be final and that every religion had its share in the spiritual development of mankind. He concluded that historical truth, which is accidental, cannot become the proof of the truths of reason, which are necessary.

Rising to the defense of Christianity, Adolf Harnack[23] pointed out the error of Lessing who had come under the influence of Rousseau. He reaffirmed the historic substance of the Christian Creed—life in God, forgiveness of sins, consolation in suffering—which had been the faith of the saints and martyrs as well as the valid experience of ecclesiastical history.

The Church is not, therefore, an ordinary development in history, but rather the community of destiny operating under a divine mandate; it is a spiritual communion which binds together men and women of every possible origin, who find themselves today members both of the Church and of our half-pagan nations.[24]

Thus, the power of the Church is made effective in the nations to which her members belong. In Great Britain and the United States, in Africa, India, China, and Russia, in Latin America, the Arab world, Europe, and everywhere else, the work of the Church

[22] Rom. 12:4 *sqq.*; 1 Cor. 12:13; Col. 1:18.

[23] *Christianity and History,* tr. T. B. Saunders, London, 1896.

[24] William Temple, *Foundations: Christian Beliefs in Terms of Modern Thought,* London, 1913, pp. 357–358.

remains unfinished. It is not preëminently the impact of one nation upon another, nor of continent upon continent, but rather of Christians upon their non-Christian neighbors.

The Christian longing to share the faith with others is at the heart of the missionary movement. For only when the glory and honor of all nations are brought into the Kingdom will the true greatness of Christianity be known. In its true expression this longing flows from the Lord's deep concern for the world. "Go ye therefore and make disciples of all the nations . . . that repentance and the remission of sins should be preached in his name unto all." [25]

There can be no element of compulsion, coercion, or worldly-wise propaganda in this plan of spiritual reconquest. Radically different from the desire to bestow the blessings of a superior culture upon backward peoples, the core of the Gospel proclamation is conceived in love for others. Here is the most unselfish sentiment that has ever stirred the followers of any one religion in their relations with those of another.

The quintessence of piety and the distillation of prayerful service, the Christian missionary enterprise would annul its central affirmation if it were to sow the dragon's teeth of strife where it ought to uphold the standards of justice, righteousness, and good will. Defined as a holy crusade, it is the only case on record of a spiritual mobilization, on a grand and exalted scale, poised to strike at the strongholds of human tragedy. In offering men the human answer, it moves to eliminate the evils of society which make for death and degradation, and emerges as the one and only genuine altruism of religious history, a practical demonstration of Christianity in action.

II. The Differential of Christianity Is in Its Making

1. *The Work of the Holy Spirit.* The chief merit of Christianity is that as a religion it is a response to the call of the Eternal, in the light of His self-revelation in Scripture and in His Son. Hence, the unique character of the Gospel, of Jesus, and of the Holy Spirit.

Christians believe that when God breathed into man the breath of life it was the Holy Spirit entering into man. Thus from the very

[25] Matt. 28:19; Luke 24:47.

beginning the relationship that existed between God and man was a religious relationship. Recalling the long record of man's rebellion and sin against God, Isaiah [26] gave the reason why the Holy Spirit withdraws His favor.

> But they rebelled, and grieved his holy spirit: therefore he was turned to be their enemy, and himself fought against them.

That disgrace, the shame of man's disorder, and the pain of his inward anxiety were not allowed to go on unchecked is the meaning of God's act of mercy and reconciliation carried out when the Son of Man actually saved the children of darkness.

The work of the Holy Spirit explicates the differential of Christianity in that it unites men with Christ and through Him with the Father. Paul enunciated this truth when he wrote:

> So then, brethren, we are debtors, not to the flesh, to live after the flesh: for if ye live after the flesh, ye must die; but if by the Spirit ye put to death the deeds of the body, ye shall live. For as many as are led by the Spirit of God, these are sons of God. For ye received not the spirit of bondage again unto fear; but ye received the spirit of adoption, whereby we cry, Abba, Father. The Spirit himself beareth witness with our spirit, that we are children of God: and if children, then heirs; heirs of God and joint heirs with Christ; if so be that we suffer with him, that we may be also glorified with him.[27]

The work of the Holy Spirit and His gifts of faith, love, hope, and perseverance, make known the reality of God in man's everyday experience and afford an incontrovertible interpretation of the novelty and superiority of Christianity.

2. Illumination of All Other Realities. An interpretation of Christianity is thus offered: God is the Father, above his people; the Son is God, among his people; and the Holy Spirit is God, within his people.[28] As surgical instruments are kept in a particular solution which makes them free from germs and prevents infection, likewise the Christian is admonished to rest in the love of God and to be illumined by the Spirit in order that worldly temptations and the evils of life may have no power over him.

> As for me, this is my covenant with them, saith the Lord: my Spirit that is upon thee, and my words which I have put in thy mouth, shall

---

[26] 63:10.   [27] Rom. 8:12–17.

[28] J. K. van Baalen, *Our Christian Heritage,* Grand Rapids, 1949, pp. 137–143.

not depart out of thy seed, nor out of the mouth of thy seed's seed, saith the Lord, from henceforth and for ever.[29]

3. *Parable of the Bridegroom-Bride.* The consent of the Christian heart to the power of the Gospel and the activity of the Holy Spirit become an objective reality in the fruits of the spirit: love, joy, peace, long-suffering, kindness, faithfulness, meekness, self-control; against these there is no law.[30]

The most glorious fruit of the spirit is the privilege to share in God's blessings. As he that has the sun has light and warmth, so he whom the Spirit guides is born into a new status of fellowship with the Eternal; he rises above the sorrows of existence and the tears of humanity in a blessed and holy relationship with the Lord of all being which sets every other relationship in its proper connection with the divine purpose.

The New Testament uses the parable of the Bride and Bridegroom in order to interpret the bond that joins the believer to God, the Church to the Saviour. Surrounded by his friends, the Bridegroom comes to claim the Bride. In like manner Christ rose in His earthly ministry to claim the believers whom He will at his final coming call by name. The joy of the new life, to which only the Holy Spirit can give true meaning, is thus like that of a bridegroom coming out of his chamber, rejoicing over the bride.[31]

Created by the Eternal and reared by the Holy Spirit, the Bridegroom-Bride bond sets in high relief an example for every other earthly communion, and beside it the brotherhoods and bonds of non-Christian religions must seem shallow and fleeting. The brotherhood of Islam, the bond that turns the Moslem believer to Allah, the Jewish vision of God, the five relations of Confucianism, the monastic order of Buddhism, and the mystical fellowship of many a sect and cult, are here eclipsed by a new creation in Christ which establishes the true pattern of faith and belonging to the Eternal.

Husbands, love your wives, even as Christ also loved the church, and gave himself up for it; that he might sanctify it, having cleansed it by the washing of water with the word, that he might present the

---

[29] Is. 59:21.   [30] Gal. 5:22–23.
[31] Ps. 19:5; Is. 62:5.

church to himself a glorious church, not having spot or wrinkle or any such thing; but that it should be holy and without blemish.[32]

This is the Spirit that dwells in the Christian, softens the cold heart, convicts the sinner, unites men with their God, safeguards the unity of the Church, welcomes those who die in the Lord that they may rest from their labors, separates those who labor for their Master, breaks down the walls of partition between races and seemingly irreconcilable camps, breaks up the congregations and assemblies of the wicked, and seals with the divine blessing all that makes for order, stability, and growth. And as Paul aptly put it, "No one can say, Jesus is Lord, but in the Holy Spirit." [33]

III. A DYNAMIC OF FAITH AND FREEDOM

Product of the Spirit, the vitality of Christianity is essentially that of the communion of saints, the fellowship of kindred hearts whose marks are manifest among all who, forgiven and forgiving, show forth the dynamic of God and the freedom of His truth. Basically and uniquely Christian, the elements of this vitality form Articles eight, nine, and ten of the Apostles' Creed and follow an impressive order of profession of faith.

I believe in the Holy Ghost; the holy catholic church; the communion of saints; the forgiveness of sins. . . .

Actually however, this logical order is subservient to the vital order which must begin with the forgiveness of sins, apart from which there could be no communion of saints.

1. *An Impact Born out of the Unity of the Spirit.* Forgiveness of the Spirit, then, is the foundation of all Christian unity, a manifestation of that love which is distinctive in Christianity because it is the love of God for man, the prodigal of earth.

Nurtured in the religions of East Asia, Kagawa set forth the relevance of God's love as it is made known in Christ and transmitted through the Holy Spirit in a dimension of religious values which Shinto, Confucianism, and Buddhism lack. Whereas Confucius recognized the way of benevolence, to him it was not the overflow of God's grace but a rationalist principle to be comprehended within the category of human relations.

[32] Eph. 5:25–27.   [33] 1 Cor. 12:3.

Buddhism pursued this matter further and made a deeper exploration of benevolence. The Buddha is reported to have forgiven the man who gave him putrid pork leading to the master's fatal illness and subsequent death. Buddhism may well boast of a doctrine of universal compassion and enlightenment but it knows nothing of the love of God which opens the unfathomable spiritual resources of the Almighty to all who come in faith.

A reasoned evaluation of Asia's religious heritage is possible from this point of vantage. For, as the ethical love of human beings rises above the instinctive love of animals, likewise and on a loftier plane the redemptive love of God restores all religious conceptions of compassion to right perspective and, revealed in Christ, fulfills and edifies where all other systems merely represent groping if not failure: "This is my blood of the covenant which is poured out for many unto remission of sins." [34]

2. *Asia's Open Mind and Rigidity.* Much has been made of Asia's toleration and religious flexibility, her open mind and hospitable intellectual mood. It is readily to be observed, however, that neither this open-mindedness of the Far East nor the Semitic rigidity of the Near East is measurable with the robust and innately spiritual determinism of Christianity.

(a) *The Compassion of Buddhism.* It is undoubtedly true that Buddhism is one of the culminating points commanding the perspective of Far Eastern religious history. Historically, it has dominated the Far East, as Islam did the South, and Christianity the West. Set at the very heart of Buddhism, the concept of compassion gave rise to what has been described as the common bond of Buddhic civilization.[35]

The normative influence of Buddhist compassion followed in Mahayana a course resulting in the substitution of the ideal of altruism on an individual level for the earlier neglect of the common layman. Thus Buddhist charity was extended to include all beings, since in everyone was recognized the aspiration for nirvana in keeping with the law of transmigration. Upon all aspirants for nirvana were conferred the attributes and prerogatives of the

[34] Matt. 26:28.
[35] Sylvain Lévi, *L'Inde et Le Monde*, Paris, 1928, p. 59.

Buddha. Like the Buddha, his disciples, and the Bodhisattvas who came after, the aspirants received a sort of common grace endowing them with a blessedness verging on the divine.

The Bodhisattvas were themselves, however, the creators of this grace for the sake of others. There was thus created among the believers an immense religious circuit, each giving to and receiving from the faith whatever was necessary in order to promote deliverance.

Yet it is a fact that this integrating element of Buddhism, consisting in the ubiquity of compassion, was eventually ascribed to the Buddhas and Bodhisattvas who ascended the ladder of hierarchical divinity; receiving prayers and petitions, they usurped the place of the Eternal in his relation to the human soul.[36]

(b) *Hinduism's Toleration and Universalism.* Hindu toleration and universalism are familiar claims, and Hindu apologists have frequently asserted that their system is the most tolerant of all religions. But the essence of Hindu toleration is the axiom that every man should live within his caste. In this sense, the much-publicized doctrine of Hindu toleration seems to oppose the doctrine of religious liberty which is the product of Western democracy, having in turn sprung from the Christian doctrine of man.[37]

Likewise, the Hindu philosophy of religion is a universalism which Gandhi, however, despite his *ahimsa* (non-violence), utilized in order to further political aims. Non-resistance, which he conceived as more humble than anyone can imagine, was nonetheless to prove the most powerful weapon the world possessed. In Gandhi's system of thought, modern Hinduism attained its highest peak, particularly in the conception of universal love and purity. To abstain from theft and earthly possessions, to engage in physical labor, the repression of hungers and lusts, fearlessness, regard for all religions on terms of equality, and a fraternal spirit toward all classes without discrimination—these form the practical implementation of contemporary Hindu universalism. Lacking metaphysical coherence, these ideals represent the rules of an elevated morality which does not, however, nerve men to creative action

[36] Th. Mainage, *Le Bouddhisme,* Paris, 1930, p. 88.
[37] John McKenzie, *Two Religions,* London, 1950, pp. 119–139.

and, cut off from the wellsprings of divine initiative, break down in oceanic ambiguity and detachment.[38]

(c) *China: Benevolence.* Whereas Taoism found freedom in submission to the universe as it is, Confucianism throve in the assurance that a man can only survive if goodness and man-to-manness governed his behavior. These two insights, supplemented by the insight of compassion, introduced by Buddhism, are the basic components of China's benevolence.

Ingrainedly ethical, Christianity constrains man to travel the way of the Cross leading to the peace of God which passes all understanding; here is, therefore, the only religion that can take hold of China's concept of benevolence and use it as an open door for the Gospel; and that is exactly what has been happening through centuries of missionary effort despite prejudice against Christianity as a foreign faith.

Offsetting this missionary thrust, however, was the survival of old deities and decadent beliefs and the perpetuation of a syncretism that set out to incorporate doctrines strange and sundry until the wars and social trends of the twentieth century forbade the acceptance of Christianity on anything like the large scale anticipated.[39]

However, Christianity, the true religion and the final revelation, claims in China many loyal adherents whose ardent faith wins daily against hostile attack and temptation. Much as in the Atlantic countries, where a strain has long existed between transcendant religion and naturalism, China's scholars and thinkers are caught in a great debate whose end the advent of Communism by no means makes nearer.

(d) *Semitic Religious Rigidity.* Compared with the apparent flexibility of the Asiatic mind, exemplified in Buddhism's compassion, Hinduism's tolerance and universalism, and the benevolence of China, the Semitic religious temper must seem rigid and intolerant. Embedded in tribal jealousy and religious parochialism, this Semitic mentality is well-attested. Of old, the servants of the king of Syria said to him when they saw the forces of Israel,

[38] J. Auboyer, *L'Hinduisme,* Lille, 1947, p. 49.
[39] E. R. and K. Hughes, *Religion in China,* London, 1950, pp. 129–144.

"Their god is a god of the hills; therefore they were stronger than we: but let us fight against them in the plain, and surely we shall be stronger than they." [40]

That Judaism, Islam, and Christianity have often erred because of the recrudescence of this form of tribal intolerance, channelled through religion, need not here be discussed. The judgment of Christ on the evils of the non-Christian religions has all too often been translated to mean the judgment of Christians on non-Christians.

The Church must watch and pray lest she fall into the temptation either of Asia's toleration or of the Semite's intolerance. Neither a Jewish legalism, intolerant because it finds its ends in racial and traditional idealization, nor a Jewish rationalism, which somewhat like Asia's open mind makes short shrift of the supernatural, is the narrow gate of God. "I am the door; by me if any man enter in, he shall be saved, and shall go in and go out, and shall find pasture. I am the good shepherd; and I know mine own, and mine own know me, even as the Father knoweth me, and I know the Father; and I lay down my life for the sheep. And other sheep I have, which are not of this fold: them also I must bring, and they shall hear my voice; and they shall become one flock: one shepherd." [41]

These words of Christ are a clear interpretation of Christianity in its attitude to other faiths and to non-Christians in general; they are also an interpretation of the Christian's solemn belief that "God so loved the world, that he gave his only begotten son, that whosoever believeth on him should not perish, but have eternal life." And this mode of religious perception is irreducible to the purely human category of tolerance and intolerance.

3. *The Essence of Freedom and Faith.* It ought to be emphasized, nonetheless, that neither the open mind of Asia nor the religious rigidity of the Semite is without spiritual significance. Yet neither is a proper interpretation of the Gospel in its outreach and attitude toward the other faiths.

In this respect, the keynote of the Gospel message is that men shall know the truth which makes free. What, then, is the essence

[40] 1 Kings 20:23.
[41] John 10:9, 14–16.

of freedom and faith proclaimed by Christianity? Upon the kind of reply which Christians give to this question must ultimately depend the validity and dynamism of Christianity in our generation.

The correspondence between our faith and dynamism is the measure of our freedom.

If "faith is assurance of things hoped for, a conviction of things not seen," [42] and if "the righteous shall live by his faith," [43] and by grace he shall be saved through faith,[44] what religion is there that can compare with Christianity which reposes all faith in the living God who justifies the penitent sinner when he professes faith in his Lord?

This positive, realistic, and eventful belief in God is the core of religion rather than human compassion, and open mind, benevolence, toleration, universalism, and mere fear or vision of the Eternal, important as all these moods and concepts are.

The unreserved commitment to God, which constitutes Christianity, differs from belief such as the Islamic in the one true God who is distant though almighty, and unredeeming though merciful and compassionate. The difference arises from the fact that Christian commitment to the Father is direct and immediate, since it is effected through the special means of grace which He provided in His Son. Christianity, therefore, maintains that faith can only be real and meaningful when it centers in Christ and issues forth as a personal, living trust in the Redeemer and Lord of man's life.

Dynamism is the attribute of all believers whose faith is strong enough to move the mountains of doubt, ignorance, and pride; that is to say, all who can match belief with action, grace with work, and prayer with love of enemies.

Before each succeeding generation, Christianity has raised the question, "When the Son of Man cometh, shall he find faith on the earth?" [45] But faith short of good works is not faith that impresses anyone. Nor is fruitless faith anything but a pretension tolerating the increase of sin in the world in the pious hope that thereby the grace and forgiveness of God may multiply.

[42] Heb. 11:1.
[43] Hab. 2:4.
[44] Eph. 2:8.
[45] Luke 18:8.

The Christian, on the contrary, prays that he may be worthy of his calling and "fulfill every desire of goodness and every work of faith, with power." [46] And being counted for righteousness, the Christian's faith bears fruit in good works, abounding in the kind of dynamism which has marked the annals of Christian history.

Finally, saved and justified by faith, and having acquired the dynamism which relates him to the major issues of his time, the Christian begins to comprehend the true meaning of freedom. For freedom is predicated upon knowledge of the truth which is this: that men may know Christ and God who sent Him. More precisely, freedom is the good life made articulate in the light of God's love and of Jesus who briefed Thomas when He specified, "I am the way, and the truth, and the life; no one cometh to the Father but by me." [47]

[46] 2 Thess. 1:11.
[47] John 14:6.

CHAPTER XIV

THE RESPONSIBILITY
OF CHRISTIANITY

THE new frontiers of knowledge, opened up during the nineteenth century and after, enriched the data available for the study of the non-Christian religions and improved our understanding of Asia's peoples and cultures. The response of the Western mind to the challenge of impressive sources bearing on religion and garnered in the fields of literature, philosophy, philology, and anthropology, was mixed and tended to alternate between two extremes. There was, in the first place, a deepening of the skeptical mood, inherited from the Age of Enlightenment, which was disposed to judge the several religions as equal, sharing in an isosthenia—that is, an essential identity of content and motivation.[1] Secondly, within the more conservative Christian circles the idea gained currency that there was hardly anything fundamentally significant in the Oriental religious heritage and that since theological weight could not be attached to Islam, the religions of India, and those of the Far East, they could be ignored with little or no serious loss to the cause of scholarship and the truth.

Christianity has not yet fully recovered from this dilemma nor reconciled itself to the existence of mighty religious forces in Asia. In failing to evolve a theology adequate to deal with the other faiths, Christian thinkers have withdrawn from an important field.

The issue is far more urgent, however, than that of keeping abreast with the events of our time and making necessary adjustments to contemporary movements abroad. Neither contempt for

[1] Joachim Wach, *The Journal of Religion*, vol. XXVII, no. 3, Chicago, July, 1947, p. 159.

other peoples' religious pilgrimage nor passive acquiescence in the so-called inherent similarity of all faiths will really meet the crisis of the hour.

Nothing less is required of us than a new consciousness and an awakened sense of responsibility, determined to interpret Christianity in terms appropriate to its genius and universality and commensurate with the relevance of God's truth to the needs of seekers throughout the entire world.

The Roman Catholic Church, at any rate since Pope Pius IV issued in 1564 the Tridentine Confession based on the Council of Trent, demonstrates a willingness to acknowledge the religious assets of the great religions as part of a natural theology. In their appeal to Scripture, however, the Protestant reformers made little provision for the norms and traditions of the Patristic Age which had upheld a concept illuminating the relation of the Gospel to other religions. That concept was itself of Stoic origin and centered in the affirmation of the *logos spermatikos* which endorsed the view that scattered germs of the truth did exist outside the pale of Christianity.

Rooted in the Lutheran and Calvinistic thought of the sixteenth century, Protestantism has generally looked askance upon any philosophy of religion that made allowance for a measurable apprehension of the truth in Asia's faiths.

I. THE NON-CHRISTIAN RELIGIONS

1. *The New Frontier of Knowledge.* Philosophy took up the task in the field of natural theology abandoned by the Reformed thinkers. Constituting a throwback to the intellectualism and moralism of the Enlightenment, this attempt was bound to fail because it laid little store by the true nature of religious experience. As a consequence, neither Christianity nor the Oriental faiths received anything like a proper treatment.

In its German expression, this philosophy laid stress upon history and ended in historical relativism; whereas in the English-speaking world it made capital of naturalism and assumed a purely rationalist garb. In opposition to the transcendentalism of Kant and Hegel, the historical school produced eminent men such as Herder and his follower, Schleiermacher,[2] who explained religion as a phenomenon conditioned by history. Doomed in the end, this incipient historicism went the way of Hegelian metaphysics, which had sacrificed individuality on the altar of the mind and will.

Deism was the British counterpart to German historical relativism. Resorting primarily to reason, it leaned heavily on psychology and rationalism. Spearheaded by Lord Herbert of Cherbury and Hume, a philosophy of religion emerged which made the religious experience of man its chief object of investigation. But through it all, reason supplanted revelation and philosophy overshadowed theology.[3]

Toward the close of the nineteenth century, the German and British philosophers of religion found in idealism a common platform. Supported by thinkers such as Troeltsch and Caird, McTaggart and Wundt, Scholz and Siebeck, this idealistic emphasis focused in the empirical method and in epistemology. Empiricism pursued knowledge by observation and experiment, whereas epistemology discovered that knowledge was subject to the limitations of scope and validity.

In the United States, the study of religion had in the meantime fallen into the hands of men determined to prosecute their task along the lines of realism, pragmatism, and naturalism. Betraying the inevitable temptation to convert the philosophy of religion into metaphysics, these American trends left the rank and file of students in the field relatively unimpressed. At long last, however, the new material concerning the non-Christian religions, enlivened by missionary and cultural contacts with the peoples of Asia, spurred some of those who had despaired of the old patterns of evaluation to more direct approaches.

Reaching the very depths of the human problem and related to the understanding of Christianity's role in the modern world, these pioneer approaches were not futile. Among the theologians who rose to the occasion were those who offered new interpretations which merited attention because they took serious note of the new data; among the philosophers with a theological bent of mind were

[2] R. B. Brandt, *The Philosophy of Schleiermacher,* New York, 1941.
[3] E. S. Brightman, *A Philosophy of Religion,* New York, 1940, pp. 22, 438.

those who gave point to their ideas with reference to Christianity in its relations with the living faiths. Of the theologians, Nathan Söderblom and Rudolf Otto, and of the philosophers, W. E. Hocking and F. S. C. Northrop, are eminent representatives.

2. *Söderblom and Otto.* Nathan Söderblom (1866–1931), the Swedish ecclesiastic and Nobel Prize winner for 1930, was one of the most creative minds among the theologians of his day.[4] In dealing with the non-Christian religions he declared that all varieties of historical religious expression—in ritual, worship, and faith— were of a positive character; and that belief in a general revelation of God is forced upon us as soon as we make a serious acquaintance with the other faiths.[5] Perhaps the most notable achievement of Söderblom [6] was his discovery of the inner unity of all positive, genuine religion.

He insisted, furthermore, that within the inner unity of all positive religion, including of course the Biblical, one encounters an element that is of divine origin. He cited Cardinal Newman's idea with approbation, namely that natural religion is also revealed. Söderblom called upon his co-religionists to acquaint themselves with the general revelation of God, long forgotten for lack of knowledge of the cultures and spiritual treasures which represent the East but at last brought to the fore thanks to scientific research and exploration.

Söderblom also maintained that, although they fall within the orbit of general revelation, the non-Christian religions are basically committed to a mystical surrender to the infinitude of God. In contrast, Christianity, while by no means the end of an evolutionary journey toward the Eternal aided by culture, may be described as special prophetic revelation.

He regarded Christianity as unique by virtue of its concept of God, His unity, and His personality, a God active in history and dynamic in human destiny. The self-revealing God, who discloses Himself in the whole history of religion, makes it possible through Christ for an experience to occur which is distinctive in its depth

[4] See Walter Sillen, *Journal of Religion,* vol. 28, no. 1, January, 1948, pp. 37–50.

[5] Nathan Söderblom, *The Nature of Revelation,* pp. 6–8.

[6] *Naturliche Theologie und Religionsgeschichte,* Leipzig, 1937, pp. 63, 67.

and extraordinary in that it is continuous in nature, history, and moral life.

Rudolf Otto (1869–1937), the German interpreter of religion whose conclusions had been partly heralded by Söderblom, conceived of holiness as the thread of meaning upon which all genuine religion was strung. His major work, *Das Heilige*,[7] appeared when the Western world was engulfed in the debilitating apathy and disillusionment of World War I. In it Otto offered an insight into man's life and destiny which was comparable to Karl Barth's *Commentary on Romans* both in its gripping character and in the breath of refreshment which it carried to those who lived through the shadow of crisis. Indeed, against the background of international anarchy and excessive theological liberalism, the achievement of Rudolf Otto stood as a tower of religious strength.[8]

In keeping with the trend of modern German theology, Otto sought to free religion from dependence upon reason and rationalistic metaphysics. He presented his views on the concept of the holy in a manner which guaranteed the autonomy and non-rational character of religion.[9] In this regard, however, he was quick to sound a warning: To discard the rational element in religion is not to deny its validity in thought and faith. It was rather his intention to stress that the essence of religion cannot be satisfactorily comprehended in rational terms. His critics, nevertheless, called his central thesis to question on the grounds that it was tantamount to the destruction of rationalism.

The lasting contribution of Otto, then, lay in his apt identification of religious essence as autonomous, holy, and non-rational. To him this holy nature of religion was something more than the universally accepted values of goodness, beauty, and truth. The holy nature of religion must include all these and something beyond, namely something inherent in the suprasensuous character of reality.

Otto recognized the suprasensuous character of reality as the numinous—that is, a quality of deity, a unique dimension of reli-

[7] Breslau, 1917; Munich, 1936; Eng. tr. *The Idea of the Holy,* Oxford, 1923.
[8] Davidson, *Rudolf Otto's Interpretation of Religion,* pp. 2, 192–193.
[9] Otto, *Idea of the Holy,* pp. 1–2, 61–62.

gious experience. It is no exaggeration to say that his concept of the holy was a remarkable interpretation of Christianity and a discovery of first magnitude in the realm of religious thought. With penetrating knowledge of Eastern, particularly Indian, religions he defined spiritual experience baldly; and where many minds had sought to describe the essence of religion without much success, he set forth in undisguised strokes his concept of the numinous as independent of and other than the sensuous, aesthetic, and moral dimensions of experience.

3. *Hocking and Northrop*. William Ernest Hocking [10] though not a theologian, treated the non-Christian religions from the viewpoint of a philosopher schooled in the post-Kantian idealism of Hegel and Schopenhauer. His partiality to the philosophies and cultures of the Orient resulted, perhaps for the first time in the history of American philosophy, in a broadening of the base of Western thought to include Oriental concepts.[11]

Concerned primarily with the problem of the universal and the particular in religion, Hocking's influence tended to sharpen the importance of the history of religions. The main incentive for his work was neither derived from the now available data on the religions and cultures of the Orient nor based upon a desire to develop a Christian theology that dealt with the cults and faiths of the East. It was rather the product of the actual living contact which a constantly shrinking world had imposed upon the followers of the several faiths.

The significance of Hocking's thought was less in the method which he proposed for the reconstruction of a world faith and more in his introduction of an illuminating philosophical jargon to describe the genius of non-Christian religions. Employing often a simple yet sophisticated vocabulary and documentary material drawn from Oriental life, he laid bare in a startling and devastating manner a number of the most characteristic peculiarities of Asia's religions.

Thus under the rubric, "plural belonging," Hocking indicated

---

[10] *Living Religions and a World Faith*, London, 1940, pp. 69–118.
[11] F. S. C. Northrop, *The Meeting of East and West*, New York, 1946, p. 150.

the syncretic character of Far Eastern religions which, for example, permit a person simultaneously to be a Confucianist, Taoist, and Buddhist. By "relative formlessness" he meant, of course, the absence of recognized ecclesiastical and ecumenical institutions; and the elusive character of religious juridical control, a striking feature of most Far Eastern and Near Eastern religions. He used the expression, "variety of personnel," to describe the many classes of lay mystics, scholars, pundits, gurus, muftis, sannyasis, fakirs, yogis, kadis, and sheikhs who seemingly monopolized the kernel of religious doctrine and, in the absence of any office remotely resembling that of the Christian pastor, excluded the common man from access to the core of the faith and limited his spiritual experience to participation in cultic and primitive observances.

Hocking's definition of "the place of thought and doctrine" in the non-Christian world took note of the vast accumulation of wisdom and learning, particularly in India, China, Japan, and the Islamic countries. With an array of sacred texts and a luxuriant literature serving as the repository of their reflective genius and exegesis, as well as with the aesthetic and exhortatory facets of the faiths, these religions presented the spectacle of formidable and enduring systems rooted in the social and cultural structures.

Finally, under the headings, "immunity to disproof" and "plasticity to change," problems were explained which related to the communication of the Gospel to the peoples of Asia. While the religions of Asia possessed a rigidity which forbade defeat in argument, they were also provided with an incalculable degree of flexibility which enabled them to borrow from Christianity without betraying the normal signs of weakness before a superior system.

Having thus analytically surveyed the religious structure of Asia, mother of all the races, Hocking explored the prospects for a new world faith. Since Christianity, according to him, is neither capable of displacing the other religions nor ready to serve as the world faith of the future, the only course open to it, if a truly universal status was contemplated, consisted in the procedure of reconception—that is, rethinking its assets and liabilities and augmenting its essence by the incorporation of new elements.

He lyrically enjoins that the joy of lifting struggling thought to a new level of self-understanding, the blessings of raising all men to the spiritual vantage point from which they can lay hold on what is eternal and true for all, that in itself is the genuinely universal faith of mankind which Christianity must promote.

Indeed, nothing ought to be written here which would in any way belittle the truth and honesty which surge from Hocking's thought; nor can we detract from the power and daring of his recommendations insofar as they conform with the Gospel. The disparity between his position and the Gospel grows out of one main consideration that is absolute and ultimate, namely, that the Gospel hinges on the centrality of Jesus Christ and that in basic Christianity the Redeemer gives a purpose and a meaningful design apart from which a world faith is unthinkable. For apart from all the resources of wisdom and knowledge with which the Eternal endows men, there is His paramount gift of grace.

F. S. C. Northrop addressed himself in *The Meeting of East and West* to the conflicting currents of modern culture and, taking stock of the political, aesthetic, economic, and religious situation in the twentieth century, attempted to indicate a general plan for integration. His main thesis was a laissez-faire philosophy which in effect maintained that in order to forestall further tragedy and woe we must understand the ideological differences that separate the East from the West.

In giving an analysis of the structure of religion and society prevalent in America, Europe, and Asia, his aim—as he intimates —was to arrive at a synthesis of value, free from the kind of provincialism which asserts that only one set of standards has the right to exist in the modern world. He broadened the sphere of religion by the inclusion within his purview of several aspects of secular life.

Professor Northrop rightly conceived the orbit of Eastern culture as one constituted by the Far East and India and comprising the traditional civilizations of the Orient in their Confucian, Taoist, Hindu, Buddhist, and Shintoist forms. Judiciously, though contrary to ordinary practice, he grouped the Hebraic and Islamic traditions with the Western types of thought and religious experience. At any rate, over against the Oriental systems he set forth those that are standard in the West, represented by the rich culture of Mexico, the free culture of the United States, British democracy, German idealism, Russian communism, and the Roman Catholic Church.

Northrop's principal contribution consisted in his brilliant definitions of Eastern and Western cultures; less incisive on account of their exhaustive and accurate character, these definitions were nevertheless remarkable for their originality and provocative nature.

At the heart of Western culture, Northrop found a determinate, theoretic, theistic religion, whereas that of the East was indeterminate, intuitive, contemplative, and aesthetic, which led the individual to express his religious genius in indefinite form and to adore an incomprehensible, infinite, impersonal continuum. Hence the goal of the philosopher is to promote a meeting between East and West through better understanding of these divergent approaches, looking toward the future synthesis of the theoretic and intuitive components of the truth.

Apart from the irrelevant character of the religious esperanto such as Hocking and Northrop proposed, the position—particularly of the latter—was fundamentally unsound because it left matters much as they were. Seeking the unification of world cultures on a purely intellectual basis, Northrop suggested that religion, for instance, would be unified by union, that men would agree by agreement; or to change the figure, that in order to avoid poverty men should have money.[12]

The basic weakness of Northrop's position is that it substitutes understanding for reconciliation and, in its distress over the problem of the one and the many, the particular and the universal, sacrifices the claim of Christianity to transcend the confusion and ambiguity of history. In support of this Christian claim, Biblical religion maintains that the confusion and disunity of mankind presage the judgment which follows where God is not loved and feared.[13]

[12] Paul Schecter, "In Quest of Mutual Understanding," *The Saturday Review of Literature,* August 24, 1946, p. 5.

[13] Paul Ramsey, "Beyond the Confusion of Tongues," *Theology Today,* vol. III, no. 4, January 1947, pp. 446–458.

Cultures, like empires, disintegrate because they put their trust in man, whose breath is in his nostrils, and are therefore confounded. The Christian view of man and history implies that only humility before the Lord, righteousness in the inward parts, love of one's fellows, and a contrite and penitent spirit will produce unity, enduring peace, and the meeting of minds and hearts.

4. *Reflection on Destiny in Crisis.* The classic affirmations and basic philosophies of the world's religions were generally formulated on the anvil of adversity, crisis providing the main spur to reflection on the subject of man and his destiny. Not only is this true of the leading non-Christian religions but of Christianity as well. Professor Pitirim A. Sorokin[14] of Harvard ably demonstrated in his treatment of the philosophies of history which are most symptomatic of our time that these are an expression of its crisis and anxiety.

It is likewise true that the humanism of Confucius, the meditation of India, the resignation of Islam, and the rationalism characteristic of so much in modern Judaism, stemmed from the quest for a deeper and more valid understanding of man and his destiny. It may be further observed that in a sensate culture, such as that of the modern world, the tendency has been to meet the challenge of crisis through an ideology based on the concept of progress-evolution; in an ideational age, however, such as the one toward which we seem to be moving, the tendency is to express a sharp rupture with the progressive, positivist, empirical norms of a dying sensate era in favor of a more critical, cyclical, creative, rhythmical, eschatological, and messianic vision of human destiny.

Neither these in themselves nor the revival of Asia's aesthetic, intuitive, and contemplative pattern of thought satisfies the requirements of a Christian philosophy of man and history. Essentially theological, the Christian viewpoint on the meaning of history is rooted in the Biblical outlook on the victory of God's truth, justice, and righteousness both in time and eternity.

Unlike Hinduism and Buddhism, the Christian interpretation of history is not negative; nor is it agnostic and humanistic like its

[14] *Social Philosophies of an Age of Crisis,* Boston, 1950, p. 9.

counterpart in Islamic, Confucianist, and Jewish thought. Christian reflection on man and his destiny is, above all, one of hope and fulfillment.[15] The paradoxical fact of the Cross, the sign of the deepest ignominy, and of the Risen Lord, victor over death and moral disorder, is significant as a doctrinal structure which presents reality in an encyclopedic and fully constructive context.

Not the figure of a rebel Prometheus but that of a ministering Christ emerges as the Eternal's projection of meaning, purpose, truth, and providence. Therefore it may be said that despite their conceded ignorance of the true meaning of history, which is hidden in the will of God, and of the shape of things to come, which is also concealed by the Almighty, Christians accept in faith the reality of God's presence with them, His purpose ever unfolding in history and, in the coming of His kingdom, perceive the miracle of His unfailing love and constant bestowal of grace.

II. Responsibility in an Age of Crisis

In a rapidly changing world and despite the many setbacks which Christianity has suffered, Christians persist in proclaiming their faith, incarnating thereby the consciousness of responsibility toward the followers of other faiths by sharing gladly what they have received.

Aware of their status as minorities in an alien world, the Christian believers realize that the Gospel works inside human lives; therefore they proclaim its standards as demands which God makes on men. In India, Japan, Africa, and the Near East, as well as amidst the multitudes in the West who are shackled by materialism, secularism, and spiritual apathy, Christian leadership is gradually passing into younger hands, and more consecrated spirits are increasingly taking the initiative. As history continues, saintly leaders rise up in more and more races and through them the leaven spreads into the lives of the unredeemed; and as they change from within, the institutions of human society are purified and blessed.[16]

Until the newly formed bodies of believers, representing the

[15] Karl Löwith, *Meaning in History,* Chicago, 1949, p. 2.
[16] R. W. Moore, *The Furtherance of the Gospel,* Oxford, 1950, pp. 134–148.

Church of Christ in her global thrust, began to shoulder the responsibility for the proclamation of the Gospel, wide disparity existed among those called to minister in non-Christian lands. And until the essence of general revelation had become widely recognized in the great faiths of Asia, their proper role in the propagation of Christianity could not be clearly described. Nor could Christianity, under those circumstances, discharge the responsibility to contribute toward the reconciliation of East and West.

Clashing theologies had come into being and although evangelism was not thus cancelled out, since it derived its vigor from a higher gift of grace, the ill-effects of radically opposed interpretations of religion proved a heavy drain on the spiritual resources of the Church.

In brief, the implementation of her responsibility toward the world led the Church to recognize that germinal truth existed everywhere and that Jesus Christ alone is Lord, apart from whom the integrity of the believers, the purity of their witness, and the basis of their responsibility quickly vanished.

1. *Appreciation and Education.* In the furtherance of the Gospel, the modern missionary has learned to avoid slurring references to other religions and harsh words about their doctrines. While the famous chapter of Karl Barth,[17] entitled "The Revelation of God as the Abrogation of Religion," has been interpreted by some to give a concept of religion which apparently violates the Biblical view of general revelation and proves inconsistent with the findings of the missionary on the field, nevertheless it has authority insofar as it refers to the essence of Christianity in Christ and the newness of life which He creates.

John Calvin[18] expressed a truly Biblical insight into the nature of the problem when he laid down the position that the human mind, even by natural instinct, possesses some sense of the Deity, and that God has given to all some apprehension of His existence, the memory of which He frequently and insensibly renews, so that as men universally know that there is a God, and that He is their

---

[17] *Die Lehre vom Wort Gottes,* vol. II, Basel, 1938, p. 304.
[18] *A Compend of the Institutes of the Christian Religion,* Hugh Thomson Kerr, Jr., ed., Philadelphia, 1939, p. 7.

maker, they must be condemned by their own testimony for not having worshiped him.

If the assertion that revelation abrogates the non-Christian religions is too unqualified and therefore fails to express the true responsibility of Christianity, it may be said then that the spirit of appreciation and the strategy of education form a plausible approach to those outside the fold whom Christians seek out in love and Christian entreaty.

In the realm of philosophy and ideas—as Professor E. L. Wenger [19] of Serampore College, Bengal, India, pointed out— appreciation may yield fruitful results leading to a more conclusive interpretation of Christianity. What God has made known in the long process of India's spiritual experience is desperately needed for the reconstruction of a Christian theology which will commend itself to the Hindu mind. Although Christianity must supplant the pantheism and monism inherent in the Hindu schools of wisdom, it need not ignore what, in the rich metaphysics of India, supports the concept of authority. Added to the inference and perception of Western logic, this principle of authority might well serve a deeper purpose, namely that of communicating God's truth for the benefit of all men.

Awakened to its responsibility and committed to the appreciation of the truth, no matter from what quarter it comes, Christianity has discovered that the Gospel message becomes instinct with meaning when channelled through education.

Laying the cornerstone of College Hall at Beirut years ago Daniel Bliss (1823–1916) said, "The College is for all conditions and classes of men, without reference to color, nationality, race, or religion. A man, white, black, or yellow, Christian, Jew, Mohammedan, or Heathen, may enter and enjoy all the advantages of the institution for three, four, or eight years, and go out believing in one God, or many gods, or no god; but it will be impossible for anyone to continue with us long without knowing what we believe to be the truth and our reason for that belief." [20]

[19] "The Problem of Truth in Religion," *Studies in History and Religion,* Ernest A. Payne, ed., London, 1942, pp. 159–180.

[20] Stephen B. L. Penrose, Jr., *That They May Have Life,* New York, 1941, p. 181.

Christianity does not seek to throw an intellectual or theological grenade at the non-Christian structures of the world but in keeping with the spirit of its Lord to build the citadel of faith through appreciation and education.

2. *The Wisdom-Religion and the Culture-Gospel Dilemmas.* The exercise of responsibility in an age of crisis imposes upon Christianity the necessity of choosing constantly between wisdom and religion, Western culture and the Gospel.

Had Jesus simply founded a school of philosophy and wisdom instead of bringing all novelty into the world when he brought Himself, the Gospel, and the religion of God's purpose, Christianity might indeed have been very different. Like the schools of the Platonists and Stoics, of Philo and his Jewish successors, of Hindu, Confucianist, and Buddhist wisdom, it would have declined in time. Influenced by the ever-changing intellectual currents and patterns of thought, Christianity might at best have merged with the general heritage of mankind. It is quite unlikely in that event that it could have succeeded in resisting the onrush of the ages, in touching the heart of man, and in entering the bloodstream of the masses.

That despite its ministration to the poor and lonely, Christianity did provide material for philosophical discussion served to give pause to those who accused it of vulgarity.[21] While it remained a religion at the core, Christianity expanded through a series of interpretations, each a venture of faith involving the sacrifice of what was once considered vital.

Thus the Cross shattered the Jewish conception of a Messianic kingdom. The Resurrection enlarged the scope of reality to include time and eternity. Pentecost caused Christianity to break through the confines of Judaism and made it plain that the spiritual and intellectual thrust of religion transcends race and geography. Nor could many of the acutest minds fail to take note of these and subsequent interpretations.

The miracle of Christianity has lost nothing of its validity nor has its responsibility in the world diminished. Ever ready to meet

[21] W. H. V. Reade, *The Christian Challenge to Philosophy,* London, 1951, pp. 183, 191.

the needs of the disinherited and humble, it is also equipped to reach the philosopher, the ruler, and the proud, a sequence which could not have been achieved had the Church been born to the ermine, catered only to privilege, and cultivated nothing but worldly wisdom and philosophy. And the marvel of it all is that holding out neither a panacea nor a sinecure, the Church without mitigating agony and uniformly unable to silence the cry of crisis continues to forge ahead. For the opening lines of Browning's *Easter Day* ring true to the genius of Christianity,

> How very hard it is to be
> A Christian! Hard for you and me.

Christianity must also make a choice between the Gospel and culture. Now it is obvious that when the missionary has established contact with the unbeliever in the name of the Church's Lord, the benefits of Western culture and the creative impulses in the indigenous heritage are released. But the oft-forgotten principle is this, that the promotion of culture in itself does not necessarily lead to the knowledge of God.[22]

It is nothing short of folly to suppose that since large segments of Western society betray little interest in theology, the peoples of the East will be deeply impressed by a presentation of Christianity that lacks spiritual vigor. Having despaired of imperialism and commercialism, and almost instinctively prone to hold materialism and communism suspect, the Oriental soul seems confident that just as evil means ultimately degrade good ends, so a purely secular strategy will rob Christianity of the initial advantage which only the Gospel can give it in Asia. In short, only a religious interpretation of the Gospel bids fair to unlock the hidden treasures of wisdom in the world and to set in proper perspective the several national cultures in the light of an eternal purpose.

3. *Preparation for the Gospel.* The late Archbishop of Canterbury, William Temple,[23] spoke of the non-Christian conscience as the voice of Christ within the unbeliever. Emergent in all that is

---

[22] D. B. Macdonald, *The Moslem World,* January, 1944, vol. 34, no. 1, pp. 6–9.

[23] *Readings in St. John's Gospel,* First Series, New York, 1939, p. 10.

sound and real in the teachings of Plato, Zoroaster, the Buddha, Confucius, and Mohammed, this inner conscience possesses a permanence and a validity which are discerned by those who preach the Gospel among the followers of other faiths.

Indeed, a proper understanding of general revelation lends a voice to quiescent and hitherto dormant truth and demands a just evaluation of the potential religious character of beliefs held by non-Christians. It is inconceivable, moreover, that the essentials of the Christian faith can be communicated in forms other than those deriving their strength from the genius of the native cultures. A discerning Asian evangelist, Daniel T. Niles of Ceylon, in a brilliant book, *That They May Have Life*,[24] attested in his appraisal of Buddhism that a study of that realistic system "can fertilize the growth of understanding of the Christian faith"; but that although such a study makes for a formulation of Christian truth in Buddhist terms, it affords no foundation on which the Christian faith can be based. This is so because of the inevitable contradiction between the self-revelation of God and all the natural presuppositions of Buddhism, Hinduism, and Islam.

Two propositions might be in order. First, that Christianity as it is communicated to men has two folds, the outer represented by the racial and cultural elements, necessary for directness of transmission, and the inner which is sublime and of unalterably divine essence. Second, that God should have intended His truth, the inner fold, to be proclaimed through any other channel than that deriving its origin from the indigenous framework, is highly improbable.

But that is not equivalent to saying that the cultural heritage of Asia is like the Old Testament in its relation to Christianity and the Gospel. An unbroken continuity of holy history and confrontation with the Eternal joins together the Hebrew Prophets and tradition, on the one hand, with Christianity and the Church, on the other. There is, therefore, an indissoluble bond between the Old and New Testaments grounded in revelation. Nevertheless, viewed within the context of natural theology, the great religions of Asia, especially with due regard to the indispensability of their

[24] New York, 1951, pp. 96–114.

forms and metaphors for the effective proclamation of the truth, rank within that peculiar category as a preparation of the non-Christian soul for the Gospel.

China and the foundation of her culture in Confucianism provide an illustration on this grave aspect of the crisis. President Francis C. M. Wei [25] of Hua Chung University, an eminent Christian thinker, demonstrated that in its popular and diversified Western character Christianity was not best suited to the needs of Asia's peoples. With its implacable and absolute affirmations, its creedal scars, and its denominationalism, this Christianity, he declared, must give way to the essence of the Gospel, the mainstay of all the inner life of Christian growth which is the true and potent soul of the Church.

That Chinese culture, as an outstanding example of non-Christian civilizations, need not be feared, has not been generally conceded. Utilizing the rich philosophical harvest of China, the Christian teaching will spring more glorious, and in contrast with the humanism of Confucius the truth will surely vindicate itself. Radiating through the Chinese insights and concepts, Christianity will be more admirably fitted for the purification of Confucianist ungodliness, the development of a new humanism balanced by faith, and the redemption of the people from callous emphasis on this world as well as the annulling of ancestor-worship. Taken for what it is worth, a national culture is an unrivaled adjunct for the interpretation of Christianity abroad and the propagation of the faith.

4. *Crisis within Christendom.* The twentieth century at midway confronts the Church with a crisis consisting in struggle with three prodigious forces, Communism, Asia's awakened self-consciousness, and Western decadence. The last of these requires a few words within our limited space.

Decadence in the West originates in least suspected quarters and consistently exacts a heavy toll upon thought and spiritual virility. To set man against darkness and to contend that even if religion can get on with any sort of astronomy, geology, biology, or physics, it cannot survive in a purposeless and meaningless universe, is to

[25] *The Spirit of Chinese Culture,* New York, 1947, pp. 25–26, 28–29.

project a distorted picture of reality and to uphold a negative, if imaginative, value of existence.[26]

Christianity is precisely that light which shatters the great Western illusion of darkness as it dispels the Hindu view that life is illusory and the Buddhist wintry negativity. Actually the Western prophets of darkness betray a flagrant propensity to bow to Buddhist pessimism and nothingness instead of directing man's vision beyond the spiritual twilight of our era to the springtime of the Eternal. A twittering world can be saved neither through a mirage which promises escape from crisis nor by the admonition that men ought to put their heads in the sand, but by critical and empirical exposure of unbelief, and profession of faith in the living God.[27]

In proclaiming that Christianity's discharge of her responsibility abroad is "a provincialism which leaves the non-Christians of the world, especially of Asia (and later Africa will come into the scene) outside the fold," [28] naturalist philosophy serves a needed warning to Christians who have not lived up to their profession. But such a proclamation is also symptomatic of that Western immaturity which refuses to come to grips with the essential incompatibility of the Gospel with the world's cultures.[29]

The basic offense of the Gospel is that in presenting a sound diagnosis of man's ailment it does not offer a worldly cure but offers instead what the Eternal has abundantly supplied for the creature's unlimited growth in grace and love. Against this design of sanctification and liberation of the human spirit no earthly expression of defeat, decadence, and pride can prevail.

III. RESPONSIBILITY AND ONTOLOGY

Intensive study of the massive data on the living religions of Asia and their modern offshoots, aided by the attempt to fathom

[26] Cf. Walter T. Stace, "Man against Darkness," *Atlantic Monthly,* September, 1948.

[27] Theodore M. Greene, "Man in the Twilight Need Not Falter," *Christianity and Reason,* Edward D. Meyers, ed., New York, 1951, pp. 3–17.

[28] John Dewey, "Antinaturalism in Extremis," *Naturalism and the Human Spirit,* ed. Y. H. Krikorian, New York, 1944, p. 16.

[29] John H. Bavinck, *The Impact of Christianity on the Non-Christian World,* Grand Rapids, 1948, p. 67.

their ontological depth, leads to the inescapable conclusion that these systems possess a certain degree of validity endorsed by the doctrine of general revelation.

The non-Christian frontier needs to be resolutely manned and incessantly extended in view of its invaluable contributions along a number of crucial lines. It will promote our understanding of religion and heighten the significance of the Gospel; it will give effective expression to the longing of men everywhere for a truly ecumenical world and the creation of a Christian community coterminous with the inhabited world; with accent upon religion as the core of all culture, it will magnify the fellowship of peoples instead of their standing feuds and differences; it will provide, on a high plane of thought and faithful endeavor, for the association of all who seek after truth and righteousness; and, above all, it will further a vibrant proclamation of the Gospel through an interpretation of Christianity that takes cognizance of the insights, spiritual vigor, and religious inquisitiveness available in the domains of the other faiths, in order to reach out both to the common man and to the intellectual.

The religious crisis of our time is partly due to the appearance in Asia of several forceful interpretations of religion that reject the affirmations of the Church. There are exponents of modern Islam who are as confident as were their medieval ancestors that largely because of its purer conception of God, which is relatively free from anthropomorphism, their religion outranks Christianity.

Neo-Hinduism has also produced in recent decades apologists who, in their fevered concern for the revival of India, saw in the greater flexibility and tolerance of their system a sign of its superiority over Christianity. The neo-Buddhist revival also reared those who contended that their own religious heritage with its greater realism regarding the centrality of nothingness, spiritual objectivity, and great compassion, is entitled to a place of honor topping Christianity among the religions of the modern world.

As for Judaism, which is today a powerful Western faith, the Christian is keenly aware of its ancient protest against Trinitarianism and the affirmation of its theistic antecedence in terms which assert the excellence of the synagogue. The Jew glories in the fact that his vision of God and the rabbinical conception of the truth are the result of a people's spiritual pilgrimage in history rather than a resort to theological dialectic and mystery.

Faced with the contradictory character of these and other interpretations, Christianity's proclamation of finality rests on the grounds that in its broader intent and deeper comprehension of man, the Gospel is truly discontinuous with all the religious phenomena of history.

The essence of Christian discontinuity springs from a holy and penitent response to the Eternal, who in a living Person confronts man with all his defections and imperfections and sets out to redeem him.[30]

It is therefore on the issue of ontology—that is, of man's total being, destiny, and place in the universe—that Christianity is moved to fix its gaze. Christianity perceives its course in the light of that sacred epic of the faith contained in Scripture which explains man as God made him, as sin and folly debauched him, and as in love and grace Christ restored him to communion with the Eternal.

In an era when great nations became churches, persecuting the Church and seeking to replace God in the allegiance of men,[31] Christianity had the singular distinction that its essence could not be reduced to moral precepts alone. Vladimir Solovyov[32] (1853–1900) had voiced the faith of Russian Eastern Orthodoxy when he maintained that Christianity differed radically from other faiths in that its content could not be limited to teaching nor even to the concept of God as Father; extinct religions had thought of their supreme deity as a father and Zoroastrianism conceived of Ahura-Mazda both as father and loving Lord.

Devastatingly arresting and extraordinary, however, is Christ's declaration of Himself as the way, the truth, and the life; hence, He is the logos, that is the living, incarnate truth. This Godman-

[30] E. C. Denwick, *The Gospel and Other Faiths,* London, 1948, pp. 12–16, 132–133.

[31] John A. Mackay, *The International Review of Missions,* vol. XXIX, 1940, p. 381.

[32] S. L. Frank, ed., *A Solovyov Anthology,* tr. Natalie Duddington, New York, 1950, pp. 39–59.

hood, involving the Wisdom (Sophia) of God and man's eternal individuality, is the essence of Christianity.

But the image of the perfect Godman was not to be only an object of worship and contemplation or of passive faith; it was the heart of a heroic religion, creative in its world ministry and in its responsibility as a receptacle of the divine order, the foundation of the believers' faith and unity.

And it is a matter of deep joy that our far journey in the intricacies of world religions should bring us back to the Church whose unity, purity, and catholicity true believers cherish. This is the Church whose Lord, the living bread of life, saves men by revealing to them the Eternal.

If the religious organization of mankind has not been inherent in the seemingly endless process of change, decay, and development within the several great religions, surely it is permissible to think that the real comfort and growth of both East and West are contingent upon heeding that One who in forgiving inspires progress through renewal.

In short, the indivisibility of all cultures, societies and politics, and of religion itself, is in the end subject to that quickening of the spirit by which the Eternal gives men tenderness to achieve peace, human rights, and social justice, and in constancy to Himself to look for a city whose foundation and founder is God.

INDEX

Abbasid Caliphate, 252, 255
Abdu, Mohammed, 258
Abel, 27, 49, 138
Abraham, 14, 47, 49, 137, 140–146;
  and idolatry, 220–221; covenant
  with, 270
Abrahamitic tradition, 139
Abydos, 70
Achaeans, 98
Adam, 27, 138, 148
Adapa and Etana, 78
Adonis, 87–88
Aegean world, 96–106
Aeschylus, 99, 115, 151
Afghani, al-, 258
Africa, 8, 24; pygmies of, 41; Ewe
  of West, 45; primitives of, 49, 67;
  ideas of God, 56–57; Ashanti, 57;
  North, 98
Agamemnon, 95–96
Agha Khan, 253
Agra, 103
Agrippa, 153
Ahab, 143
ahimsa, 277
Ahmad Khan, 260
Ahmadiya, 260–261
Ahriman, *see* Angra-Mainyu
Ahura-Mazda, 65, 90–95, 148, 301
Ainu, 119, 122, 127
akbar, 246
akh, 71
Akhenaton, 68, 71, 80; monotheism
  of, 143–144
Akiba, 227–228
Akkad, 73–74
Albright, W. F., 9
Albo, Joseph, 230
Aleppo, 89
Alexander the Great, 90, 97, 99–100,
  148–149, 176

Ali, 253
Aligarh, 260
Allah, 34; in primitive Arabia, 53–
  54; sovereignty, 241–265; union
  with, 255
Alpine, 42, 106
Amarna, 84
Amaterasu Omikami, 13, 121–124,
  129
American Indians, 67; Crow, 39, 41,
  44; California, 3, 45; culture of,
  54–56; Andean, 55; Algonkians,
  61
American Protestantism, 264
Americas, the, 24, 255, 261; indige-
  nous population of, 45, 54–56
Amerinds, *see* American Indians
Amitabha, 209, 213, 217
Ammianus Marcellinus, 112
Amon, 68, 71
Amon-Ra, 67
Amoraim, 229
Amorite, 74
Analects, 6, 174
Anan ben David, 229
Ananda, 203
Anath, 83, 87
Anatolia, *see* Asia Minor
Anaxagoras, 99
Anglo-Saxons, 11
Angra-Mainyu, 91; as Adversary,
  147
Anointed, the, 147
Anthropocentrism, 23–27
Antiochus Epiphanes, 149
Anu, 75
Anubis, 69, 72
Apennines, 106
Aphrodite, 87–88, 100, 101
Apiru, 84
Apocrypha, 148, 231, 243